About The  D0617827

The Silhouette Man is the 'expanded' version of *The First Thirty*.

The two stories begin in the same place, and they are based on the same story. *The Silhouette Man* includes nearly 100 additional pages along the way -- expanding on the characters, twists and turns in *The First Thirty* (and introducing new ones as well).

You do not have to read *The First Thirty* before reading *The Silhouette Man*, but it might be fun to do so. In some cases, *The Silhouette Man* answers questions purposely left unanswered in *The First Thirty*.

In terms of grammar and content, *The First Thirty* is intended for students (and adults who simply prefer to read shorter stories). *The Silhouette Man* is intended for adults (and students who prefer to read longer stories).

A Place To Sit is the journal companion workbook. It can be used in conjunction with *The Silhouette Man* or *The First Thirty*. It is filled with hundreds of questions and projects which readers can consider and complete as an individual or as part of a group.

www.TheSilhouetteMan.com

www.TheFirstThirty.com

www.APlaceToSit.com

www.GregForbes.com

To Ann,
Connect the Dots

THE SILHOUETTE MAN
The Story of a Dreamer and His Reflections

───────────────

ISBN: 978-0-9758794-2-9
Library of Congress Control Number: 2004109673

About the Cover:
Concept & design by IdeaList Enterprises Inc.
Photo by Vincent D. Johnson

This book has been printed
and bound in the United States of America.
DBTFISF11-10-02NRRIP E2
Published by IdeaList Enterprises Incorporated

ideaList enterprises inc.

*"If life was nothing but straight lines,
it wouldn't be worth living."
-- Greg's Grandma*

———————————————

To the parents, grandparents,
teachers and substitute teachers
who encourage their kids to dream

To our reflections

- JNP

The Tempo Cafe
November 10, 2002 - 11:48 p.m.

For the record, the meeting was scheduled to begin at eleven-thirty, and for what it's worth, I arrived twenty minutes early to be safe, so by the time it was 11:48 p.m., I'd already been waiting thirty-eight minutes for Greg to walk through that door so I could interview him for the book I was writing about the first thirty years of his life.

Frankly, a mid-afternoon meeting in a conference room with an unobstructed view of the skyline would have been my personal preference, but it wasn't up to me. It was, after all, his story. And, at this point, I was just glad to finally have a meeting.

You see, a month ago, after I'd been selected to write the book, I *tried* to arrange an interview, but it had turned out to be easier said than done. Instead of meeting with me, Greg sent me a list of names and instructed me to contact them all first.

I presumed they were people who could serve as sources for the story -- so I eagerly started at the top and began to work my way down -- but it didn't take long to realize there was a slight problem.

Of the first seventy people I called, some -- former students, old neighbors, ex-girlfriends, relatives -- did provide some anecdotes and background information that would prove helpful, but a dozen others said they had no idea who Greg was and/or what I was talking about, and hung up on me. Another thirty-eight *weren't even real*.

It was a discouraging exercise, but I kept looking up the names -- all 142 of them. Rumor had it Greg already turned down five other authors who wanted to tell his story. I wasn't about to give him a reason to add me to the list. If I had to spend two months calling wrong numbers to prove I was grateful for the opportunity and devoted to the project -- if that's what it was going to take to earn his trust -- then so be it.

Speaking of those other authors, the ones who got turned down, I'm sure a few of them are *still* wondering why Greg chose the person with the *least* impressive resume to write his story. It's a fair question with an ironic answer. Life isn't always fair.

The fact of the matter is that only one person on the list of people hoping to tell Greg's story used to play catch with him in his backyard twenty-five years ago.

And that would be me.

Given that I've known Greg since I was little, you might wonder why I need to interview him in the first place. After thirty years, I should pretty much be familiar with his story, right?

Well, the fact is my old bond with Greg is just that -- an *old* bond. We had not seen each other since we were little, so the connection might have been enough to help get me chosen to write the story -- but it certainly isn't enough to make me an expert on it.

Let's face it. I knew Greg when he wet himself on a regular basis. What are the chances the boy I knew and the man he has become are even remotely the same? I doubted I'd even recognize the guy.

And yet, when he did finally show up at five minutes before midnight, I spotted him right away. It was actually quite easy. I mean, who else *but* Greg would show up at a restaurant with a lunchbox in one hand and a gold-painted milkshake glass in the other?

Not that I gave either much thought.

Once I got a good look at the man himself, I forgot all about what he was holding. The same boy who used to run around the backyard until the sun went down now walked *delicately* -- like a banged-up athlete trying to avoid any sudden movement after the game. His skin was pale and lifeless, and he needed a shave. The bags under his eyes looked out of place on the face of a thirty year old -- except that they matched the bags above them. Even the eyes themselves, once described in a magazine as *penetrating*, looked worn and tired -- as if they'd spent far too many nights fighting to stay open. His shirt and pants were wrinkled and at least two sizes too big (in a he-must-have-lost-ten-pounds-since-he-bought-them kind of way). His thick mop of brown hair was even gone -- replaced by, well, *nothing*.

During a brief talk by phone a few days ago, he said, "If you don't recognize me when I walk in, just look for the big ears."

At the time, I figured he was joking -- his reputation for self-deprecation preceded him -- but as he sat down at the table, I realized he actually meant it. His ears really did seem to be the only thing that had *not* changed since he was little -- the sole remnant of the kid I once knew.

I started to ask the first question on my mind -- *What happened to you?* -- but before I could get out the words, he offered seven of his own.

"Mind if I take off my shoes?"

I was going to object, for the sake of the other customers, but before I could respond, he had already leaned over to remove them, revealing two distinctly mismatched socks in the process.

I stared at (and smelled) his feet in silence until he spoke again.

"Sorry I'm late," he said, "I went to a film and lost all track of time."

I didn't appreciate him being late -- especially not when his excuse turned out to be something as trivial as seeing a movie -- but I wanted to get my mind off his feet, was equally anxious to get started with the interview and this seemed like as good a topic as any to break the ice, so I asked, "What did you see?"

He laughed and said, "You really want *that* to be your question?"

"Excuse me?" I asked.

"Did I forget to mention that?" Greg asked, as he fiddled with his ears. "You're only allowed to ask me *one* question."

"Says who?" I protested.

"Says me," he replied matter-of-factly.

He had to be kidding. He couldn't possibly expect me to solicit all the information I needed to write an entire book by asking just one question. And yet, judging by the expression on Greg's face, it was clear that he was serious. After making me call a bunch of imaginary people (not to mention, summoning me to a twenty-four hour cafe in the middle of the night), he was only going to let me ask *one question.*

"I can't do it," I said with a shrug. "I give up."

"Oh, come on," he pleaded. "You can't give up *that* easy."

Despite my frustration, I couldn't help chuckling. It was much like when we were little. Greg wanted to win as much as the next kid, but more than anything, he just liked to play the game.

"Fine," I said with a smile, "but I'm going to have to think about this for a second. It's not too easy reducing thirty years to just one question."

While the waitress came over and took his order -- a vanilla milkshake and a grilled cheese sandwich -- I sat quietly and thought about his riddle.

What one question could get you all the information you need to write a book about the first thirty years of someone's life?

Unfortunately, I couldn't think of a good one off the top of my head, but I knew that with most problems in life, as long as you don't get too exasperated and quit, the solution will eventually come to you. And, sure enough, that's what happened in this case. By the time Greg had his meal, I had my question.

"Greg," I said, while he cautiously dipped the tip of his straw into the shake to measure its thickness like a little boy using his big toe to check the water temperature in a pool before jumping in.

"Yeah?" he asked, after finally deciding the shake worthy of a sip.

"I've come up with my question."

"Oh yeah?" he replied, as he shifted his attention to his sandwich and began nibbling on its edges. "What is it?"

"Will you start at the beginning?"

Judging by the smile on his face, I apparently solved the riddle.

And so, as the clock struck midnight and the first thirty years of his life came to an end, Greg sat up straight, wiped a couple crumbs away from the corner of his mouth, cleared his throat and did as I asked -- he started at the beginning.

****

On November 10, 1972, a 30 year old stockbroker named Mark and his wife, Rose, had their first child.

The boy's first name, Gregory, was chosen in memory of a late relative (whose name started with a G). The middle name, Forbes, was thought up by Mark in deference to billionaire Malcolm Forbes and the magazine bearing his name.

Like so many young professionals who coveted wealth but had not yet experienced it, Mark was convinced that affluence was a prerequisite for true happiness -- and he hoped the famous financier's name would one day inspire his son to pursue it, too.

Some of Mark's friends -- mostly other men in their thirties who shared both his humble beginnings and his quest for upward-to-the-point-of-being-perpendicular mobility -- seemed particularly taken by his idea to choose a name that (however vicariously) linked his child to the uppermost levels of the socioeconomic stratosphere.

But that's not to say everyone approved.

Susie Atner, who met Rose while both were pregnant and had been comparing child-rearing notes ever since, said, "Most of the literature on parenting says to avoid making your children feel weighed down by what you hope they will achieve. And yet, that's exactly what Mark did by attaching that name to their son. Some kids are burdened with high expectations. This boy was *branded* with them."

A year later, Mark and Rose had a baby girl named Michelle. They intended to divide their time evenly between their two kids, but that plan changed -- and with good reason. Their new baby was gravely ill.

Day after day, Rose kept a vigil at the hospital while her husband trekked back and forth to work in between visits.

For Mark, the daily commute was difficult, but his daughter's bedside was far more strenuous than rush hour traffic.

His friend, Barry, said, "Mark was six foot three, two hundred thirty pounds, an Army vet, a gun collector, an athlete -- he took a lot of pride in being a *man*, in the *very* traditional sense of the word. You know, providing for and protecting his family, that kind of thing. And yet, in this instance, his baby girl was near death and there was nothing he could do except to step back and let someone else take care of her. Even when you know the doctors are doing their best -- for a guy like him, that was a tough pill to swallow."

With his parents so focused on Michelle's health, Greg was usually dropped off at his Grandma's. Given his age, the two didn't have any substantive conversations -- but as Greg's mother's mother rocked him back and forth, an unspoken bond did seem to develop between them.

Michelle eventually pulled through, things got back to 'normal' and the family of four moved into a two story home on a quiet cul-de-sac in a suburban enclave called the Shore.

The three bedrooms were upstairs -- one for Greg, one for his sister, and one for their parents. The latter two rooms had windows facing the driveway. Greg's window overlooked the backyard -- a modest-sized square plot of land. In the far corner of the yard, across from Greg's window, there was jungle gym equipment.

One piece was a horse standing on its hind legs. Its back was a ladder that could be climbed up and down. The other piece was a fifteen foot tall, multi-colored stick figure man with his arms stretched out to the side, a swing hanging down from each one. Greg was especially fascinated at night when darkness reigned and the brightly-painted man transformed into a towering, pitch black silhouette rising up into the sky.

Sometimes, Greg swung on the swings or climbed the ladder, but on most afternoons, he seemed content to just sit in the grass cross-legged and barefoot (he almost never wore shoes) and watch them -- waiting for the epochal moment when The Silhouette Man and The Ladder Horse finally *moved*. The rest of the time, he played with his father's dogs or sat up in his room, learning to read.

The fantasy that The Horse and The Man might move like real people was the tip of the iceberg when it came to Greg's imagination.

Grandma often joked, "Figure out a way to charge admission to see the world inside that head of yours, and you'll be rich."

In fact, the boy day-dreamed so often -- so distracted was he by the ideas floating through his head -- that he literally ran into things. At one point, his father even gave him a helmet to wear around the house, so he'd stop hurting his head when he bumped into the walls.

Mark said with a shrug, "It seemed like the easiest solution."

When Greg's father came home from work each night, the family sat down for dinner -- but it was never much of a unified event.

Rose and Michelle chatted away like two old friends, while Mark listened intently to the business gurus on TV (and thumbed through his trusty stack of financial papers during commercials).

Greg, in the meantime, stared out the kitchen window, engaged if not altogether engrossed by his imagination -- interrupted only by occasional directions from his mom ("Honey, pass the salt.") or lectures from his father ("Do you see this man?" Mark would say, while poking his fork at a CEO flashing a just-went-IPO smile on the front page of the paper. "I want you to be just like him, son.").

Even when it came to the actual meal, Greg was odd man out. Regardless of what Rose cooked for the family, he wouldn't eat it. In fact, no matter how hard anyone tried to convince him otherwise, Greg stubbornly insisted on eating just six things: hot dogs without mustard, peanut butter and jelly sandwiches without jelly, bagels without lox, pancakes or french toast without syrup, cereal with milk (but the milk had to be separate, so he could eat the cereal with his hands) and grilled cheese sandwiches (which he insisted on calling *meatless cheeseburgers*). And that was it.

Every meal of *every* day, it had to be one of those six things.

Perplexed by their son's abnormal diet, Mark and Rose took Greg to see a local doctor named Dr. Adamson.

After the evaluation, the doctor explained, "When you have a second child, it's common for the first one to feel like yesterday's news -- and that's under normal circumstances. In this case, your new baby was ill and required undivided attention for the better part of a year -- so it's almost a given your first child is going to feel left out and may resort to an attention-getting measure like refusing to eat to try and reclaim that lost spotlight. Now that things at home are back in order, your boy should be eating again in no time."

The diagnosis made sense -- except that, months after Michelle was released from the hospital, Greg's diet still remained spartan. Apparently, he had been on his little hunger strike for so long that he simply stopped liking most foods.

(Rose did eventually manage to get a seventh item added to Greg's diet -- vanilla milkshakes -- after convincing him they were filled with special paint that kept teeth bright and shiny. But that was it. Other than the shakes, Greg's menu would remain virtually unchanged for years to come.)

Once Greg started school, some older kids seized upon his eating habits as something to ridicule, but it was hardly the only thing they mocked. He also was teased about the way he looked.

He had buck teeth and chubby cheeks. He also had *enormous* ears

-- the type normally seen in cartoons. He tried to comb his hair over them or hide them under hats, but nothing ever worked. Sooner or later, they always popped back out.

And then there was that middle name. Forbes wasn't like John or David. It was *different*. Greg's parents tried to explain it was different *in a good way*, that he had the *world's greatest name* -- but it was no use. To Greg, it was just one more thing on a never-ending list of things that people needled him about (if they caught wind of it). He eventually started to pretend he had no middle name at all.

To top it off, whenever he got nervous, he peed on himself.

He truly was an easy target for teasing if there ever was one.

Despite Greg's problems with some of the older kids, there *was* one thing that did go his way. His teachers. Year after year, he had some of the nicest ones a boy could ever hope for. They were kind and patient and never ridiculed him about anything (or let anyone else do so in front of them, either). Other than his bedroom and the backyard, the classroom quickly became his favorite place to be.

But that's not to say the teasing stopped completely.

Before and after school, when the teachers weren't there to protect him, Greg still had to fend for himself against the older kids who called him names and poked fun at him on a daily basis.

Sometimes, they worked in tandem -- one flapping Greg's arms, while another grabbed his oversized ears and hollered at him to "start flying like Dumbo!"

Greg turned to Grandma for sympathy, but she offered him little.

She said, "You got big ears. Looks like two pancakes were glued to the sides of your head. *So what?* Would you rather have none?")

Over time, Greg began to appreciate the peace and quiet of his backyard more than ever. It became his own private sanctuary -- the one place he could go outside without having to worry about running into the older kids who picked on him.

Before long, perhaps borne out of solitude, Greg began talking to the swing and ladder. At first, it was just a polite greeting -- a way to acknowledge their presence -- but eventually, The Silhouette Man and The Ladder Horse became Greg's *friends*, and he talked to them for hours at a time. (In later years, people teased Greg about his tendency to treat conversations like soliloquies -- unaware that his penchant for rambling could be traced directly to the fact that, as a child, he spent hours and hours talking with two 'friends' who never said a word.)

When Greg first befriended The Silhouette Man and The Ladder Horse, he did not plan on introducing them to anyone -- but the secret didn't last long.

One night, Rose walked Mark over to the kitchen window and said, "Look outside. I think Greg's talking to the swing."

Mark was none too pleased. He installed jungle gym equipment so his son would have somewhere to play with his friends. He never expected the swing and ladder to *become* those friends.

Concerned there was something 'wrong', Greg's father consulted Dr. Adamson. After meeting with the boy, the doctor assured Mark that there was little cause for worry -- just your run-of-the-mill young child with a vivid imagination.

The diagnosis did little to pacify Greg's father.

Hoping to see his son put his time to better use, Mark rummaged through some boxes, pulled out a smock and some brushes, handed them to Greg and said, "Instead of talking to the ladder and the swing, why don't you paint some pictures of them?"

In the days that followed, Greg did as his father told him, but the results were not too impressive. No matter how hard he tried, he could barely draw a straight line. He was on the verge of giving up when his Grandma stepped in.

"You're right, you *stink* at drawing," she said in her no-nonsense way, "but so what? Work twice as much as the people you think are twice as smart and eventually, you'll catch up. And besides, you learn more from your mistakes than you learn when you get it right. So all that really matters is you don't quit. Don't ever forget -- if life was nothing but straight lines, it wouldn't be worth living."

He followed her advice -- and not only with drawing. When he first tried to read, the words got all scrambled up in his head, but instead of giving up, he just kept trying. And sure enough, over time, the words started falling in place and the pages started turning.

Once Greg learned to read, he never wanted to stop. He read in the morning before anyone else woke up, and he read late into the night -- hiding beneath his covers with a flashlight.

On the weekends, he hid deep within the stacks at the local public library. He arrived there early in the day, and other than a break for lunch at the hot dog place across the street, he remained there until closing time -- going through one book after another.

At times, reading was a struggle for him -- words still got

scrambled in his head, and he was such an easily distracted kid -- but he felt it was worth the time and effort. He truly loved the stories.

The people Greg read about, and the things they did, and the places they went filled his imagination with extraordinary dreams that carried him far away from the 'real' world where he never felt quite like he belonged.

Of the books he read, one of his favorites was a book about a pro athlete. After he read it, Greg wanted to play sports, too. He started running around the yard, wearing that helmet his parents gave him, playing games against imaginary people.

Mark had seen enough. He declared that Greg was old enough to play *real* games with *real* people and signed him up for tee ball (which is when he first became friends with a kid named Charlie).

Shel Silverstein's books of poetry captured Greg's attention, too. With a different poem every few pages, they were a perfect fit for a boy who became distracted so easily.

Curious George and *The Little Engine That Could* were also near the top of the list. The classic stories reinforced two of the messages Grandma always emphasized -- ask lots of questions, and don't quit.

Another one of Greg's favorites was *Where the Wild Things Are* -- the tale of a boy who is transported from his bedroom to a faraway land populated by giant creatures. After reading the story, Greg became *convinced* The Silhouette Man and The Ladder Horse in his backyard could come to life -- no matter what anyone said about them being just metal and paint. And so, at night, he sat in bed, staring out the window, hoping and watching and waiting for the moment they began to move like other real people.

Greg's *absolute favorite* was a book about Harriet Tubman -- partly because it was the first book he ever purchased himself (at a grade school book fair), and partly because he was so inspired by her story -- escaping slavery, then risking her freedom to help others.

Obviously, the son of a white, suburban businessman could never *really* understand let alone replicate the heroics of a black woman who helped others flee from oppression, but in his own little-kid-kind-of-way, Greg aspired to be like Harriet.

He wanted to help people, too.

So when, quite fortuitously, just a few weeks later, a visitor came to his class and talked about a program in which kids could help fight a disease by getting people to donate money for every book they read, he eagerly volunteered to do it.

Rose was not quite as quick to jump on board. She thought it was a nice charity, and the chance to read books to help it did seem tailor-made for her library-loving son -- but the idea of him actively solicit-ing money for every story he read? There was no way. She figured he was simply too shy to do it. Or so she thought.

Without so much as a stutter step, Greg set aside his insecurities, laced up his shoes and marched outside -- walking all over town, knocking on doors, asking anyone and everyone to make a pledge.

Friends, neighbors, strangers, old, young, it didn't matter who they were -- if they crossed his path, he asked for their support.

It was a side of his personality that, up until that point, few had ever seen. And despite his age and inexperience, he proved to be quite the little philanthropist.

Rose recalled, "He had a real knack for inspiring other people to see value where he saw value."

Of those Greg convinced to help, some gave a one-time lump sum donation like twenty dollars. Others pledged a certain amount for every book he read -- usually between ten and fifty cents per book -- which motivated him to read more than ever. While other kids fin-ished a book a week, Greg knocked out one *a day*. He was suddenly raising hundreds of dollars...*at the age of six*.

The Read-a-Thon was the first time Greg ever felt like he did something well. Once the ball was rolling, there was just no stopping him. He was a shake-slurping, book-reading, fund-raising machine. By the time he was eight, he had raised thousands of dollars.

Champ Reader declared the headline in the newspaper after the charity honored Greg at a special luncheon.

The experience -- being able to help others by sitting and reading books -- taught the young boy a valuable lesson: Anyone at any age can make a difference. All you need is time, the willingness to spend it and a place to sit.

There seemed to be nothing that gave Greg as much satisfaction as his foray into philanthropy. Until, one day, his mom took him to the theater where his godfather worked and introduced him to a whole new universe -- the world of movies.

At first, he was scared to death inside the theater, but he soon became intrigued by its darkness. Invisible to those around him, Greg felt a sense of freedom he had never experienced outside his home. It was the one place where he didn't feel like he needed to have a parent, a teacher or a librarian keep a protective eye on him. After all, in the theater, nobody -- bullies included -- could see him. Sitting in the dark, he felt safe, liberated, *free.*

Not that it really mattered. When the previews started, he forgot about everything and everyone around him. The wall had come to life, and he was positively *hypnotized.*

Greg returned every weekend, munching down box after box of buttered popcorn and watching the latest releases over and over again -- memorizing entire sections of dialogue in the process.

When he got home, he'd beg his parents to let him stay up late and watch old films playing on TV or on video.

All day long, Greg imitated his favorite characters -- running up and down the stairs like he was Rocky Balboa training for a bout, or pacing in front of The Silhouette Man in the backyard like he was Atticus Finch talking to the judge in *To Kill a Mockingbird.*

Greg's father was not entertained by the antics.

A deeply driven man who had little time for such silliness, Mark longed to hear his son quoting stock market analysts -- not characters from films. He wasn't particularly good at expressing these feelings, however, so he turned to an unlikely source for help -- cartoons.

When he wanted to try and coax Greg into caring more about finance, for instance, he gave him a cartoon that featured a father telling his son: *'Life is not about whether the glass is half empty or half full. It's about who owns the glass.'*

The manner in which Mark 'gave' Greg the cartoons further underscored the impersonal nature of their relationship. Instead of, at least, handing them to his young son face-to-face, he would have his assistant send them in the mail -- complete with an 'I thought you might find the enclosed of interest' card.

A defensive Rose said, "Greg was a hard kid to reach. Mark thought appealing to his imagination might be the way to do it. So he did the best he could to do that, even though he personally wasn't the creative type. I'm sure having his secretary mail the cartoons wasn't exactly out of the father-son handbook, but come on, at least give the guy credit for trying."

Not surprisingly, the cartoons -- absent any conversation to explain their meaning -- had little impact on the boy who received them.

Still determined to dash his son's big-screen dreams, Mark turned to Greg's godfather (the one who worked at the theater) and asked him to take the boy up to the projectionist's booth and spoil the illusion.

He said, "Make him realize the wall doesn't *really* come to life."

Greg's godfather did as asked, but one look at the expression on the boy's face and it became clear Mark's plan to take the magic out of movie-making not only failed -- *it backfired.*

The concept of one man in a little booth running the entire show left Greg even more awe-struck than the films themselves -- it was like a bonafide *Wizard of Oz.*

He still hoped to be like the people he saw on screen, but if he never did possess a physique like Rocky or the intellect of Atticus Finch, he now had a new dream to fill the void. He was going to be the one who told the stories of those who did.

Mark was beside himself. This was *not* a path to the lucrative future he envisioned for the son he named after a business mogul. He had his assistant mail another cartoon: A typewriter-toting man standing on a street corner with a sign: "WILL WRITE FOR FOOD."

Undeterred, Greg continued to insist storytelling was his destiny. And not just any old stories, either. One day, he insisted, he would tell stories about underdogs like *Rocky*, about people who stuck up for others like *To Kill a Mockingbird*, about places where it's okay to dream like *Willy Wonka and the Chocolate Factory.* He said he would tell stories that change the way we think.

Greg insisted his stories would be told *so* well that he would win an Academy Award ® for his very first one.

And night after night, while his mom and sister watched on with amusement, and his father shook his head in frustration, Greg got up from the dinner table, lifted his milkshake glass like it was a trophy and practiced the first six words of his acceptance speech again and again: "I'd like to thank the Academy...."

**

Between the films, the books and his friends in the backyard, Greg seemed increasingly content in his own little world -- and increasingly lost in the real one. If he had even thirty seconds to himself, his mind drifted off in a dozen different directions.

Within ten minutes of learning how to ride a ten speed bike, he got distracted, crashed, went sailing through the handle bars and cut his head wide open.

On a family trip to Washington D.C., he wandered off when his mom wasn't looking. Three hours later, he was found on a city bus, nose pressed against the window, staring in awe at all the towering buildings -- blissfully unaware of how long he had been gone, let alone the panic caused by his disappearance.

Another time, at a local pool -- well, the home video captures the story better than words ever could. A little boy with giant ears, by himself, spinning around in circles -- too preoccupied with pretend friends to realize the real ones had paddled over to the deep end.

Even at that luncheon where Greg was honored for his reading, despite being the guest of honor and despite being sandwiched between his father and an All-Pro from the NFL up on the dais, he said nary a word for a full ten minutes, focused intently on the picture he was trying to draw on the back of the afternoon's program.

Rose insisted, "It wasn't that he was a loner. It was just that he got so wrapped up in his imagination that he lost track of who or what was around him in the real world."

Over time, the potential harm of that became increasingly, painfully clear. On a family vacation in California, Greg ran through the lobby and out the hotel's front door -- except that the door was closed. He went flying backwards, getting a bump on the front of his head from the collision and a bump on the back from the landing.

Time and time again, he got so distracted by the goings-on in his head that he literally ran nose-first right into something. (By the time he turned sixteen, he would have already cracked his head open twice and broken his nose four times -- requiring two operations.)

However Greg incurred them, the cuts, the bumps and the bruises always healed in a matter of weeks. It was the emotional repercussions that were far more lasting. After each incident, he withdrew further and further into his own imaginary world -- a place where nobody got teased, got lost or crashed into anything.

Again and again, Mark urged his son to snap back into reality.

"Do you know what two things these people all have in common?" he'd say, pointing impatiently at the well-heeled execs gracing the cover of a business magazine. "These people make a lot of money, and *none of them* talk to swingsets."

But it was easier said than done. Everywhere Greg looked in the real world, there was someone or something that made him nervous.

Even on his own street, where all the neighbors and their kids treated him nicely, the boy still found plenty of excuses to be afraid. Three houses to the left, there lived a girl with captivating blue eyes. Whenever Greg saw her, he started to stutter. Three doors to the right, a new couple moved in, and they had an ominous-looking dog who always seemed like he was about to pounce. Whenever Greg saw the dog or heard it growl, he started to pee on himself.

Sometimes, Greg hopped the fence and played catch with the boy who lived next door. Other times, on weekends, he slept over at the houses of some of the other kids his age. But more often than not, he was content to put up a tent in his backyard and stay up late talking with his friends, The Silhouette Man and The Ladder Horse.

At home, he just felt *safe*.

At least, he did until the burglar broke in.

One night, Greg came face-to-face with a man who broke into the house. The intruder ran back down the stairs and out the door as soon as he was spotted, but Greg was still trembling with fear two full hours later. His parents tried to convince him there had been no burglar -- it was just your shadow, they told him (and they were probably right, given the absence of any sign of a break-in) -- but it was no use. The damage was already done.

Night after night, Greg insisted on sleeping in his parents' room -- terrified that the 'burglar' would come back to get him.

Determined to reclaim his domain, Mark surprised his son with something that could keep him company at night -- his own dog.

The idea worked.

Even though the eight-week-old puppy was tiny, Greg felt like he now had a 'bodyguard' and finally returned to his own room.

He named his new pal 'Tug' in honor of a favorite athlete.

As time passed, the two became attached at the hip.   In the afternoon, they watched TV together. At dinner, Tug sat loyally by Greg's feet. At night, the miniature bodyguard slept on the edge of Greg's bed. There seemed to be nothing that could pull the two apart.

Rose recalled, "When Tug began to grow, we put a cage in the laundry room and told Greg that the dog had to start sleeping down there. Without missing a beat, he literally crawled in the cage with Tug and refused to come out until we reconsidered our decision."

(And eventually, they reluctantly did.)

Over the next few months, the puppy continued to grow rapidly. By the time summer came, with such a sizable friend to protect him, Greg not only felt safe inside the house -- he felt safe outside, too.

Mark noted, "That really was the grander plan we had in mind when we got Tug. It really had nothing to do with a phantom burglar. It was done to help Greg get over his fear of the neighbor's dog."

And the plan worked like a charm. With his canine companion by his side, Greg gleefully roamed the neighborhood, smiling and happy.

Until, one afternoon, just seven months after he first trotted into a young boy's life, Tug was suddenly gone.

It was a sunny Saturday in July. Mark and Rose were hosting a barbeque for Greg's Little League teammates and their families. When one of the kids opened the front door, Tug dashed outside and ran down the street. Three blocks later, he was hit by a car and killed.

At the time it happened, Greg was in the backyard with his team-mates -- oblivious to the terrible news that awaited him.

Greg's parents hoped to delay the inevitable until after the party, but it was not to be. The boy and his dog were truly inseparable. Within minutes, Greg noticed Tug was missing.

As her eyes welled with tears, Rose knew she had to share the news that would break her little son's heart.

In a voice barely above a whisper, she managed just three words. "Tug is gone."

It was the first time Greg ever lost a friend to violence, and he was, as expected, devastated by the news. He ran up to his room and collapsed to the floor while the tears began to flow uncontrollably.

Under normal circumstances, Mark would've followed his son up the stairs and chastised him for "crying like a baby." But this wasn't a normal circumstance, and he knew it.

Dogs had always been a constant in Mark's life. He had one as a child, worked with them while in the military, and spared no expense caring for his own as an adult. And now that he'd succeeded to a modest degree in business, he gave money to organizations that helped care for animals who had been abandoned by others.

He knew dogs as much more than mere pets. He knew them as loyal friends and trusted confidantes. As a result, no matter tough he seemed on the outside, Mark understood the bond that can exist between a boy and a dog.

And so, on that tragic summer day, instead of berating Greg for displaying such emotion, he went upstairs, and without saying a word, sat down beside his son and began to cry, too. It would be the first (and only) time Greg would ever see him shed a tear.

A couple days later, as they buried Tug's ashes, as tears once again streamed down Greg's cheeks, he turned to his dad and asked him why this had to happen to such a great dog.

Mark replied, "Sometimes, friends come into each other's lives, and then, when you least expect it, they move on -- and there's no real explanation for it. So instead of trying to figure out why they left, all you can do is try and appreciate them while they're here and make sure to remember them once they've gone. To treat everybody you meet like they came into your life for a reason."

Mark's tears had helped -- and now his words did, too.

It also gave Greg comfort knowing Tug's ashes were buried some place he could keep an eye on them (in the backyard beneath a small headstone behind three small bushes) — but he just wasn't the same without Tug by his side. Weeks turned into months, and Greg still seemed as despondent as the day his beloved dog died.

Hoping that some time away from home would help their son put the tragedy behind him, Rose and Mark signed Greg up for overnight camp in Wisconsin. His pal, Charlie, was signed up by his parents, too.

At first, as he boarded the bus, even with Charlie there, Greg was reluctant to spend eight weeks away from home with a bunch of strangers. After just a few days, though, he decided summer camp in Wisconsin was just about the greatest place ever.

The chance to shoot a bow and arrow, run in the woods and swim in the lake was the closest thing he'd ever experienced to the adventurous world inside his head. To be sure, the kid from the white-picket-fence suburbs was not exactly a skilled outdoorsman -- Robin Hood actually hit the target and Tarzan never needed a life preserver -- but he really did seem to enjoy his new environment.

He also appreciated the way he was treated by the others who were at camp with him. Even though Greg was different (and *never* seemed to stop talking), the kids in his cabin tried to include him in their plans.

The counselors were supportive, too. When Greg was nervous about trying new things (which was almost always), they were there to encourage him. If he failed at something (which was almost always), they picked him up, dusted him off and convinced him to try again.

The Camp Director was especially thoughtful. When he heard about Greg's eating habits, he made sure there was always a cheese sandwich waiting, just in case his finicky camper didn't eat what was being served. And when Mark sent up a box of weight-gain powder to mix in his skinny son's shakes, the Director let Greg drink the shakes in his office, so he didn't have to feel self-conscious about it in front of the other kids.

Given all the different activities the camp had to offer, Greg even found one where he could excel -- The Spelling Bee. Thanks to all those books he read, he outlasted kids nearly twice his age and won the entire thing. As the weeks passed, his confidence grew by leaps and bounds. At a Social with a girls' camp on the other side of the lake, he even got his first kiss.

[As the story goes...at the Social, there was a girl with big blue eyes. All the boys liked her -- none more than Greg. She reminded him of the blue-eyed girl who lived on his street back home. As the other boys egged him on, he reluctantly walked over to speak with her -- certain she would laugh him away. But, to their astonishment (and Greg's as well), the girl smiled warmly when he said hello and started to talk with him. And when the Social was over, she leaned in and kissed him -- as the other boys' jaws dropped. It would be nearly twenty years -- a chance meeting at a health club -- before he would see or speak with her again and learn it was a kiss given more out of sympathy than attraction. In the meantime, as he and the other boys boarded the bus to head back to their camp, Greg felt like he was walking on air.]

He would return to Wisconsin every summer until he could drive.

When Greg came home that first year, his parents were thrilled to see the impact that camp had on their son. He was finally going outside again and socializing with other (real) people again. He even started rambling on and on about his dreams again.

Knowing how easily Greg got distracted, Grandma told him to commit those dreams to paper to make sure he didn't forget them.

And so, that's exactly what he did -- writing down each new dream that crossed his mind. He kept the scraps of paper with his ideas in a box by the side of his bed. When his Idea Box filled up, he smooshed his socks into his underwear drawer so he could have a whole drawer to house his idea papers. When *that* quickly filled up, Grandma suggested he consolidate a bit.

He went through all the scraps of paper, picked the ideas he cared about most and put them together into a single, concise list. He en-titled it *My Idea List: The First Thirty.* It contained the thirty goals he aspired to reach by the time he was thirty years old.

The First Thirty included many of the typical dreams a boy his age might hold dear. He wanted to go on a date with the blue-eyed girl three doors down. He dreamed of writing a best-selling book and winning his first argument in the Supreme Court. He hoped to be a pro athlete and become President, too (which he changed to just 'live in the White House' once he remembered you can't run the country until you're thirty-five). And somewhere along the way, he also hoped to travel to all the continents. And on and on his "Idea List" went.

He even took the time to list the goals alphabetically. So, it was only a coincidence that the first one happened to be the one he cared about most: *An Academy Award for his first film.*

Greg's parents were not surprised by the list of wide-eyed dreams that their son compiled. Most of them were things he'd been talking about (and talking about, and talking about) for years.

They knew, of course, that most of the goals were *so* grandiose that he would probably never reach them -- at least not any time soon. But mixed in with the dreams about game-winning scores and kicking up his feet in the Oval Office, there was one goal on the list that seemed a lot more immediate and at least *a little* more reachable: *Going to the Ivy Leagues for college.*

Mind you, Greg didn't actually know anything about the schools that comprised the elite group. He didn't know about the kind of classes they offered, or the professors who taught there, or what their campuses looked like, or even where they were specifically located. But he did know the man he was named after (Malcolm Forbes) was a card-carrying Ivy League alum, and he knew the mere mention of such a school always seemed to send his father into a stuttering tizzy ("Did you hear that, son?" Mark would say at a holiday get-together. "Brian here goes to Dartmouth. *Dartmouth!*").

Charlie had a similar interest in the Ivy Leagues -- Harvard, to be specific -- but he cringed when he heard Greg broach the subject.

Charlie scoffed, "I had *reasons* for wanting to go to Harvard. I'd already done all kinds of research on the place. But Greg didn't know anything about the schools. He didn't even really know what *Ivy League* meant. He used the term like it was an adjective. According to his logic, a school like Stanford was 'just as Ivy League' as Brown -- and, as far as I could tell, he didn't really seem to care which one he went to."

Charlie was right. In truth, Greg didn't care where a college was located (or, for that matter, what majors were offered or anything else of the sort). He didn't even care if a school was actually in the Ivy Leagues. As long as it was a school known for accepting 'really smart' kids, then it was 'Ivy League enough' for him and made his list. He wanted to prove he was good enough to be *one of them.*

And what made him so sure he was?

Among other things, *Risky Business.*

In the film, the main character, Joel, gets accepted into Princeton despite turning his parents' house into a makeshift brothel on the very weekend a school rep pays him a visit.

To Greg, the movie was much more than mere entertainment. It was *evidence* -- irrefutable proof his own lofty dreams were *not* out of whack. After all, just about the worst thing he'd ever done was put his feet on his Grandma's couch. If an amateur pimp like Joel could get into the Ivy's, how could he *possibly* be turned away?

He seemed to have a good point, except for one not-so-small detail -- *Joel didn't actually exist.* The guy was a made-up character in a made-up movie. Of course, there was no telling Greg that.

He even went so far as to look up Joel in the phone book to ask him for advice. (When he couldn't track down the number, he still refused to admit Joel was fictitious -- suggesting the number must be unlisted to keep the fans and media at bay). Whenever someone brought up Joel's strictly celluloid existence, Greg offered the same, stubborn response: "The guy got in Princeton. I can, too."

It may be hard to imagine someone believing so strongly in the stories he read and saw on screen, but Greg really did believe Joel and the others existed -- or, at the very least, were symbols of what could exist if someone pursued a dream. He still didn't understand -- or just didn't care -- that there was a difference between what was real and what was not.

Over the next few years, Greg began pursuing the thirty goals that he called *The First Thirty*, but he fell flat on his face trying to reach them. A part of him wanted to rip up the Idea List like it never existed, but Grandma urged him not to do it.

"Don't you remember anything I ever taught you?" she huffed, "It's okay to get knocked down once in a while. If life was nothing but straight lines, it wouldn't be worth living."

It was an important lesson to remember, and the timing could not have been better -- because Greg was about to face his toughest challenge yet: *High School.*

**

Other than some occasional, garden variety teasing by upperclassmen, Greg's freshman year seemed to go okay. Nothing spectacular to report, but nothing to be too concerned about either. He studied hard, received good grades, stayed out of trouble and participated in three sports. (At his size, he didn't exactly play, but he did at least get to

suit up for the freshman 'B' teams). He also seemed to be developing
an interest in the kind of careers that would make his father proud --
having signed up for a program that helped kids learn about business
in a fun way, and getting excused from classes on occasion to spend
time observing trials at the courthouse.

On the surface, everything seemed fine -- but, in truth, beneath the
weight of Mark's expectations, Greg felt like an abysmal failure.
He knew that, deep down, his father wished he had a son who did
more than stand on the sidelines and pick mud out of his cleats. A son
who was not merely doing well in class, but who was excelling. There
was a part of Greg that wanted to live up to those lofty standards, but
increasingly, there was another part of him that wanted to run away
and escape them. And then, one day, he learned about a place that
seemed to give him a chance to do both.

Named after a quartet of nineteenth century financiers, Mortimer
Dowhill Crest Randolph High School was notably smaller than most
schools -- its entire student body could fit inside a typical freshman
class -- but it was hardly provincial. Students migrated to MDCR from
no less than ten states and six countries. And by all appearances, their
long-distance commute was well worth it. From the world-class
resumes of its instructors and the state-of-the-art technology in its
classrooms to the tennis courts and its own body of water, Mortimer
Dowhill was truly an oasis in more ways than one.

And while, admittedly, there were more than a few students on the
roster with familiar if not altogether famous names and sizable inherit-
ances awaiting them, the school was hardly some exclusive sanctuary
for the offspring of old money. Contrary to what some might assume,
MDCR had students from all kinds of backgrounds.

Cynics said the multicultural mix was nothing more than a superficial attempt to 'brighten up' the school brochure a bit. Others gave the
benefit of the doubt, saying the school's powers-that-be had a positive,
progressive view about the value of diversity. Whichever the case, the
undisputed result was an institution that consciously funneled tens of
thousands of dollars into financial aid and exchange programs to help
ensure students from different cultures and socioeconomic backgrounds were aware of the school and able to enroll there.

All in all, the MDCR literature painted quite the impressive
picture -- a sprawling campus, top facilities, learned instructors, a
diverse student body, a wide range of extracurricular activities and a

challenging curriculum -- but what caught Greg's eye most was the fact that students could live on campus, and the claim that its prized pupils matriculated into the nation's most selective universities at a demonstrably disproportionate rate. In an instant, he was *sold*.

If he could cut the mustard in class, he'd have the inside track on a slot at an Ivy League-level college, and, in the meantime, by living at school, he could get a slight reprieve from the microscope he felt his father placed him under on a daily basis.

The chance was just too tempting to pass up. The case was closed. Greg's mind was made. He was going to be a Mortimer Man.

Rose did not exactly leap to get on the bandwagon.

She said at the time, "For starters, our local high school is a highly regarded one, and plenty of its students go to great colleges. Secondly, I just don't think he'll fare too well if he's away from home. I mean, he's a teenager, and he still talks to a swing. I'm afraid the other kids might be tough on him, especially in a situation where he lives at school and doesn't have parents around to look out for him. Overall, it's a wonderful opportunity for many students, but it just isn't a good fit in *this* case."

Mark was not quite as quick to dismiss the idea. An entirely self-made man who had gone from making cold calls at thirty to making tee times at forty, he salivated over the prospect of rubbing elbows with the sophisticated set whose kids attended Mortimer Dowhill. This was, after all, the same man who chose FORBES as the middle name for his first child, and FOR D EGO as the vanity plates for his first Mercedes.

But, in the end, just as he did when contemplating any transaction, the conservative investor calculated risk versus reward -- and he decided to play this one safe.

Mark concluded, "It *was* a tempting proposition, but even if it was true that Mortimer Dowhill sent a greater proportion of students to the elite colleges, that statistic surely only applied to the upper echelon of its graduates. What happened if Greg had a little trouble adjusting to a new environment and ended up with a 'C' average? You think a Penn or Stanford is beating down the door then? And let's be honest, Greg wouldn't just have 'a little trouble' adjusting to the environment at Mortimer Dowhill. It was going to eat him alive. If we let him go, he'd be home in two weeks with his tail tucked between his legs, begging us to let him have his room back. And then where would we be?"

Greg was deeply disappointed with the decision, but his parents felt certain the feeling would pass.   It always did.

Mark explained, "One day, Greg comes across Channel 26 [the Spanish-speaking channel] and decides he wants to learn Spanish and move to Mexico. The next day, he sees a book on NASA and decides he wants to be an astronaut. You know, just about every day, he had the *world's greatest idea,* until he came up with another one the next day and forgot about the one he was rambling about the day before."

Except, apparently, in this case.

Days turned into weeks, and Greg was still waving the brochure around the dinner table and harping about all the benefits that Mortimer Dowhill had to offer.

His parents -- knowing they were clearly never going to hear the end of it if they turned their son down now and the Ivy League-level schools turned him down later -- decided to call his bluff.

Mark admitted, "I still felt it was a risk, but sometimes, a kid has to learn things the hard way.   And it was about time mine did."

And so it was, at the age of fourteen, Greg packed his bags, said goodbye to his friends in the backyard and headed out the door.

**

From the start, Mortimer Dowhill was a struggle for Greg -- and, for the most part, he had only himself to blame.

The teachers were great, and they assured him he was doing well, but he never seemed willing to believe them -- working himself into a panic over each and every assignment. The progress reports to his parents almost always said the same thing.

"Your son is a gifted student. I just wish *he* realized it."

Outside of class, he had his share of problems, too.

A scrawny kid who rarely if ever stopped talking about all the seemingly ridiculous dreams in his head, he continued to be an easy target for older kids looking for someone to tease.

To add to his troubles, he kept getting hurt.

A cut lip here, a busted nose there.

A friend joked, "The guy was a walking infirmary."

The decision to branch out beyond the tightly protected cocoon where he lived all his life meant Greg also had to confront a new kind of conflict -- one that went beyond mere bumps and bruises.

One of the school's few Jewish students, he was called anti-Semitic names for the first time. It did not happen often, but it was still enough to affect him deeply. Back home, where virtually everyone shared the same background, religion was a topic even the bullies did not touch.

To make matters worse, since Greg lived at school, there was nowhere for him to hide when the bell rang at half past three. And thanks to the luck of the draw, he had been placed in a dormitory with dozens of upperclassmen and just two freshmen -- not exactly offering him strength in numbers.

To complicate Greg's efforts to 'fit in', even though he received good grades during his freshman year, he was now repeating it. Mark and Rose had been persuaded their son would benefit from "four full years of the Mortimer Dowhill experience". Whether or not that would prove to be the case, the decision added, in the short term, to Greg's sense that he was out of place -- as he looked around at new classmates, all of whom he considered a year younger than he was.

On top of everything else, he was just plain homesick -- missing his old neighborhood and his friends in the backyard.

At times, he felt like giving up and going home, but he couldn't bear the thought of admitting his parents were right about him being unable to cut it on his own.

He *had* to stick it out.

While he maintained a brave front with his parents, Greg bared all to his Grandma -- including the part about the kids who made the anti-Semitic remarks and how much it upset him.

She was much slower to condemn them than he expected.

She said, "Some of those fellas are probably just repeating what they've heard other people say and have no idea what those words mean. So, they're probably not bad kids -- *just stupid*. You go talk to them and set them straight and if any of them will actually listen to you, then maybe they just might stop."

Greg reluctantly did as instructed -- asking the guys if he could talk to them. As he figured, they mostly ignored his request, but one was willing to listen, and after doing so, he confessed that he truly didn't realize what he was saying was so hurtful. Admittedly, the kid knew he wasn't being particularly nice, but he honestly didn't seem to know the words he was using cut any deeper than words like 'dork' or 'goof'. Now that he understood, he promised to stop.

After hearing how it turned out, Grandma nodded and said, "You know the best part? The guy who stopped, he isn't gonna just stop calling you those names. I'll bet he won't make fun of anyone else's religion, either."

It was an experience that would help shape decisions Greg would make in the years to come: Treat intolerance as *hatred* and avoid it, and you may be less likely to endure it again. Treat it as *ignorance* and address it, and others may be less likely to endure it all.

As the year progressed, the circumstances at school improved.

This was Greg's first significant exposure to people of other races and backgrounds, and over the course of six months, he found that the benefits of having so many diverse classmates were well worth the discomfort caused by an isolated one or two of them.

And, in a sense, even those isolated cases had a silver lining. Since he lived at school, Greg no longer could run to his parents or retreat to the safe confines of his backyard every time things didn't go his way. He had been sheltered and coddled most of his life, but now he had to start learning to deal with the people or the problems in his path.

In short, he had to start to grow up.

He was doing well academically, too. Despite his early self-doubts, he had continued to work hard and was ranked number one in the entire class (to the simultaneous shock and joy of his father).

Away from the textbooks, Greg had pursued his interest in writing through the school paper and its literary magazine. His love of sports led him to join the cross country and basketball teams. He was even elected by his peers to student government.

Rose concluded, "He had surpassed every possible expectation we had for him. It truly seemed like nothing could go wrong."

Except that, inevitably, something always did.

In the spring, despite being just a freshman, Greg impressed the coaches and earned a spot on the Varsity baseball squad.

Given Greg's youth and his frail frame, some questioned the decision, but on the very first pitch in his very first at-bat in his very first game, he knocked the ball all the way to the lake.

As he trotted around the bases, his head started to swell with vindication, but the joy did not last long. X-rays confirmed that in the process of shattering the ball, Greg also shattered his thumb -- an injury that sidelined him for the rest of the season.

Working tirelessly to reach a goal and prove people wrong, only to come crashing to the ground just as he was starting to celebrate his success -- it would be a recurring theme throughout Greg's life.

In fact, the same scenario repeated itself just a few months later.

In the summer, after his thumb healed, Greg got his first job (as a busboy) and worked six days a week to earn enough money to buy a car (his father agreed to match one dollar for every dollar he earned).

In the fall, when he turned sixteen, Greg got his license and started showing off his brand new, shiny black car all over town. But less than two days later, he got distracted, ended up in a horrible accident and the front of his beloved new car went up in flames.

The crash was not the only off-campus setback during Greg's second year at Mortimer Dowhill Crest Randolph High School. One weekend, while he was off-campus, he found himself in a neighborhood where he'd never been and was beat up by what could best be described as a gang of thugs.

He recalled, "They saw me talking to a girl, and apparently, she was dating one of them. And I guess, they viewed it as a form of disrespect to them when another guy had a conversation with one of their girlfriends. So they surrounded me and started beating me up."

When people back home heard Greg was attacked by a *gang* for simply speaking to someone, there were some who saw it as a chance to speak ill of an entire race of people.

One such observer, who requested anonymity, said, "It's not *politically correct* for me to say this, but what happened to Greg, it proved my point. Black people are just so damn violent."

Such remarks upset Greg almost as much as the incident itself.

Without a doubt, racially-charged issues can be very complex, but as far as he was concerned, this one was straightforward. How can the actions of a few isolated people tell you something about other people just because they happen to have the same color skin?

As Greg told one friend, "If a guy with dark hair does something bad, it doesn't mean all guys with dark hair are bad. So if it's a guy with dark skin, why would it be any different?"

Simplistic as such logic might be, Greg had a valid point.

More importantly, he also knew there was a larger point to be made. For there was one not-so-small detail he had not yet shared with those making the remarks he found so offensive -- a fact that made their ignorance that much more ironic. A fact about which they'd never even inquired before making their remarks.

The people who beat him up were not even black.

**

In the weeks that followed, one positive thing did come out of the incident. Greg *finally* started going to the gym.

His father could not have been happier.

In the past, humiliated by the sight of his only son being pushed around like a leaf caught in a crosswind, Mark had repeatedly urged Greg to start lifting weights. At one point, he even offered him cold, hard cash as an incentive.

Despite going to such lengths, Mark insisted, "It had nothing to do with his body per se. He was still my son, no matter what he looked like. It was just a case of self-esteem. I knew from experience if he'd just give weightlifting a try, it would help his confidence ten-fold."

For his part, Greg always did want to get bigger, but he was *so* puny that he had been afraid that he'd get laughed out of the weight room if he ever dared step inside.

After getting beat up, though, he no longer cared about the kind of reception he received. This was about self-defense. He *needed* to get bigger in case he ever had to protect himself.

As it turned out, once Greg did go to the health club, nobody there laughed at all. In fact, most of the big guys went out of their way to help him. They taught him how to use the weights and offered words of encouragement, too. One of the guys even sat him down, outlined the proper diet and explained how weightlifting meant nothing if you don't eat right, too (a lecture that once and for all spurred the finicky eater to taste chicken, fish and other foods).

When Greg admitted he was surprised by how nicely they treated a skinny kid just getting started, one of the bodybuilders patted him on the back and said, "We all started somewhere."

Before long, the health club unexpectedly joined the theater, the library and the yard on the list of places where he felt most at ease.

Greg was excited to have a new circle of friends from the gym, but he still couldn't stop thinking of the assault that led him there. From his perspective, it was another example that proved he had to over-come more setbacks than most -- that his life just wasn't *fair.*

Mark had mixed emotions about the situation. He certainly didn't like to see his son beaten up, but he took it as a personal insult when his pampered boy complained about his 'tough' life.

Mark said, "Sure, Greg faced setbacks, but we all do. There were kids whose lives were a thousand times tougher than his. I provided a good life for him, and I felt it was about time he realized that. That's why I introduced him to Kahzti."

If *Ernest Kahztinrets Universe* doesn't seem like a typical name, that's because, well, it's not.

Then again, Ernest (Kahzti to friends) was not a typical person.

As a boy, Kahzti grew up in a dangerous part of Southeast Asia. When he was ten, his parents snuck him onto a boat and, they hoped, on a voyage to a better life.

Somehow, some way, he eventually made it to the United States -- a teenager in a foreign land.

Soon after arriving, the young man rechristened himself in a not-so-successful effort to blend in. He chose *Ernest* as his first name -- in deference to the legendary author whose books he'd been reading to learn English. He adopted *Universe* as his last name because that's what he had seen on his globetrotting journey to America. As for the middle name, *Kahztinrets* -- it was a tribute to the landlord who had provided him a room -- Stan Kahztinrets.

And so there he was, a kid with a truly one-of-a-kind name, in an anything-but-ordinary situation. He was on his own and far from home -- no family, no friends, he didn't know the language and lived alone in a small, windowless apartment.

Yet, despite all those hurdles, Kazhti somehow managed to scrape up enough money to get by, survive the loneliness, adapt to a new culture, enroll in high school, learn English *and* graduate school ranked up at the top of his class.

Mark heard about Kahzti and had such respect for him that he quietly cut a check to help pay for the young man to go to college.

And now, Mark hoped that Kahzti would repay the gift by giving Greg a check -- *a reality check.*

The idea worked.

After meeting the soft-spoken, humble young man and hearing about his struggles, Greg knew he had no business complaining about the supposed 'obstacles' in his own life.

Greg returned to Mortimer Dowhill in the fall more determined than ever. And by year's end, in and out of class, he was *thriving*.

He was an appointed Student Leader, a Varsity athlete, an editor for the school paper and Editor-in-Chief of the literary magazine. In his free time, he lifted weights and coached a Little League baseball team. And other than Art (as much as he wished otherwise, he still couldn't draw well), his GPA had remained nearly perfect.

In his mind, the Ivy's had gone from a fantasy to a certainty, but the lessons of the past few summers remained with him. So, instead of slacking off, Greg swore he would stay focused and work even harder -- using his final year of high school as a chance to test himself and try new things he had never done before.

Among the challenges he tackled was Varsity football.

After drinking all those shakes with the weight-gain powder, spending all those hours in the gym and finally eating regular foods, Greg had filled out his six foot frame. And now that he was grown, the boy who once ran around the yard wearing a helmet wanted to finally play football *for real.*

So, a few weeks before his senior year, to get ready for the upcoming season, Greg took an all-day bus ride to attend a four day football camp with hundreds of other players from dozens of other high schools around the country.

On the field, he proved to be a quick study -- named one of the camp's all-stars during closing ceremonies. Off the field, he made a new friend. A kid named Bailey.   On the surface, the two seemed different, but that's all most of their differences were -- *superficial.*

Despite their different races and backgrounds, and growing up in very different towns, they actually had a lot in common. The two hit it off right away and stayed in touch even after camp ended. In fact, Bailey was the only other player in the entire camp with whom Greg exchanged phone numbers. It seemed to be the beginning of a genuine (albeit long-distance) friendship.

For Greg, the season itself got off to a great start, too. He scored a touchdown in his first game and a 90 yard TD in his second. While the team didn't ultimately come in first place, just being an integral part of it felt like a victory for a kid who used to be teased about his size.

By December, Greg was feeling on top of the world. After four and a half years of high school, he was finally just one semester shy of graduation, and his college applications had all been submitted. The way he saw it, his road to a prosperous future was set in stone.

He packed his bags for vacation, convinced that he had finally navigated his way through the rough waters of life. Little did he know, the smooth sailing was just the calm before the storm.

**

The tempest began on Greg's very first day back at school after the holidays, when a classmate delivered some terrible news. While Greg was out of town, his buddy from football camp, Bailey, was murdered.

It was the first time any person Greg knew had been shot let alone killed, and he was overwhelmed when he heard about it.

Make no mistake, it wasn't that he lost a *lifelong* friend -- the two met just seven months earlier and only spent a few days together in the interim -- but in a sense, *that* was what struck Greg most.

The fact that, while he *thought* he made a new good friend, he now realized that he really didn't know much about Bailey at all.

When they were together, Greg had simply never felt any sense of urgency to learn much about him. He just kind of assumed that was what the next sixty or seventy years were for.

His dad had taught him otherwise when he was little -- when Tug died -- but Greg obviously lost sight of that lesson over the years -- making it all the more painful to have to learn again.

If Greg knew precious little about Bailey's life, he knew even less about the young man's death. He didn't know where the tragedy took place, or how it happened. Since he had been out of town at the time, he didn't even know the exact date.

In the days that followed, despite a natural instinct to ask the questions that would help fill in those gaps, Greg made a conscious decision not to do so.

There were some who thought it was odd for him not to ask how or when or where a new friend died -- callous, even -- but Greg insisted his decision was well-intended.

He said, "I knew it was not going to bring Bailey back if I found out the details. He was gone, and nothing was going to change that. And the second thing was, whenever people asked me about Bailey, I was forced to admit I didn't really know much about him at all -- his life or his death. Every time that happened, it made me think about making more of an effort to get to know other friends before it was too late to get to know them, too."

A few weeks later, hoping it would brighten Greg's spirits a bit, Rose gave him pictures from their recent vacation. After all, the annual trip to Hawaii was always his favorite part of the year.

Every December, they stayed at the same hotel with seven or eight families. The trip was the only time of the year they all saw each other -- making it as much a reunion as it was a vacation.

At first, as Greg flipped through the stack from the most recent trip and looked at all the familiar faces, he couldn't help smiling. He really did love Hawaii.

Until, that is, he saw a photo of himself on the hotel balcony.

At the time the photo was taken, he was on the verge of tears because he had just been told he had to share a hotel room with his sister -- his mom specifically taking the picture so she could later show him how infantile an eighteen year old looks when throwing a tantrum (let alone, throwing one *on vacation*).

From where his mom was standing when she took the picture, Greg's head happened to be blocking the sun -- causing his entire face and body to be draped in darkness. His shadowy image in the photo instantly reminded him of The Silhouette Man in his old backyard.

Since the image turned out as it did, the petulant look on Greg's face was mercifully concealed. But he didn't need to see it to know that photo cast a spotlight on much more than the view from the balcony. It also captured an inescapable, uncomfortable truth: At the same time Bailey was killed, Greg was in the middle of paradise -- *and complaining.*

It was a stark contrast that prompted him to call his parents and swear that he would never complain about anything ever again.

The promise lasted about two months.

For most high school seniors, spring is that time of great anxiety when they find out if they've been accepted to the universities of their dreams. For Greg, it was a time of great *anticipation.*

Over the last five years, he'd faced one hurdle after another. And now that he had cleared them -- with the coveted Mortimer Dowhill stamp of approval on his resume no less -- his entree into Ivy League-level schools appeared to be a foregone conclusion.

As he waited for the acceptance letters to arrive, he could hardly contain his excitement about the road ahead. His old pal, Charlie, had made it to the promised land (Harvard Charlie, people started calling him) and everyone thought he was brilliant because of it. Greg assumed he would be looked at the same way once he was accepted. He was going to be *one of them.*

He boasted, "The hard work is over. I made it. The only suspense left is figuring out which one of their offers I'm going to accept."

His Grandma warned him about celebrating so prematurely, but he promised her this was one time there was nothing to worry about.

As usual, Grandma was right.

One by one, the responses from the schools began to arrive in Greg's mailbox, and they all seemed to say the same thing.

No.

In the end, Greg was rejected from every college he wanted to attend. His fast track to success had been *derailed* and he had no idea why. He'd worked so hard and achieved so much that it just did not seem possible. He called each school, desperately hoping there had been a mistake, but they insisted there'd been none. Greg felt like the world was collapsing around him -- and yet, things were about to get even worse.

After the rejections arrived, Greg went to see Avery P. Welton.

On staff since the early days of the Jimmy Carter Administration, Welton was something of an institution at Mortimer Dowhill. An Ivy League grad who'd traveled the world a few times over, he always had an adventurous tale, a pearl of wisdom or some advice (occasionally solicited, usually not) to share with students.

Some kids were intimidated by Welton's blunt demeanor, but Greg was instinctively drawn to it. In some ways, the approach reminded him of Grandma, and he eagerly sought out Welton's opinion on a regular basis. So much so, after four years, the guy had become the closest thing Greg had to a father figure (or, perhaps, more aptly put, grandfather figure) at school.

During the college application process, Greg asked Mr. Welton to write a recommendation letter. But to his surprise and dismay, his instructor actually turned him down. Welton said that he knew Greg had his heart set on the Ivy Leagues, but he didn't feel those schools were the right 'fit' for him. Simply put, he didn't think Greg had the brains to succeed at that level and was only applying there to please others, and he didn't want to do anything that would help Greg get into a university where he would inevitably fail.

Rather than ask another one of his instructors to write the letter, Greg stubbornly insisted on trying to win over Welton.

When it became clear the young man would not give in and set his sights lower, Welton finally relented and wrote the letter -- which, in turn, was sent to the schools without a student review (a fairly standard practice at that time).

Now that the universities had responded -- and all apparently agreed with Welton's initial analysis -- Greg sought him out for some kind of insight into what went wrong.

"What did you know that I didn't?" Greg asked, as he waved around a fistful of rejection letters.

Welton replied that there was no way to know with certainty what tipped the scales against him, but he noted he did have an idea what probably did it. And it was then that Welton sat him down and gave him a copy of the 'recommendation' letter.

The letter did say Greg was hard-working and succeeded at most everything he tried -- but that praise was weaved within a web of criticism and ridicule. Welton claimed Greg had poor diction, little charm and asked questions that suggested he had no idea what was going on. He mocked Greg's interest in poetry. Welton even wrote that Greg, who was being recruited by some of the colleges for sports, had a complete minimum of athletic talent.

The words would have hurt coming from anyone at any time. But to come from someone he looked up to so much? In a letter that could impact the rest of his life? Greg didn't know whether to scream or cry.

When pressed for an explanation, Welton insisted he did it for the kid's own good. When Greg applied to Ivy League-level schools over his objection, Welton said he felt compelled to take the matter into his own hands -- writing a letter of 'recommendation' actually designed to hurt Greg's chances of getting in. He said he knew Greg would be upset when he first saw the letter, but he insisted that, in the long run, he had done the kid a favor because Greg was now 'free' to enroll somewhere more suitable to his intellectual capabilities.

Harvard Charlie rushed to his old buddy's defense.

He argued, "If Greg wanted to go to a school because it impressed his father, or even if he simply liked the school colors, that's his choice. The bottom line is that he busted his [expletive] for the chance, and it wasn't this guy's place to interfere and [expletive] up that opportunity. Greg deserved a shot at getting in like the rest of us."

His parents were ready to sue.

The usually reserved Rose snapped, "We didn't pay a fortune in tuition to have our child's future sabotaged."

Grandma understood her daughter's anger, and she understood her grandson's pain, too, but she knew litigation wouldn't get him any closer to his dreams -- and curling up in a corner wouldn't, either.

She told her grandson, "How many times have I told you not to dwell on things? You gotta just get up, dust yourself off and keep going."

Greg tried his best to pick up the pieces by contacting the colleges he wanted to attend and urging them to reconsider. When none of them were willing to reverse their decision, he threw up his hands and said he just couldn't take any more.

Once again, Grandma stepped in.

"Stop your crying and find a college!" she barked.

"But all the ones I wanted to go to said no," he wailed.

"Then find one where you *don't* want to go!"

"Or else what?" he asked, in a defeated voice.

She looked him squarely in the eye and said, "Or I'll kill ya."

In the days that followed, Greg swallowed his pride and called other schools -- some he knew little about, a few he'd never even heard of -- begging them to give him a chance. Until, finally, he found a school that would take him. A school located in...*Louisiana?*

In actuality, Louisiana was a highly-rated university. And under the circumstances, Greg was very fortunate they agreed to make space for him at such a late date.

It was just that there was no convincing him of that.

He didn't care what 'experts' ranked the school in some survey. All he knew was that he never heard its name discussed around the dinner table growing up, and *that* was the standard by which he measured such things.

In the days that followed, he even went so far as to publish his own obituary in the form of a poem -- with the cause of death listed as 'Graduation'. He insisted it was merely a metaphor for the end of his innocence -- how he wished he could just go back to being a kid playing in the backyard -- but others were not so sure and became gravely concerned about his depressed state of mind.

Charlie said, "What Welton did, it didn't just *impact* Greg -- it *changed* him. And I don't just mean it changed the direction Greg's life headed. I mean it changed *him*. Forever."

And that was never more clear than on his final day on campus.

By all accounts, Graduation should have been the proudest day of Greg's life. He had left home, acclimated to a new school, navigated his way through a seemingly never-ending series of bumps and bruises (both literal and figurative), balanced a schedule packed with all kinds of sports and extracurricular activities, maintained a near-perfect GPA, and earned a degree with honors.

But, as far as he was concerned, it all meant nothing now.

An MDCR diploma was supposed to be his golden key to an Ivy League future. What good is a key if it won't open the door?

Greg was so upset he didn't even want to attend the ceremony where he was to receive it. He reluctantly broke the news to his parents. He would not be going to his own graduation.

His parents refused to entertain the idea. Members of their family had made arrangements to be at the event. And Rose had planned a post-graduation party at a posh restaurant. The Ivy League rejections upset them as well, but they'd be damned if their son's detour to Louisiana was presented in anything other than a favorable light.

"You are going to your graduation," Mark said. "And you are going to act like you are the happiest kid on the planet. Period."

Greg went to the ceremony and did his best to manufacture a smile as ordered for as long as he could. But after his name was called and he crossed the stage, it became more than he could bear. He tossed his diploma to his parents and bolted out the back of the auditorium.

By the time Mark and Rose were able to make it through the crowd and into the parking lot, Greg had already disappeared -- and he never did show up at the restaurant for the party (evidenced by the group photo that featured everybody but the guest of honor.)

His parents were furious about how he handled himself. Grandma was even angrier -- and let him know it a few days later.

She said, "All those grades you got. People won't remember that now. They'll just remember you're a brat who threw a tantrum because life threw him a little curve. And, on top of that, I didn't get the pictures I wanted with you at your graduation holding your diploma."

Greg didn't know what to say -- other than to meekly apologize and promise that he would pose for all the pictures she wanted in a few years when he graduated college.

Grandma glared at him, wagged her finger and said, "You better."

**

In the fall, Greg boarded a plane with his bags by his side and a chip on his shoulder. After what he'd just been through, part of him was happy to escape to a place where he didn't know anyone, but he had never been to Louisiana (or anywhere else in the Deep South for that matter) and had no real desire to be there now.

He also had no intention of staying too long.

Night after night, Greg stayed up late studying for his classes -- so he could get the grades he needed to "get back on track" and transfer to one of the schools where he was "supposed to go."

(While the Welton mess obviously ended Greg's tenure at MDCR on a sour note, he'd be the first to admit his high school experience had prepared him well for the academic rigors of college. At Louisiana, like any university, a student could find plenty of reasons to procrastinate if he or she wanted. But Greg had minimized the impact of such temptations with a self-imposed two hour study hall every night -- just as was standard practice at Mortimer Dowhill.)

When he wasn't studying for his own classes, Greg was helping kids at a local grade school study for theirs. He took the time to volunteer partly because he liked helping others. But, in truth, his desire to give back was not entirely altruistic. He saw it as a distraction, however temporary. Every minute spent helping those kids was a minute not spent dwelling on the detour he felt his own life had taken.

Between classes, homework, volunteering and his daily visits to the gym, Greg had packed his schedule to the hilt.

And yet, there was still one thing clearly missing. *Friends.*

While other students were getting to know each other and enjoying the freedom college brings, the Ivy League reject was acting more like a wrongly imprisoned man. He even went so far as to hang up a Martin Luther King, Jr. poster outside his door, pull his mattress into the hall and stage his own version of a sit-in -- convinced he had been denied the "constitutional right" to attend the college of his choice.

After observing Greg's demonstration from a distance, Galloway Roarke decided to walk down the hall and meet her new classmate.

Born and raised in West Texas, Galloway had a story and a point of view unlike any Greg had ever heard. She was accepted to the Ivy Leagues but chose Louisiana instead. When he asked her why, Galloway said she picked the school that was a better fit.

Greg didn't want to be rude, but this was just about the most absurd thing he ever heard and he felt like he had to say something.

Galloway listened to him politely as he rattled off reasons her decision was such an ill-advised one. When he finally paused to take a breath, she replied, "Look, just because we didn't have the same dream doesn't mean one of us is wrong. It just means our dreams were different. The Ivy Leagues *are* good schools, but so is this one. And if you opened your mind a little and gave the place a chance, you might see why so many of us wanted to come here."

It was the attitude adjustment Greg sorely needed.

One classmate observed, "After Galloway confronted him, it was like a 360 degree turnaround. Almost immediately after that, Greg began making an effort to get to know us."

Which is still not to say he blended in completely.

When it came time to take mid-semester exams, for instance, most guys -- exhausted from a long night or two of cramming -- wore a baseball cap, t-shirt, shorts and flip-flops.

Greg showed up in a suit.

The first time, it was just a case of old habits dying hard (after four years of Mortimer Dowhill's formal dress code). But after realizing the suit gave him a sense of confidence at a time when he otherwise might get rattled by nerves -- and after hearing the reaction from his teacher ("It looks like we have at least one 'A' in here," she said as he strolled into the room) -- he decided to do it for every exam.

[Funny side note: The first time he did it in Louisiana, some of his classmates teased him. After they saw his grade on the exam, a couple of them showed up in suits the next time, too.]

The hallway conversation with Galloway was just one of several events over the next few months that made Greg stop and think.

His first semester of college also was an election season, and it was certainly no ordinary one. Of the two men trying to become the next governor of Louisiana, one was an alleged racist and the other had a long history of alleged corruption.

The election brought the issues of race, ethnicity and abuse of power front and center -- and it would not be the only time.

During that same period, Native American groups around the country were gaining national attention for their protests against sports teams with Native American-based names and mascots. The teams' supporters said the names and mascots were a 'tribute' -- that the protesters were being too sensitive and politically correct -- but many Native American groups disagreed. They said the teams' names and mascots degraded their culture and history -- insisting the owners would never dare do the same thing to ethnic groups with more 'economic leverage' in the world of sports.

Native American groups voiced these feelings many times in the past, but the issue was in the spotlight like rarely before.

And then, there was the case of Rodney King and the police officers in Los Angeles. Even before the infamous verdict that triggered the riots, the incessant television replays of the videotaped beating forced much of America to confront the reality that our nation was still a racially divided one in many ways.

With all of these events taking place in a short period of time, Greg began paying more attention to the climate around him.

In the process, he observed that there didn't seem to be any tension between students of different backgrounds on campus -- everybody seemed to get along fine -- but he noticed that, in many cases, there didn't seem to be much interaction, either.

He said, "We all seemed to be *co-existing side by side* instead of *co-existing together*."

And nowhere was that more clear than it was by The Benches.

In the middle of campus, there were two sets of benches a few feet apart. Every day, hundreds of students spent time there between classes -- catching up with friends. And every day, almost without fail, the white students hung out by one set of benches. The black students hung out by the other.

The separation was completely voluntary -- it wasn't like there were signs "Whites Only" and "Blacks Only" -- but there might as well have been.

Rest assured, it was not as tense a situation as it sounded. In fact, it wasn't tense at all. The students hanging around The Benches laughed and joked, listened to music, and tossed around a football and a frisbee or two. And it wasn't that Greg thought there was anything wrong with people having friends who looked similar. (Make no mistake, he was no different than the rest. Every day, he visited The Benches and sat with the students who looked like him.) It was just that he figured everyone's lives would be much more interesting if they expanded their circle of friends. So, he couldn't understand why nobody, himself included, ever seemed to do something to bridge the gap between the two groups.

As the days passed, the questions continued to swirl around his head. How can the choices for Governor come down to a man who appears to be corrupt and one who appears to be racist? Why are so many white people shocked by the taped assault of an unarmed black man by some white cops when so many black people say the only thing that is surprising is the fact it was caught on tape? If the names and mascots based on Native American heritage really are a 'tribute' to their culture, then why aren't there teams with names like 'Blacks',

'Hispanics', and 'Jews'? Aren't they worthy of 'tributes', too? On the other hand, what if some Native Americans *aren't* offended? Does that matter? How come students seem to divide into groups when they sit by The Benches? Why doesn't anyone ever try and bridge that gap? Wouldn't they all understand each other better if someone did? And even if they were going to divide into groups, why did it always seem to be based on race?

With all of these questions running through his mind, Greg became more interested than ever in exploring issues like diversity and multiculturalism. He took courses like Civil Rights, History of Anti-Semitism, and Race & Gender. He also began writing research papers on Native American heritage and culture, the use of stereotypes by the media, and the role of race in the justice system.

In the process, his own sense of being "denied a constitutional right" was put back into proper perspective, and the image of Martin Luther King, Jr. outside his door began to take on a whole new meaning. Instead of seeing the poster as a symbol of what he *personally* endured, Greg began to see it as a symbol of what one man could do to address what *others* endure. A symbol of what one man could do to bring people of different races and backgrounds together. What one man could do to build a bridge where none exists.

And the more he contemplated that, the more he began to think about what *he* could do to help further that idea. What could he do to build a bridge between The Benches? What could he do, in his own small way, to bring people of different races, cultures and backgrounds together?

And it was right then and there, sitting on a mattress in the heart of Louisiana, with the poster of Dr. King looking over his shoulder, that a no-shoe-wearing, cereal-straight-out-of-the-box-eating, milkshake-drinking, Ivy League reject began to hatch a *Dream* of his own.

It would be years until Greg pursued his *Dream* -- or revealed what it was, or even that he had one. In the meantime, he became more and more involved in the community.

He joined the campus group focused on service and successfully ran for class office. He also began recruiting his classmates to come with him to the grade school where he volunteered.

Most were happy to help, but some were reluctant.

A guy from Mississippi named Earl recalled, "I knew it'd be nice to do, but being honest, I was away from home, no parents watching over me, and when I got free time, I wanted to do something fun."

Despite Earl's disinterest, Greg stayed on his case, until the young man from Biloxi finally agreed to go one time. As it turned out, Earl actually enjoyed it and ended up going back every couple weeks or so. In the weeks that followed, Earl even began asking *his* friends to come volunteer, too. And just like that, the ripple effect had begun. Students who Greg didn't even know approached him about his 'program' and asked how they could take part in it.

It did not take long for school administrators to take notice of Greg's efforts. When it was announced a search had begun for a new Dean, he was one of two students asked to serve on the Committee.

It was quite a statement about how quickly things had evolved. A kid who had not even formally applied to the school through the traditional process was now being asked -- just a few months later -- to share his thoughts on the academic leaders twice his age who were seeking to run the place.

It was also deeply ironic. After all the rejections Greg endured as a high school senior, he was now in a position to subject others to a similar fate. He became especially excited when he discovered one of the candidates had graduated from the Ivy Leagues years earlier.

Greg confessed, "Before I even met the guy, I made up my mind that I was going to vote for someone else."

At least, that was the plan. After meeting the candidates, Greg felt Mr. Ivy League was the best one for the job. And, in the end, he didn't have the heart to mess with a qualified person's future just because someone messed with his. (Not that it would have mattered. The man turned out to be the hands-down favorite and was selected as the new Dean shortly thereafter.)

Emboldened by his freshman experience, Greg spent his summer delving even deeper into service -- accepting an invitation to intern for a U.S. Senator on Capitol Hill.

In stark contrast to the race for governor, the internship exposed Greg to the good side of politics. Stereotypes about special interests and bureaucratic quagmires to the contrary, he found the Senator and his staff to be hard-working and genuinely devoted to their constituents' concerns.

Not surprisingly, Greg's stint in D.C. was also marked by a number of memorable adventures. On one occasion, he went to the White House to visit with a staffer he'd met -- and somehow soon found himself at a podium reading off announcements to military officials.

Another time, while attending the Presidential Convention, Greg was asked to help out by going on stage and checking the microphone. He did as asked, except that, instead of saying 'Testing 1-2-3', he began delivering a full-fledged speech, accepting the party's nomination, and pledging to do his very best to "lead the nation onward and upward into the 21st century."

A staffer later laughed, "This was going on in the morning before the Convention started, so the kid was giving his 'acceptance speech' to a sound check guy and about 15,000 empty seats."

The internship motivated Greg to expand his civic efforts when he returned to college in the fall. Instead of just volunteering in the community, he began "bringing the community to campus" as well -- arranging for local kids to visit the university, attend events on campus and meet his classmates and professors.

"It's just like with The Benches," Greg told Galloway when asked about the impetus for his new idea. "One group is here. Another is there, but nobody ever seems to walk over and see what's on the other side. Here are these kids, and people tell them why college is so great and here's a great university across the street just a few minutes away. Why not just walk them over here, and let them see why it's so great with their own two eyes?"

The idea was warmly received -- even the Dean volunteered his time to visit with the kids when they came to campus.

By the end of his sophomore year, Greg had come a long way.

His efforts to encourage others to volunteer had led the Dean to appoint him Chairman of Community Service for the entire college.

Academically, he had excelled -- an A in every course. A feat made even more impressive when considering his course load.

Rose recalled, "As part of his never-ending effort to prove Welton wrong, he stubbornly signed up for classes in all kinds of different majors, just to make things even more challenging than need be."

Socially, considering his rocky start, he'd come a long way. He'd made a conscious effort to do a better job of trying to get to know his classmates, and many of them had reciprocated in kind. In fact, he'd been elected twice to class office by his peers and invited to join a fraternity.

His decision to accept the latter offer surprised many. Given the stereotypes about frats, it hardly seemed to be the place you'd expect to find a textbook-toting kid who didn't like to drink and usually kept to himself. But in this case, the stereotypes just were not true.

The fraternity Greg joined in Louisiana *did* host some parties, but its members were hardly one-dimensional. They studied for classes and did their share of philanthropy, too. And while the guys did have a lot in common, they were hardly identical. Some liked sports, others liked politics. Some were from New York, others were from Georgia. Some were preparing to be lawyers, others were focused on physics.

(Still, as much as they all walked to the beat of their own drum, Greg clearly was listening to an altogether different song. When he was given his own paddle, per fraternity tradition, he couldn't resist the urge to etch a thunder bolt and the word *'Wonderboy'* along the side -- a tribute to Roy Hobbs, who did the same to the bat he hand-crafted out of a fallen tree in *The Natural.*)

Of all the lessons Greg learned from being in the fraternity, the one he probably needed most was taught to him by Deric.

Nicknamed 'Red Juice' (and 'Red' and 'Juice' and 'RJ' and a never-ending list of other derivations) for his cranberry-colored hair, Deric was just about the funniest person Greg ever met. At least, that's what Greg thought until he started to realize that Red's one-liners always seemed to be about *him*. Still as sensitive as ever, he angrily demanded his new fraternity brother stop making fun of him.

"You gotta lighten up," the easy-going Southerner said with a laugh. "I'm not making fun of you. I'm just cracking jokes."

Greg said he wasn't so sure he understood the difference.

Red explained, "Nobody else is here but us when I tell them."

It was true. In others' presence, Red never made fun of his friends.

As much as he would've never dreamed it possible when he first stepped off that plane in Louisiana two years earlier, Greg had come to like the university. His classmates, the courses, the teachers, the Dean, the fraternity, the extracurricular activities. And, in general, he'd come to appreciate the region. The food, the music, the diversity, the down-home hospitality (and the Southern belles didn't hurt, either).

The Deep South was a long way from the life he knew growing up in the North Shore, but to be clear, Greg didn't merely *come to accept* where life had taken him. He *liked* it.

They even had good milkshakes in Louisiana.

In a word, he was *content*.

As the days passed, thoughts of the Ivy Leagues faded further and further from Greg's mind, and he began echoing Galloway's belief that The Big Easy was not so easy after all -- that it meant just as much to succeed in Louisiana as it meant to be a success elsewhere.

So much so, he couldn't resist thumbing his nose at good, old Mr. Welton just one time. Halfway through his sophomore year, Greg sent his former instructor a letter, boasting of all the ways he was proving the man wrong.

He expected a quick reply -- a humble "I'm sorry" from a guy who underestimated his potential -- but no response ever came.

Not an admission of guilt for doubting Greg's ability. Not an apology for overstepping his bounds and altering a student's future. Not a letter commending Greg's achievements in Louisiana. Not an invitation to sit down face-to-face and bury the hatchet. Nothing.

In all likelihood, the 'slight' was the result of ego -- whether it was the mentor's (unwilling to apologize to someone less than half his age), or the pupil's (sending a self-righteous 'I told you so' letter that offered little in the way of an olive branch) -- but Greg thought there was much more to it. He believed Welton's silence was the man's way of saying he was still unimpressed and unconvinced.

Before long, that familiar thought crept back into Greg's mind and lingered there for days: For all the things Louisiana was, there was one thing it wasn't and never would be.

The Ivy Leagues.

And more than anything, he wanted to make Welton eat his words.

And, so, just like that, despite knowing his detour to Louisiana had actually turned out to be an unexpected blessing, despite the fact he still had never visited the campuses of Cornell or Berkeley or the others he had in mind (or even done any research to determine which if any of them would be a good fit), Greg decided to stick with his original plan and transfer in the fall.

The Dean insisted he was making a *huge* mistake. He said that Greg was doing so well in Louisiana that he should really think twice before giving it up just to start over at some other school.

"It's not *some other school*," Greg railed. "It's *the Ivy Leagues*."

The Dean held firm, offering him advice that echoed the words of Galloway two years earlier.

"The Ivy's *are* great schools. Personally, I enjoyed it there. But this is a great school, too, and you of all people should know that by now. You're flourishing here, and you'd be crazy to give that up."

The Dean's advice fell on deaf ears.

"I've made up my mind," Greg said emphatically.

And it seemed like nothing was going to change it.

Until, that is, the Dean brought up the idea of Junior Year Abroad -- the program that lets co-eds study in another country.

He said, "It'd give you a change of scenery and a new challenge, and then, right around the time you realize how much you miss us here in Louisiana, it'll be time to come back for your senior year."

Other than a short trip when he was a boy, Greg had never crossed the ocean and was intrigued by the idea of going overseas.

"What do the students study when they're in the program?" he asked, feigning indifference.

The Dean explained that was the best part. Depending on where a student chose to go, there was a wide range of subjects he or she could study -- from how to speak another language to how to make movies.

Greg had already learned another language (Spanish), but the moment he heard those four magic words -- *how to make movies* -- he lit up like a Christmas tree. In an instant, he scrapped the plan that had just seemed so set in stone. Instead of seeking a transfer to the Ivy Leagues, he decided he would spend his junior year in Europe learning about filmmaking and then come back to Louisiana to wrap up college and get his degree.

His mom later said, "It was like when he was little. Every day, a different idea. One day, he says he's happy in Louisiana. The next day, he's going to apply for a transfer to the Ivy Leagues. Day after that, he's going to England. After all these years, I was no longer surprised, but it was still stressful for a parent."

When summer arrived, Greg went home with a sense of excitement about the road ahead and the trip to Europe in the fall. But as always, with time on his hands, his mind began to wander. So, as the summer wound down, second thoughts started tiptoeing into his head. Was the trip abroad about learning to make films? Or was it just a way to avoid finding out if he actually could cut it in the Ivy Leagues?

His mother urged him to let those doubts go -- to focus on the promising future instead of the painful past.

She said, "What's done is done, no point looking back now."

Her words were spoken with compassion, but in the heat of the moment, Greg became convinced that what she was *really* trying to say was she didn't think he was smart enough for the Ivy Leagues.

He stormed out of the house and went for a drive to calm down. He intended to go see his Grandma, but as always, he got distracted and lost. A left turn here, a u-turn there, a stop sign here, and before Greg knew it, he suddenly found himself driving right through the campus of Vernon Froehmann Whitfield University.

Since it wasn't on the East Coast, VFWU was not part of the Ivy Leagues, but it might as well have been. By all accounts, it was one of the most highly regarded universities in the nation (and of, perhaps, even more specific relevance, it was viewed as an 'elite' school by Mark, Rose and the others who lived in their community).

As Greg sat in his car and watched the students pass, smiling and happy, wearing t-shirts and shorts and hats with the school's name and colors, he became consumed with jealousy. He knew the students walking down the sidewalk were probably much brighter than he was, but he refused to believe they were *better*. In his heart, Greg knew he would have outworked them all if only he'd been given the chance.

He knew he should stop dwelling on it, but now that he was this close, he just could not walk away. He had to know, if only for a few seconds, what it was like to be *one of them.*

He got out of his car and slipped into the crowd of students. He only meant to walk a couple feet, but with each step, he became more convinced he fit in, and it became harder to walk away. He *was* one of them. And once and for all, he was going to prove it.

His heart racing, his confidence growing with every step, he veered off the sidewalk, into a school office and declared he was there to enroll.

"Young man," said the woman behind the desk, after it became clear Greg was serious, "*this* is Vernon Froehmann Whitfield University. You cannot show up one day and get in the next."

"Well, that's good," Greg shot back, "because I don't plan on starting *tomorrow*. I'm ready to start *today*."

When Greg got home a few hours later, Rose was in the kitchen.

"Your Grandma says you never showed up. Where have you been all day?"

"Vernon Froehmann Whitfield University," he said.

"Visiting friends?" she asked.

"No," he said, with tears in his eyes. "I go there now."

**

As impossible as it seemed, Greg had shown up unannounced at one of the top-ranked universities in the country, spontaneously decided he wanted to go there and literally talked his way in.

Greg's parents were not sure what to think.

Rose concluded, "The whole thing was *crazy*. That was the only word to describe it. The kid goes for a drive, gets lost, and next thing you know, life is turned upside down. There was a room waiting for him in England."

Mark said, "On the one hand, it was all so sudden and not-well-thought-out, and that made me a little uneasy. On the other hand, how upset could I be? He'd just talked his way into Froehmann Whitfield."

Harvard Charlie was fascinated by the turn of events.

He said, "Forget that it was crazy that he did it. The fact that he convinced the school to *let him* do it -- now *that* was crazy. It's one thing to convince people to donate a dime for every book you read. I mean, this was *Vernon Froehmann Whitfield University*. You can't just walk in off the street and talk your way into a school like that. It just doesn't happen."

Except that it did.

When pressed for details on how he pulled off such a feat, Greg played coy, shrugged his shoulders and said, "I asked nicely" -- but, in fact, as you might guess, there was much more to it than that.

Apparently, Greg had convinced school officials this was an emergency and struck something of a deal. As the story goes, the school had agreed to let him attend classes for one year as a 'special' student. He could sign up for classes just like the 'real' students, and he would get grades just like the 'real' students. If he did well, he could stay, and retroactively, they'd go back and give credit toward a VFWU degree for the courses he'd taken -- as if he had been a 'real' student all along. If he didn't do well, he'd have to leave -- with no credit given for the courses taken, and no refund, either.

For the school, there really was nothing to lose.

For Greg, on the other hand, his entire future was at risk -- but, in his mind, it was a gamble worth taking. A gamble he *had* to take.

He wanted to prove he never should've been rejected from all those schools three years earlier. He wanted to prove Welton was wrong. He wanted to prove, once and for all, he was good enough to be *one of them*. And, the way he saw it, if succeeding far away in Louisiana wasn't enough, this was his shot to do it back home.

Vernon Froehmann Whitfield University seemed to have everything a student could want -- brilliant professors, interesting courses, talented classmates, a beautiful campus -- but for Greg, the opportunity to go there came at a very steep price.

Just as his old Dean warned, he was like a freshman all over again. In the blink of an eye, Greg had gone from being a big fish to feeling hopelessly lost at sea. Just finding his way to class was a challenge, never mind the assignments already piling up on his lap.

And it wasn't just the workload weighing him down.

Within days of setting foot on campus, Greg began to butt heads with the people in charge.

Rose recalled, "Shortly after he started classes, he requested a meeting with a school official and was told he would have to make an appointment, and he wasn't too happy about that."

"The lady told me to take a number," he muttered angrily, at the time, "They would *never* say that to a real student!"

In fairness to the school official, Greg *wasn't* a real student. And even if he was, it was clearly unreasonable to expect someone overseeing thousands of students to meet with one at the drop of a hat, but in his defense, that level of access was all he had ever known.

Mortimer Dowhill was a small high school with an 'open door policy' that gave students the chance to talk directly with school officials with little else required besides a knock when they entered. Louisiana was obviously bigger, but Greg served in several student leadership positions so the Dean and other administrators always made time for him if it was important.

When he didn't receive the same treatment at Froehmann Whitfield, he insisted it was *personal* -- that it had to do with his 'Special Student' status.

Greg didn't fare too well off campus, either.

He got a weekend job delivering food, but not surprisingly, he kept getting distracted and lost. He was let go after just one night.

The chip on Greg's shoulder began to grow bigger and bigger by the day. Instead of putting up the poster of Dr. King in his new room, he literally put up a giant poster of a snarling pitbull.

As the weeks passed, Greg was angry, lonely and overwhelmed, but he refused to quit. Just as in Louisiana, he retreated to the gym to work out his stress and volunteered at a local grade school in the community to distract himself.

Of course, nothing put Greg in a better mood than his Grandma. And now that he was going to college just ten minutes down the road from her apartment, he was able to see her in person on a more regular basis -- cementing the bond that was already the strongest one he had.

But that was it.

Exercising, volunteering and visiting Grandma. Other than an occasional date or two, virtually every other waking minute was spent going to class or studying for one -- whatever it took to get his work done. And, in the end, that tunnel vision paid off. Despite the odds against a guy showing up out of nowhere, adjusting to a new environment and acing all his classes, that's exactly what Greg did.

With an A in every course, he had passed the test with flying colors and earned the right to stay at VFWU. And yet, for the most ironic of reasons, he planned on walking away.

Greg missed friends like Galloway and fraternity brothers like Red, to whom he'd never properly said goodbye. He missed his old professors and the Dean. He missed the local school where he volunteered. Not to mention, the culture, music, food and hospitality.

In short, for all the great things Vernon Froehmann Whitfield University was, there was one thing missing -- one thing it wasn't and never would be. *Louisiana.*

And so it was that he placed a call to the Dean. A good man with the kind of understanding heart that comes with working with young people for many years, he never gave Greg an 'I-told-you-so' lecture -- just a 'we'll-be-glad-to-have-you-back' pep talk.

Not surprisingly, Mark and Rose were beside themselves.

His mom said, "He had risked everything...for nothing."

If Greg's parents were upset about the twists and turns, they nearly threw up from motion sickness after what happened next.

At some point during the summer, their son decided he was going to stay at VFWU after all. He claimed he'd had a "change of heart."

A change in heart *rate* might have been a better way to put it.

Despite now being halfway through college, Greg had never had a girlfriend for more than a month. It was a combination of several things. Up until his junior or senior year of high school, girls rarely gave him a second look -- so he had no girlfriends. Once he started working out, things changed dramatically. At that point, it was partly just a case of a guy trying to 'make up for lost time' -- wanting to date around and see what he had been missing out on -- and partly that he had such little experience that he was an awkward, stumbling, bumbling mess, even if he now looked confident on the outside.

Whatever the reason, the result was a never-ending string of first dates, brief flings and short acquaintances.

That unimpressive track record notwithstanding, he still hoped -- and expected -- to cross paths with The One some day.

And then, one summer afternoon, it happened.

The One crossed Greg's path. Literally.

As the story goes...he was walking down the sidewalk with a friend, drinking -- what else? -- a protein milkshake, when he saw a complete stranger walking in his direction. The moment Greg saw her, he dropped the shake and said, "That's my future wife."

As vanilla splattered in every direction, Greg didn't even flinch. His body was frozen, his gaze transfixed -- concerned that she might disappear if he looked away for even one single, split second.

He wanted to say so many things to her -- about their future wedding and future home and future children -- but he was so excited he found it impossible to speak. In the end, as The One strode by him -- a moment that felt like it was occurring in slow motion -- all Greg managed to do was to point down at the shake puddle and say, "Watch your step."

Without breaking her stride, she glanced down, shifted her path one step to the right, winked, said "Thanks", and kept walking.

The conversation consisted of four words and lasted less than three seconds. But for Greg, it was enough. So much so, he decided on the spot to change his plans for the coming school year.

Charlie said, "I'd like to reiterate, in case you missed it, Greg was giving up his plan to move back to Louisiana to pursue a potential relationship with a woman he didn't actually *know*. He didn't know her number, or even her name. In fact, for all he knew, she didn't even live in the area. Maybe she was just visiting for the day, never to return. And even if, by some miracle, he did run into her again, what's to say she wasn't already with someone? It was insane."

Charlie may have been right, but Greg did not care. He was convinced this was The One he was meant to marry. And so, despite how much he missed Louisiana and the people there, he decided he was going to stay where he was, in the hope that he and his 'future wife' would cross paths again and start building their life together.

Even after Greg became a 'real' student at Froehmann Whitfield, he didn't seem to fit in with his peers. Some went out of their way to try and include him in their plans, but he rarely accepted the invitations. When the other students went to eat, he stayed home to study. When they went to basketball games, he studied. When they went to parties, he studied. It was as if he was still more interested in *proving* he should be one of them than actually *being* one of them.

To make matters worse, Greg actually did run into his 'future wife' again, and the two even dated for a while -- only convincing him further that she really was The One -- but the seemingly predestined relationship fizzled out after a few weeks, just like all his others.

Charlie joked, "Gee, imagine that. I mean, their first meeting was so *meaningful*. A four word conversation about spilled milkshakes. And it turned out they weren't lifelong soulmates. Go figure."

Greg was beyond miserable about the turn of events. He had thrown away a chance to get back what he already loved (Louisiana) for a woman he thought he would. Now, he had neither and was stuck somewhere he didn't want to be. To top it off, as Greg's second year at VFWU got underway, he continued to clash with school officials.

Charlie recalled, "There were a whole list of things they did that upset him -- like when he felt they were messing with his credits."

Even though Greg received an A in every course in Louisiana, the decision-makers at Froehmann Whitfield ruled that some of his credits would not carry over -- meaning he would have to take a fifth year of college courses. It may well have been perfectly routine, but when it happened to Greg, he again became convinced he was being singled out. He started firing off angry letters demanding administrators leave him alone.

The officials at VFWU were not the only authority figures in town who Greg felt were crowding his space. More than once, as he made his way back toward campus from the local public library, a police officer would stop him and tell him to head the other direction.

It was a classic case of guilt by assumption and association. Greg didn't sport the school colors so many of his classmates favored -- so the officers did not realize he was an undergrad. And he hung out at the public library with young men who were known to have criminal backgrounds -- so, put two and two together, and the cops apparently figured, he was trouble, too.

What the officers didn't know was the young men in question were actually *former* gang members hoping to get their high school equivalency degrees and Greg was just their volunteer tutor.

In fairness, the mistaken identity only happened a couple times, the officers were not looking to bother anyone as much they were trying to protect the local co-eds, and, by all accounts, they always treated Greg nicely once he cleared up the matter. But the brief encounters left a lasting mark.

The experience intensified his belief that no matter how good his grades, he would never be perceived as a *real* member of the Froehmann Whitfield community. On a broader level, it reinforced his belief that any accurate measurement of a person's character requires more than a first impression. The young men he tutored still may have *looked* like stereotypical gang members -- the style of dress, the tattoos. But these guys sincerely seemed to be trying to turn the page, one small step at a time -- starting with the weekly visits to the library. And the only way to know that would be to get to know them.

As the weeks passed and the conflicts on and off campus continued, Greg spent even more time in the weight room working out his frustration -- and before long, it started to show. By the time his fifth year of college rolled around (an extra year to make up those credits), the skinny boy afraid of the neighbor's snarling dog had transformed into a young man bench-pressing 300 pounds. Instead of ribs poking out of his sides, veins now bulged out of his arms.

A college neighbor named Kim laughed, "He'd stand in the mirror and flex over and over, but it wasn't in an I'm-so-tough kind of way. It was more of a where-did-these-muscles-come-from kind of way. In all the time I'd known him, I'd never seen him so happy."

Just like always, though, his joy was short-lived.

It was only a matter of time until skeptics rained on his parade -- howling about the steroids he *surely* must have taken to change his physique in such dramatic fashion.

He knew he should just shrug off the remarks.

While it might've *seemed* like Greg exploded into a whole new person, he still only weighed 180 pounds. It was not as if he'd turned into a middle linebacker. And there was really nothing sudden about it. If anything, when you factored in his workout regimen (an hour or two a day, six days a week), his newly expanded diet (chicken, fish, and anything else healthy he could get his hands on), his dedication (he'd now been lifting weights for over seven years), and genetics (his father was six foot three, nearly 230 pounds), not to mention, all those protein shakes, Greg's transformation was probably more inevitable than it was unbelieveable.

Not surprisingly, the guys at the gym were as supportive and encouraging as ever. Still, the rumors upset him to no end.

"How can people say stuff about me when they don't know me? I don't even know what steroids look like, let alone how to get them."

Grandma offered him little sympathy.

"Quit whining, shut up and listen. *You* know how hard you work, and that's what matters. If anyone else hassles you, just tell them you'd love to respond but you can't because you gotta save your breath so you can go to the gym and exercise some more."

Her advice helped. He resumed his workouts, as focused as ever, and did his best to just ignore those who questioned him.

Greg's success in the weight room was outmatched only by what he achieved in the classroom. Five years after being told he wasn't good enough for the Ivy Leagues, and three years after walking into Froehmann Whitfield University right off the street, Greg somehow managed to graduate with Highest Distinction -- a title bestowed upon the select few who finished at the top of the class.

In all, he completed college with 37 A's and a B.

He had every right to feel proud of what he accomplished.

Despite all the detours and obstacles, Greg just kept chugging along, until he got exactly where he always dreamed he would be -- the cream of the crop at a school he felt people back home perceived as 'Ivy League level'.

And yet, at what should've been his crowning moment, all Greg felt was *regret*. Having been at Froehmann Whitfield for three years, he understood why so many students thought it was a great university and wanted to go there -- but *he* had gone there for the wrong reason...and he knew it.

For more than four years, he insisted that 'recommendation' letter could not define who he was or what he could achieve. And yet, he gave up what he loved in Louisiana -- not to mention, the plan to study film in Europe -- for the chance to get a diploma with a name on it that he thought would impress people more. (A decision made all the more painfully ironic as he finally came to realize that most people were impressed by Louisiana's reputation in the first place.)

The kid who insisted he should not be measured by a piece of paper sacrificed everything for...*a piece of paper*. And now, that's all his diploma seemed like. Instead of symbolizing the success he achieved at Froehmann Whitfield, it served only as a painful reminder of what he foolishly sacrificed (and endured) to be there.

He felt *so* strongly about it that he said he never wanted to see the diploma a single time and said he would not even attend the graduation ceremony where the degrees were handed out.

His Grandma was *beyond* furious.

First and foremost, she believed Commencement was an essential part of college -- tantamount to crossing the finish line in a marathon.

On a more personal level, Grandma had flown all around the country to see the other three grandkids graduate -- and had the pictures to prove it. [Greg's cousins were older and had gotten their degrees a few years earlier. And due to Greg's extra year of high school and extra year of college, his younger sister, Michelle, had passed him by and already gotten her degree as well].

After flying around the country to see the other grandkids graduate, she'd be damned if the one going to school ten minutes from her apartment was the only one she didn't get the chance to watch go through this rite of passage.

And, of course, there was The Promise.

Grandma may have been getting older, but her memory still worked just fine. The very specific pledge Greg made about attending his college graduation was still fresh in her mind -- and she was more than happy to remind him about it.

"I know," he said softly, "but I just can't do it."

Grandma wagged her finger in his face and bellowed, "You're going to that ceremony, you're crossing that stage, and you're gonna smile in some pictures!"

Despite how strongly his Grandma felt, Greg defied her orders -- offering her little more than another empty promise that somehow, some day, he'd get her a picture of him in a cap and gown.

His parents, surprisingly enough, didn't seem too upset.

Rose explained, "We were disappointed that we wouldn't get to see him cross the stage. But frankly, we were so pleased with his grades that we didn't want to belabor the issue if he really felt that strongly about skipping the ceremony."

Indeed, they had every reason to be in a flexible mood. They knew, despite all the bumps in the road, Greg was 'back on track'.

Mark boasted, "As one of Froehmann Whitfield University's top graduates, he could have his pick where to go next -- whether it was an elite law school or a high-paying corporate job, whichever his goofy, little, wandering heart desired."

And it was right about then when Mark and Rose found out their son and his 'goofy, little, wandering' heart no longer desired either.

Despite being branded with a business mogul's name, despite twenty-plus years of high expectations, despite his degree and the honors that came with it, Greg decided he would not be interviewing with any company for any position -- and he wouldn't be applying to any law school, either.

He told his parents that his up-and-down road -- combined with five years worth of racially and culturally charged events around the nation -- from the Rodney King case when he started college to the O.J. Simpson trial as he was finishing it -- caused him to reconsider his future, his purpose and what it meant to be a success.

[Side note: Even as Greg *thought* he'd become more aware of the world around him, he was still living in a relative bubble. During the same period, the decades-long fight against apartheid in South Africa was coming to a head...and he was largely oblivious to it.]

Going forward, Greg still thought business and law were worthy pursuits -- just not for him. At least, not right now. Simply put, in the process of getting back on the fast track to the corner office, he discovered that he'd rather be somewhere else -- in a school, working with students who are overlooked and underestimated like he had been, and trying to bridge racial and cultural barriers.

"And that," he explained, "is why I've decided to set my goals on hold and spend one year teaching."

His parents were absolutely stunned.

Rose later said, "Teaching is wonderful -- it just wasn't for Greg. He didn't know the first thing about it."

Mark was a bit less diplomatic. He'd invested a great deal of money into his son's education -- and as with every other investment in his portfolio, he expected financial dividends.

He said, "If Greg wanted to donate some income to help teachers, that would've been fine. But the notion of *him* teaching? It was assinine. Not that I was surprised. He used to run into walls and talk to a swing. He'd been doing assinine things his whole life."

Hoping some time in the sun would bring his son to his senses, Greg's father gave him a ticket to California as his graduation gift.

Mark said, "He always got so easily distracted, and it used to frustrate me a great deal, until finally, I realized I could use it to my advantage. When he wanted to do something crazy, instead of putting up a fight, all I had to do was wave a little carrot in front of him and he'd forget all about his idea. So, in this case, I said, 'Okay, teaching sounds great, but before you start, let me send you on a vacation."

The chance to be near Hollywood did cause Greg to think once again about pursuing his lifelong dream to write stories and make movies. He had even signed with an agent and picked out an apartment -- indefinitely postponing his plan to be a substitute teacher.

The plan seemed to be working.

Until, that is, he got his first roll of photos from California developed, and he saw something that truly jolted him. In one of the pictures, his head blocked the sun -- casting his image as a silhouette.

The reappearance of his old friend, The Silhouette Man, triggered a memory of that photo taken on the hotel balcony in Hawaii six years earlier. In turn, that made Greg think about Bailey -- his friend from football camp who was killed during that same period of time. And that made him think about Tug, his other 'friend' who had been killed. And once those tragedies crossed his mind, Greg couldn't stop thinking how naive it was to assume he'd have a chance to pursue something later on in life. If he really wanted to teach, he had to do it now.

He knew it was a far cry from the traditional path most kids in his position chose to follow. It certainly wasn't going to bring him a salary like the one Charlie was getting from the global consulting firm that hired him -- Charlie's *holiday bonus* was probably more than a teacher's annual salary -- but this was what Greg wanted to do. He wanted to spend one year working with kids, and he wanted to do it now rather than later on in life -- just in case later never came. So, just like that, after the unexpected visit from The Silhouette Man, Greg packed up his bags and headed home.

"Maybe, one day I'll go back to California. Maybe, one day I'll go to law school. Maybe, one day I'll join corporate America. But none of those one days are today," he told his mom (who looked faint) and father (who looked sick). " They're all good places, but they're not where my heart is right now. And I've just gotta follow my heart, and my heart's telling me to be a teacher."

As always, it didn't take long for Greg's plan to hit a snag.

To become certified as a teacher, whether someone planned on doing it for one year or fifty, certain credentials were required -- and, apparently, he lacked them.

He explained, "I think the problem, according to the powers-that-be, was that, in college, I had not majored in Education. [In fact, of the thirty-eight courses he took, a grand total of *none* were in the field.] I did take one class about the evolution of the education system in urban communities throughout history. But that was a class about schools, not how to teach in one."

Still determined to work as an educator for one school year, he researched other options and discovered that he *could* get certified to be a substitute teacher. As far as he could tell, the position required no experience whatsoever. Just a clean background and a degree.

His father was mortified.

Mark said, "Some of the boys from the neighborhood were in law school or med school or business school. Many of them went to Wall Street. A couple took positions at family-owned firms. I'd see them at Nordstrom getting their new suits. And then there was Greg. My son, the substitute teacher. It was embarrassing."

**

In preparation for his new job, Greg moved into a one bedroom apartment in a high-rise building in The City.

The City was less than an hour or so from the Shore -- the suburban enclave where Greg was raised -- but they were distinctly different worlds.

In the Shore, the residents were mostly wealthy and almost entirely white. It felt like everyone knew everyone (and everything about everyone). The City, on the other hand, had millions of residents from every race, culture and background imaginable. One could ride the train every day for a year and never see the same face twice.

Each community had something special to offer.

The Shore provided a certain sense of peace and calm. Neighbors had keys to each other's homes just in case one got locked out. There were luxurious country clubs and first-rate golf courses. Random acts of violence were virtually nonexistent.

The City felt *alive*. There were expansive parks, iconic cultural institutions, Fortune 500 corporations, nightclubs with lines around the block, skyscrapers rising fifty stories high, and major sporting events attended by tens of thousands of roaring fans at a time.

Of course, neither place was perfect.

The City had pockets of extreme poverty. And while it was a

profoundly diverse place, it was also true that those different groups sometimes co-existed *side by side* instead of *together.*

The Shore, on the other hand, could give kids a skewed sense of reality. More than a few grew up with the belief that it was 'normal' to have a pool in the backyard.

(Even among the ones who thought they were mindful of the fact their upbringing provided opportunities others would never experience, there could still be a tendency to take some things for granted. Greg was a prime example. After meeting Kahzti, he did become more appreciative for some of the luxuries in his life. And yet, before he applied to college, he never had a conversation with his parents about the cost. He just assumed they could and would pay his bill.)

While Greg waited for the call to get started as a substitute teacher, he decided to use the extra free time to teach himself a skill that had eluded him all his life -- how to draw.

"How do you teach yourself something you don't know?" Harvard Charlie asked with a laugh.

His longtime friend did seem to have a point, and in fact, Greg's new sketches were profoundly unimpressive -- but he stuck with it anyway. Despite his apparent lack of skill, Greg truly loved the field of art. So, each night, long after the rest of the world went to sleep, he continued to work on his drawings -- and somehow, over time, they actually started to improve. They still weren't *good*, mind you, but they were good enough to motivate Greg to keep on trying.

To fill the rest of his time, he started helping his father with finance work during the week, kept lifting weights at the gym at night and began working at a brand new, upscale restaurant/bar called The Club on weekends.

The latter was Grandma's idea. She felt he had become cocky as a result of his success in school, and she thought a job that involved serving others in some capacity would be a good, humbling experience for him.

As it turned out, even the interview process served that purpose.

When Greg walked in to apply for the job, he proudly handed over his resume to The Club's Boss. He expected to be praised for his sterling academic record, but that's not exactly what happened.

The Boss turned the resume into a paper airplane, launched it into the air, and said he had just one question: "Can you tell people to [expletive] off diplomatically?"

Grades, Greg quickly learned, are an important thing, but they are not *every*thing. The ability to deal well with people mattered, too.

He started at The Club two nights later. His role was to stand by the door, greet customers, tell them to "[expletive] off diplomatically" if it was too crowded inside to let them in, and check the bathroom once an hour to make sure it was clean.

It seemed easy enough, but just like always, there were bumps in the road. He was fired after one night.

(To add insult to injury, he was fired in front of a group of well-heeled, young professionals who arrived moments earlier to scope out the new locale and enjoy a bottle of merlot -- a group that included none other than Charlie.)

Needless to say, Greg was humiliated beyond words.

"I felt badly for the guy," Charlie later said. "But, let's be serious, he was a part-time doorman. It wasn't like he lost a *real* job."

The alleged transgression was a relatively minor one -- The Boss at The Club thought Greg had accepted ten dollars from a guest trying to sneak in ahead of the line -- but, even as a first offense, he decided it was enough to justify terminating his new doorman right on the spot.

In reality, Greg had not taken any pay-off, but the matter hardly seemed worth disputing. The job only paid a few bucks an hour, he'd only worked there one night, he was planning on quitting once he began substitute teaching, and The Boss clearly had already made up his mind about what he thought he saw -- having reached his verdict without asking a single question to determine what happened.

The logical thing for Greg to do was to just walk away. There were hundreds of clubs and restaurants in The City. If he still wanted to work on weekends, he could always get a similar job at another place. But he stubbornly refused to move on until he wrote a note to The Boss to clear things up. He had not done anything wrong, and he was determined to prove it.

Within hours of getting the note (all nineteen rambling pages of it), The Boss realized a mistake probably had been made -- "Who writes such a long letter about a part-time job they've held for one night unless they really didn't do anything wrong?" he reasoned -- and called to apologize. He even offered his former doorman the job back.

Greg was stunned. He never expected The Boss to call up and

admit it was probably a misunderstanding. When The Boss did, Greg knew this was someone he could learn from. So much so, he immediately accepted the job back and even decided he would keep working there on weekends after he started substitute teaching.

**

It was a cold January morning, when a 24 year old, part-time restaurant doorman strolled out his apartment building's front door, past the train tracks and into a section of The City called The Green for his first day on the job as a substitute teacher.

[Amusing side note: Not knowing any better, the stockbroker's son had donned his best suit -- briefcase in hand. This was, after all, how 'everybody' dressed for their first day on the job.]

Greg had never before stepped foot in The Green, but he had certainly heard of it. He saw the stories in the paper and on TV. Stories about drugs and violence and despair. He'd also heard that white people were not too welcome there.

At one point, those myths might've been enough to cause him to stay away, but after his positive experiences in the weight room and in Louisiana, he knew not to pre-judge a place where he had never been.

As it turned out, Greg did have problems that first day in The Green -- but it had nothing to do with the neighborhood.

It had to do with teaching.

He didn't know how.

That first day, after being greeted graciously by Blue Academy's Principal, Mr. Brooks, and warm-hearted clerk, Ms. Boggs, Greg was given a room number and sent on his way. He assumed it was the room where he'd be trained -- but when he walked in, it was an *actual* class with *actual* students expecting him to teach them something.

The kids behaved fine, but Greg quickly found himself over-whelmed -- the day, a complete disaster.

On Greg's second day, things did not go much better. He mistook an unusually tall, mature-looking kid named Junior for a graduate student (and presumed he was there to do a classroom observation). Greg confided in him that he was clueless, and offered to let him teach the class in his place -- an offer Junior happily accepted -- to the great amusement of his pre-teen classmates.

In the weeks that followed, Greg's job didn't get much easier -- as he found out the hard way that knowing something and actually being able to *teach* it were two different things (especially while monitoring twenty or twenty-five students at once).

The experience frustrated Greg to no end. The full-time teachers made it look so effortless -- like jugglers gracefully tossing around six bowling pins at once with their eyes closed -- but when he tried to step in their place and do it, he always seemed to drop everything.

Night after night, Greg stayed awake, staring out the window, thinking about Blue Academy, wishing he could be as good as its full-time teachers.

Not that he could avoid thinking about it even if he'd wanted.

As fate would have it, Blue Academy sat exactly four blocks due west of his window, and its front porch light stayed on all night every night -- even as the others around it were darkened. So, as Greg sat in bed and gazed out his high-rise apartment window, Blue Academy was impossible for him to miss. Some nights, he succesfully distracted himself by focusing on his sketches. But the rest of the time, he just sat there, looking out the window, staring at that one, single, unavoidable light and the school attached to it, thinking about how inept a teacher he was proving to be -- until finally, one night, tired of not sleeping, he literally threw out his bed.

It would be seven long months spent sleeping on the floor until he got a new one.

On the bright side, there was one thing Greg did do well as an educator -- *names*. He could memorize an entire class full of them in minutes. The kids seemed amazed he could do it, but more than anything, they wondered why he bothered. After all, he was a sub. It's not like he'd be with them all year.

He always responded the same way -- telling them whether he was there for one day or forever, he still wanted to know them as individuals instead of assuming they were all the same.

"And the first step," he told them, "is knowing your names because names are the first thing that set us apart from each other."

It was a saying he repeated so often that one kid drew a cartoon of him saying it. And years later, the same girl sent him a note thanking him for the difference he made in her life -- a note that ended with one simple phrase: "Thank you again for knowing my name."

As he got to know the students better, Greg found the biggest obstacle for some of them had little to do with confidence in themselves. It had to do with confidence in *others*. Having seen people in their community treated poorly just because of where they live or the color of their skin, some of the kids questioned whether they would get a fair shake to succeed when they got older even if they did put in the time and effort.

Searching for a way to convince them they could accomplish anything they put their mind to -- even if they had to create their own opportunity to do it -- Greg told the kids about his lifelong struggle with art. He told them how he could barely draw a straight line as a kid, and how instead of giving up, he just kept practicing.

The kids seemed skeptical when they heard his story, so he pulled out the portfolio where he kept his sketches, letting them see his progress with their very own eyes.

A twenty-four year old man, twenty-five kids and a book of drawings. Little did anyone know that just a few weeks later that moment in time would trigger a chain of events that would change Greg's life -- and thousands of others -- for years to come.

**

It started simply enough, when Greg walked out his building's front door to go pick up his sister for brunch. At the very same time, two boys from Blue Academy happened to be heading down the very same street on their way to get some sodas.

The moment they saw Greg, they recognized him and hustled ahead to say hello. (They later admitted they didn't actually remember his name -- just that he was the new substitute at school with big ears who could draw.)

After learning the boys were on their way to get sodas, Greg offered to get them milkshakes if they wanted to save their money and join him and his sister instead. The students happily accepted, but as it turned out, Michelle changed her mind -- upset that Greg had gotten sidetracked, and added two complete strangers to what was supposed to be a brother-sister lunch without her permission.

So off the three went, a new substitute teacher and two students, for some impromptu milkshakes at Gordon Birchwood's Terrace -- a popular, casual restaurant located in an upscale part of town.

When the trio arrived, they were seated at a table next to a couple of middle-aged white women. As they sat down, one of the ladies gave the two boys a look of disdain and moved her purse to the far side of her table in a way that suggested she was afraid one of the boys might steal it.

Greg was infuriated. How could this lady make a presumption about two kids she never met? As far as he was concerned, it just made no sense. He was tempted to say that right to her face, but he never uttered a single word in her direction. Instead, he decided to just use the negative moment as an excuse to do something positive.

He rose from his seat, approached the head of the restaurant, and said, "Do you see those two kids? I'm coming back with *ten*."

When people first heard about the incident at the restaurant, most presumed the lady with the purse was guided by preconceived negative stereotypes about African-Americans. But in later years, as Greg's civic efforts received increasing attention, that 'milkshake moment' did as well. In the process, some observers pointed out the customer's motive might have had less to do with the color of the kids' skin and more to do with the fact simply that they were kids. Since she didn't *say* anything, how can we be so sure?

It was a valid point -- an important one, even -- making it that much more significant Greg had chosen to respond as he did.

One teacher observed, "History tells us that, more likely than not, the race of the students *was* a factor in that customer's decision to do what she did, but the valuable lesson comes from realizing that the way Greg chose to respond makes the whole debate moot. Had he said something to the lady about her being a racist and turned out to be wrong, that'd be one thing -- but he chose a response that focused on helping others instead of hurting her. As a result, we find ourselves able to focus on the benefits of what he did without fretting about what caused him to do it."

Grandma concurred, "That teacher is right. People don't remember how you are treated. They remember how you respond."

Initially, Greg's plan was to return with ten black kids -- to try and prove a point to the woman with the purse and people like her -- but he quickly decided to take a different tact. His new plan was to return with ten people from *different* races and backgrounds.

He said, "I realized the lady with the purse was only as relevant as we allowed her to be. So, instead of worrying about her, I decided to just make it about us. To use the event as a chance to bring people together from diverse backgrounds, let them meet each other and hopefully get beyond the stereotypes that divide so many others."

Greg was excited about the idea and anxious to make it happen, but reality began to settle in a short time later. Before the return visit could take place, he needed to find kids who wanted to go, get permission from their parents *and* come up with a way to pay for it.

The first part proved easy -- plenty of students were interested in taking part in the brunch. Getting permission from parents, on the other hand, was understandably more difficult.

"Let me get this straight," said one mother, "some guy I don't know wants me to let my child -- *my baby* -- go to a restaurant where I've never been with a group of people I've never met?"

Greg paused, then replied, "Well...uh...yes."

She hung up without saying another word.

Another parent recalled, "He seemed like a polite man, and I appreciated what he was trying to do, to step out on a limb like that to try and disprove such a hurtful stereotype, but as a parent, I just simply don't let my child eat with strangers."

Others said they were interested, but their kids already had week-end plans -- be it church, work, sports, babysitting or chores.

Given the lukewarm response, Greg decided to approach the schools and ask them to step in and vouch for him. He thought that might help reassure parents this was a worthy idea to be part of.

Unfortunately, with the notable exception of Blue Academy, the initial response from the various schools was not much better.

And in all fairness, their view was a perfectly reasonable one.

With all the issues already faced by overworked, underfunded school administrators, the last thing they needed was a new substitute teacher -- however well-intended -- starting a program that would inevitably generate a flood of calls from inquisitive parents.

In one instance, a school was so concerned about all the potential pitfalls that they told Greg in no uncertain terms he would no longer be brought in as a substitute teacher if he went through with the plan.

"But it's on the weekend, and everybody would have their parents' permission, and they'd understand it isn't a school trip," he pleaded.

"If you do it, you won't be called to sub here again," the school official warned.

Another Principal said she admired Greg's passion and would be open to the idea *if* he waited until second semester to pursue it.

"It's a wonderful gesture, but you've only been here for a few weeks," she explained. "We hardly even know you."

Her point was valid -- and Greg knew it -- but he wouldn't budge.

"Look," he replied, "I get what you're saying, but the lady who moved her purse didn't wait until second semester, so I can't, either."

The Principal said, "Then, I'm sorry, but we just can't get behind it. I'd love to, but we can't. I'm afraid you're on your own on this."

Unable to line up enough attendees, Greg was on the verge of giving up on the idea -- when he was extended an unexpected lifeline.

Junior (the tall, mature-looking middle school student who Greg mistook for a post-grad on hand to do classroom observation) had told his mom about the brunch idea, and the incident that inspired it. And she was impressed by the young substitute teacher's effort.

"I like what you're trying to do," she told Greg. "So if you decide to do it, my son can go...and I'll come, too."

Greg's eyes started to well with tears of relief. He excitedly began phoning other families with the news. Each call started the same way:

"I'm going to brunch, Junior's Mom is going, too."

The presence of a parent meant all the difference in the world.

Within ten days, six other parents gave their blessing for their kids to take part -- including one who had previously said no.

That parent said, "Once another student's mom was going, I was happy to let my child be part of it. I thought it was a powerful, positive example -- addressing intolerance in a nonviolent way."

Except for the fact that Greg was indeed banished from one of the schools where he'd been a sub for defying the edict to drop the brunch idea, everything seemed to be going smoothly.

He said, "The only real obstacle left was financial. I had to come up with a way to pay for it."

With two days to go until the big brunch, he still had no solution. As he headed over to The Club for another night on the job as a doorman, he was convinced that the only option was to dip into his own savings to cover the tab. Until, suddenly, a seemingly laughable idea popped in his head: What if he convinced one of The Club's wealthy clients to foot the bill?

Greg knew the chance that a customer would grant that kind of request from a doorman was virtually nonexistent, and he knew he could (and probably should) lose his job just for asking -- but he decided it was a risk he had to take.

After carefully scoping out The Club's interior, Greg singled out a forty-something, well-dressed executive who appeared to be enjoying a night out with some friends.

The young doorman recognized The CEO as a repeat customer, but the two had never exchanged anything more than a polite greeting.

After taking a here-goes-nothing deep breath, Greg marched up to the table of four and asked if he could speak privately to the man.

Thinking that, perhaps, the doorman was about to deliver some bad news about his car getting wrecked by the valet or something of that sort, The CEO quickly rose to his feet and asked if everything was okay. Greg assured him everything was fine at The Club -- before proceeding to tell him about the two kids and the milkshakes, the woman who moved her purse and his pledge to return with ten people.

As improbable as it might seem, after hearing what the doorman wanted to do and why he wanted to do it, The CEO not only said he would pay for the entire brunch -- *he agreed to join them.*

That Sunday, Greg made his triumphant return to Birchwood's Terrace just like he vowed he would. The ten people who came with him ended up being Junior, his mom, six other kids, The CEO and one of The CEO's friends.

The brunch was everything Greg could have hoped for and more. The food and shakes were delicious, the staff treated them wonderfully, and everyone at the table had a great time.

And it was likely at that moment -- sipping a vanilla milkshake, surrounded by a diverse group of people all getting along -- that Greg knew he stumbled onto the world he always wanted to be part of -- a world where people of different backgrounds co-existed *together* instead of *side by side*. And he knew he didn't want to see it end as quickly as it started. And so, he decided it wouldn't.

A week turned into a month and Greg was still returning to Birchwood Terrace every Sunday. Each week, he brought five to ten of his friends -- adults from every walk of life -- and an equal number of students -- kids from different races and backgrounds. The adults each paid for themselves and one kid. The students each paid a dollar to remind them "nothing in life is free."

In many ways, Greg was following the blueprint he mapped out in Louisiana -- creating a forum for kids to meet people who could mentor them about college and careers. But this time around, there was one significant difference. He was now also focusing on giving kids a chance to meet *each other* -- going out of his way to invite students from all different backgrounds to attend.

Some people questioned the value of including so-called *rich kids,* but Greg insisted on it. He said the only way to truly get people from different backgrounds beyond the stereotypes they hear and read about each other was to bring them all together, face-to-face.

"And besides," he said, speaking from personal experience, "those kids need just as much guidance and help as kids from The Green -- maybe even more."

The all-inclusive philosophy wasn't just limited to the students. Week in and week out, Greg tried his best to invite adults from different racial, social, cultural and economic backgrounds, too.

People who heard about the outings frequently asked, "What do you guys discuss?"

Greg always chuckled, knowing the answer he was about to give would be a letdown to anyone hoping for something profound.

Rather than dictate topics of conversation, the hope was the group's members would talk about the same things they always discussed -- college, careers, music, sports, fashion, politics. What made it special was simply that they were discussing those things with different people -- and, as a result, they were hearing a new set of perspectives and opinions.

One adult, Cresta, said, "That concept is really what drew me to the table. Brunch wasn't divided into *volunteers* and *beneficiaries.* We were all just *new friends.* It was an environment based on mutual respect, where people treated every other person at the table as a potential source of wisdom -- and I valued that."

In the process of bringing these multicultural groups together, Greg had created a full-fledged program. He even gave the group a name. *The Brunch Bunch.* It wasn't too fancy-sounding, but neither was the group. They were just a bunch of people going to brunch. Nothing more, nothing less.

Until, that is, Mr. Landers learned of them. The head of a company that runs a fleet of top health clubs, Landers appreciated what Greg was trying to do and offered to let the group come play basketball after brunch since one of his health clubs happened to be just a few blocks from the restaurant.

From personal experience, Greg knew sports had a unique way of transcending otherwise powerful divides. People from completely different backgrounds setting aside those differences in the name of team spirit and unity. He hoped that would be what happened in this case, too -- and it did.

Greg said, "The kids not only got along, and not only didn't worry about who was on which team, they didn't even keep score. They were just happy to play. It was awesome."

After seeing how well the kids behaved and how much they enjoyed themselves, Mr. Landers said Greg could bring them back for an hour every week.

And just like that, The Brunch Bunch suddenly had a *routine* -- eat at Birchwood's every Sunday, then head over to the health club for an hour of fun.

As one kid said, "Milkshakes and basketball, it doesn't get much better than that."

[Side note: There was actually one additional activity each week. Thank you notes. Greg was adamant about them being written -- and being written immediately just to ensure they didn't get lost in the shuffle. And so, each week, after basketball ended, but before the kids all went home, they would each write a thank you note to one of the adults who attended (and helped pay for) that week's brunch.]

**

Birchwood's Terrace was not the only restaurant Greg visited every week. A true creature of habit, he always stopped by the same bagel shop to get lunch on Tuesdays.

The shop's manager, Cleo Hamilton, recalled, "He always ordered the same thing. I still remember. It was turkey and lettuce on a plain bagel, plus a muffin and a can of juice, to go."

One week, as he picked up his order, the young substitute teacher told Cleo that he'd love to give bagels to the kids at school if she ever had leftovers.

"They keep thinking bagels are doughnuts," Greg sighed. "I want to help them understand the difference."

A week later, the manager gave him three bags full of them.

The kids loved the bagels, and Cleo loved helping kids, so she began giving Greg more and more to pass out each week. Until, one time, she gave him more bagels than there were students. He thought about just throwing away the extras, but then he decided against it.

He said, "I figured it would be hypocritical of me to throw away extras since the only reason I had any in the first place was that the store manager was kind enough to not throw out *her* extras."

He walked around the neighborhood looking for a place to bring the leftover bagels. In a matter of minutes, he found one.

The Center already provided food to its residents, of course, so they didn't need the bagels, but the elderly men and women who lived there did seem to enjoy the company of an unexpected visitor.

Wheelchair-bound or not, they were young at heart. They wanted to argue about politics, hear jokes and cheer on their favorite teams. More than anything, they loved to tell stories. They didn't just know history -- they had *lived* it -- and the presence of a new set of ears meant they had a chance to share their favorite chapters again.

For his part, Greg was in Grandkid Heaven. Despite his busy schedule, he began carving out enough time to visit The Center every Saturday afternoon.

The more Greg got to know the residents, the more he liked them. They were respectful and worthy of respect, and above all else, they were kind. In one instance, after he said his Grandma was sick, one resident surprised him with a bag containing seven greeting cards so he could "send her one every day of the week."

Before long, just as he did in Louisiana, Greg began asking his friends to come volunteer with him. Some were happy to do it. Others, frankly, were not too crazy about the idea of spending their free time with a "bunch of old people." But Greg stayed on their case until they went at least one time to The Center. And once they did, it usually didn't take long for them to realize why Greg liked it there so much. By the time the hour was up, many of his friends were already asking if and when they could come back.

Of all the residents, Greg was drawn most to Mrs. Goldmill.

He recalled, "There was just something about her, like she was someone worth knowing."

In the beginning, the feeling was anything but mutual.

"Go visit someone else," she huffed, when he first walked in.

Her words anything but ambivalent, their message loud and clear, Mrs. Goldmill assumed the young man would turn and leave the room -- but, to her great dismay, he eagerly pulled up a chair.

He gushed, "You're just like my Grandma!"

Mrs. Goldmill was neither impressed by his persistence nor flattered by the comparison.

Perfectly content to spend her golden years talking with her own grown children, reading books, watching TV, playing Bingo, practicing her faith and thinking about her late husband, she had no interest in making the acquaintance of a complete stranger who was "younger than my socks" -- but it was clearly too late.

Whether Mrs. Goldmill liked it or not, she had a new best friend.

Greg began visiting the woman reminiscent of his Grandma every week, and every week, Mrs. Goldmill did her best to convince him to make that visit his last.

"I'd sit there in silence and watch TV, and I *know* these were shows that he didn't watch, but he'd never complain," she later recalled. "He'd just sit and watch the show with me, with that big grin on his face, like it was the most interesting thing he'd ever seen."

Mrs. Goldmill soon resorted to name-calling.

"I'd call him Twerp - who could possibly like that? -- but he'd laugh and call me Bully, and say how much he liked the fact that we were such close friends that we had given each other nicknames."

The Bully even tried a good, old-fashioned bribe.

She said, "Twerp reminded me of Forrest Gump, so I offered him a box of chocolates to never come back, but he said he didn't like chocolate -- started rambling on and on about vanilla shakes."

Before long, she resigned herself to the fact Greg wasn't going anywhere, and her tough exterior slowly but surely began to melt away. She even began to greet him with a smile.

The Bully joked, "What choice did I have? I was stuck with him... like glue."

As the weeks turned into months, the two began to talk at length. She told him about her political views (staunchly Democratic), her religious faith (a devoted Catholic), her family, the Depression, segregation, and other topics that crossed her mind. And he sat there by her side, an hour at a time, fascinated by it all, never running out of questions.

**

In June, Greg's stint as a substitute teacher was scheduled to end.

For weeks, he carefully mapped out his final day. Instead of teaching, he planned to stop by each of the schools he worked at throughout the year -- giving out donated books and supplies to the students. He even convinced his mom to join him so she could see firsthand that his tenure as a sub had been time well spent.

The day went even better than hoped. At one school after the next, starting with Blue Academy, people approached Rose to tell her what a positive impact her child had on theirs.

At the sixth and final school, the Principal -- finishing his first year on the job -- loaned Greg a wheelbarrow so he could push the remaining books into the playground and pass them out to the kids who were about to head home for summer.

For Greg, whose philanthropic efforts began with a charity read-a-thon nearly twenty years earlier, the chance to give away hundreds of children's books seemed to be a perfect way to bring his journey full circle. Until, just like always, as he began to celebrate reaching the finish line, things went horribly awry.

A student's aunt -- apparently thinking Rose was one of the many parents picking up a child on the last day of school -- encouraged her to keep her kid away from the young man giving away books.

The comment stunned Greg's mom, but she didn't reveal who she was -- instead asking the lady what caused her to say such a thing. According to Rose, the lady said that nobody shows up at a school, acts nicely to the kids, gets them books and invites them out to brunch with his friends unless he has ulterior motives.

The comment was *such* a predictable stereotype -- the notion that a young man from a 'good' neighborhood must have some nefarious reason for helping others -- but Rose refused to turn the other cheek.

Ever the protective mother, she marched over to the Principal and demanded that something be said to the woman slandering her son.

The rookie administrator meekly refused. The very same man who had been calling Greg regularly to substitute teach at the school -- *the same man who'd just been so appreciative for Greg's support that he lent him a wheelbarrow to lug the books into the playground* -- was now suddenly unwilling to say a single thing in his defense. It was the ugly side of school politics -- something Greg would witness more than once before all was said and done.

As for the remark itself, it was not the first time such a comment had been made since Greg started working at the schools.

Sometimes, his supposed 'ulterior motive' was ambition -- "He is just here so it'll look like he cares about the community when he runs for Senate some day." In the eyes of others, his alleged motivation involved his social life -- "He's just trying to impress the ladies with all his do-gooding." Other times still, the supposed motive was far more sinister -- "You watch, he's gonna kidnap a carload of students and run off to Mexico. He speaks Spanish fluently, you know."

It hurt Greg to have his intent questioned, but he tried his best to just dismiss such sentiments. The remarks were mercifully isolated, and patently ridiculous -- not to mention, inherently contradictory (Kidnapping a bunch of kids and fleeing the country is probably not the best way to woo women or win over future voters.).

But this time was different. The comment was made *to his mom*. And in the final moments of what was supposed to be his final day.

He just couldn't walk away. Not on that note.

And so, with the same prove-'em-wrong impulsiveness that led him to transfer to Froehmann Whitfield instead of studying film in Europe as planned, he suddenly decided to take yet another detour -- once again delaying the pursuit of his own dreams in the process.

He vowed, "I'm going to substitute teach again in the fall."

He sounded certain about his decision, but deep down, he knew it was easier said than done. Months earlier, he promised his parents that he'd interview for a corporate job after the year was up. There seemed to be no way out. Until, that is, he came up with a loophole.

Technically speaking, he promised his parents he'd *interview* for a job. He never guaranteed he would actually *get* one.

So, over the next few weeks, he went on job interviews as he pledged he would -- but he purposely ruined each opportunity. In one interview, he stood up and jumped an imaginary rope right there in the man's office. In another instance, Greg brought a bag full of bagels to the meeting -- *and started juggling them.*

In between bungling interviews, Greg continued to help students -- and continued to learn from them as well.

In one instance, Greg, his girlfriend at the time (Sloane) and his pal (Charlie) took some kids to their first pro baseball game. One boy, Elliott, wanted to bring his glove so he could catch a foul ball. At first, Greg refused to let him -- saying the glove would inevitably get lost.

Elliott complained, "But if I don't bring the glove, I'm gonna hurt my hand when I catch the foul ball."

Greg, himself once a boy with wide-eyed dreams, couldn't help but be amused by Elliott's certainty that 'the' foul ball would come his way -- unaware or unfazed by the odds of it actually happening.

"Okay, Elliott," the substitute teacher said with a grin, "you go ahead and you bring your glove. And when that foul ball comes your way, you just reach up into the air and grab it."

Ever the student, Elliott did exactly as instructed.

In the 7th inning, as 20,000 other fans watched on, Elliott
from his seat, hoisted his glove into the air and caught his foul

In the fall, having successfully sabotaged every interview he went
on, Greg dusted off his substitute teacher badge and returned to the
classroom. (Not to that school where his mom was treated poorly,
mind you. In fact, after that day, he vowed to never set foot inside that
building again until his mother received an apology).

His first day back as a sub was certainly a memorable one.

During third period, a seemingly drunk man wandered into the
school parking lot, climbed on top of the first car he stumbled upon
(which happened to be Greg's) and began to bash it with a brick.
When a Hall Monitor delivered the news, Greg dashed outside, but the
man quickly rushed off -- leaving only the brick in his wake.

An individual sitting on some nearby steps, who had witnessed the
incident, encouraged Greg to keep the brick so nobody else picked it
up and wrecked other cars.

The guy meant well, but the comment seemed absurd. The Green
was rapidly gentrifying -- its infamous housing projects uprooted in
favor of upscale townhomes. As a result of the ongoing construction,
there were hundreds if not thousands of stray bricks throughout the
area. Taking away just one seemed pointless.

"What good is one brick?" Greg asked.

The man's response became the basis for another life lesson: One
brick might not be much, but it's one brick better than none.

The damage to the car was unfortunate, but the incident was an
exception. Despite all the supposed dangers lurking in The Green,
Greg rarely had a problem in the neighborhood. In fact, most residents treated him with respect -- especially as time went on, and they
saw his commitment lasted far beyond a convenient photo op.

Of course, that's not to say everyone in every neighborhood
viewed his undertaking with such deference.

From time to time, when he said he was a substitute teacher -- at a
dinner party back home for instance -- there were people who asked if
he was going to become a *real* teacher at some point.

They didn't mean any harm, but the question made Greg wince.

He knew subs weren't *full-time* teachers. And he'd be the first to
admit he wasn't a *great* one. He'd even agree with those who thought
he was an *odd* one -- frequently taking off his shoes and teaching in

his socks, more likely to quote Rocky than Shakespeare when explaining something to the students. Still, being told he wasn't a *real* educator hit a sore spot for the guy who spent much of his life being told he didn't understand the difference between fiction and reality.

**

The bell rang around three o'clock, but Greg's daily routine lasted much longer. After school, he worked out at the gym and then spent an hour or two on the phone putting together that weekend's brunch. (The brunch usually took place on Sunday, but it occasionally took place on Saturday instead -- so that kids who attended religious services every Sunday could still participate).

The program was taking up more time than Greg ever dreamed it would, but there was no turning back now. The Brunch Bunch had become a part of people's lives. Kids were becoming friends with other people they would've otherwise never met. They were learning about all kinds of different careers. A few of the students even got offers to work part-time or during the holidays from the adults they impressed at brunch. And speaking of the adults, so many were now offering to volunteer that the program had a *waiting list.*

Make no mistake, The Brunch Bunch did not magically erase the barriers that have divided society for centuries. From time to time, there *were* moments of awkward silence -- and once in a while, there were people who felt downright uncomfortable sitting next to others from such different backgrounds -- but the majority of people who attended the brunches got beyond their hang-ups, got to know the others at the table, realized their similarities far outweighed their differences and happily signed up for another outing.

At the very least, just about everybody agreed on one thing -- the restaurant. The food and shakes were great, and the staff treated the group like true VIPs. Waiters knew their names and greeted them warmly. After so many weeks, Birchwood Terrace had become akin to the set of *Cheers* (with milkshakes instead of beer, of course).

To Greg, it was no longer 'the restaurant where that lady moved her purse when she saw two kids'. That sentiment had long since been replaced by hundreds of wonderful memories and new friendships. In a word, Birchwood Terrace had become *home.*

Still, after fifty-two weeks of eating there, the easily distracted guy who started it all was itching to branch out.

And so it was, upon reaching the group's first anniversary, Greg decided to stage the brunches at other eateries around the city.

As with most of Greg's plans, this one faced an obstacle or two.

For one thing, it was quite an assumption to make that other restaurants would be enthusiastic hosts. Given the group's size and strict time limitations (it was always important to have the program end at the same time so parents were not kept waiting), it was necessary to have a large table set aside for them. What if some of these restaurants had no-reservation policies? To convince them to make an exception might be easier said than done.

The other issue was price. Some of the restaurants Greg had in mind were four or five star establishments, and they charged a small fortune for a modest meal. In those cases, even if management accommodated the group and reserved a large table, the bill for brunch would be hundreds of dollars more than the equivalent meal at a casual place like Birchwood's Terrace.

As it turned out, the restaurant community truly *got it*. They embraced the mission -- using food as common ground to bring diverse people together -- and really did welcome the opportunity to be part of it with open arms.

Restaurants all across The City agreed to reserve the group a table -- and to absorb any difference in cost between their prices and Birchwood's. In some cases, they liked the Brunch Bunch concept so much that they even agreed to waive the bill altogether.

The Brunch Bunch Tour was off and running.

Some assumed the patrons of these establishments would not be as receptive as management had been -- and admittedly, there was an occasional glare or a whisper that reminded Greg of the woman who moved her purse -- but the great majority of the customers at these other restaurants were courteous and kind.

In fact, in one or two cases, they approached the manager and anonymously paid the entire bill for The Brunch Bunch. And every so often, they approached the table to introduce themselves and ask if they could participate in a future outing.

The latter gesture in particular meant a lot to Greg. These people were crossing that imaginary yet powerful boundary that keeps different segments of society eating at separate tables, co-existing side by side instead of co-existing together.

Most of the students who took part in the program were invited to every fourth or fifth brunch -- often enough to feel like they were part of a *group,* but not so often that they took it for granted. And indeed, some kids found out the hard way the invitation could be rescinded as quickly as it had been extended.

In some cases, they lost their seat because of misconduct.

Greg quickly clarified, "We never had a kid act up at a brunch, but once in a while, we'd hear one of the students misbehaved at home or at school. And if that happened, and we learned about it, they were not invited again -- or, at least, for a long time."

Some wondered why he was so adamant about that policy. Why not use the brunches as a way to help those students clean up their act?

Greg always answered the same way.

"Some programs focus on working with students who misbehave -- and that's important -- but this just isn't one of those programs. Our mission is to bring diverse people together to help break down stereotypes and to learn about each other -- not address misbehavior by an individual student. That's not to say our program is *better.* It's just that it's *different.* And the adults who are part of our program have volunteered to come talk with the kids about school and careers and that kind of thing. That doesn't mean they want to -- or are qualified to -- address any of the underlying issues that may be at work when a kid acts wrong. And don't forget the restaurants and the health club. Without them, we'd have nowhere to go. If a kid misbehaved on their property, what are the chances they'd keep supporting our efforts?"

For the most part, the kids' families sincerely appreciated the program, and they tried their best to show it -- a card, a cake, a smile -- but there were exceptions.

There was a grandfather who smoked and used foul language in front of the other kids. There was an aunt who said the brunches were good for the kids, but a 'donation' to her bank account would be nicer. There was a parent who frequently decided at the last second her child had to do chores instead of going to brunch -- which would've been fine, except she never bothered to call and cancel. In the meantime, having not been informed, the rest of the group sat around and waited for them to show up before departing for the restaurant.

When such things happened -- and if they continued over time -- their kids were no longer invited.

Greg explained, "I know that might seem unfair -- a kid no longer being invited because of something one of their family members did --

but I think it's important to remember we didn't actually have to invite anyone to any brunches. We were all volunteers, sacrificing a lot of time and money. And all we asked from the kids' relatives was that they were respectful to us and to the other kids and parents involved. That's really not asking much. It's also good to keep things in perspective. It's not like this happened on a regular basis. In fact, of all the kids who were part of the program, we only took this step a couple times. Most of the parents, aunts, uncles, grandparents -- they were kind and supportive and appreciative -- and that meant a lot to us."

**

Greg's Saturday afternoons were always spent volunteering, too -- at The Center.   After a few months there, he was even given an unofficial role -- Bingo caller. His role was straightforward -- sit at the head of the table and shout out the numbers for an hour -- but just like always, nothing in Greg's life went as simply as it should have.

One afternoon, he got banned from the game.

His friends were astounded when they heard the news.

"How could you mess up Bingo?" Cresta asked.

Greg shrugged, "I like the residents so much that I just couldn't stand to see them lose. So, I started calling out numbers that ensured each of them got a chance to win, and they eventually caught on to what I was doing."

The Bully knew he meant well and did her best to help him understand what he had done wrong by taking the competitiveness out of the game she and other residents loved to play.

She said, "We might not get around as quick as we used to. But we still like the blood to flow."

The folks in charge seemed to know he meant well, too -- so they said he was still welcome to visit The Bully and his other pals each week. Just no more calling Bingo.

Greg's finance work wasn't going any smoother. His father 'hired' him in the hope it'd spur an interest in the world of economics -- and Greg accepted the role because he hoped it would bring them closer together -- but it didn't seem to be working on either level.   The two remained as unable to understand each other as ever.

Greg's time at The Club had its bumps, too.

He enjoyed working there, but after several months, he was

anxious to prove he could do more than just stand by a door and greet people. So, as time went on, he started to take on more responsibility. Seating guests. Serving bread. Clearing dishes.

He thought he was doing a great job, and when The Boss asked to talk to him about all the tasks he was doing without being asked, he thought he was on the verge of getting a promotion and a raise. As it turned out, he almost got fired.

"I know you mean well," The Boss said politely, "but you're so busy trying to help everyone else do their jobs that you're not doing your own."

Greg just didn't get it.

"Aren't I doing a better job if I'm running around and helping everyone instead of just standing by the door and greeting people?"

The Boss said, "Not when I pay you to stand in one place."

Greg quietly went back to doing the job he was hired to do -- stand outside and greet customers. Not that he really minded.

The Club had quickly become *the place to be* for The City's movers and shakers (and had a line down the street to prove it). As its doorman, Greg was in a unique position to interact with all kinds of interesting people. Prominent people. The kind who graced the pages of his father's favorite papers. He got to watch them, to study them, to try and figure out what made them so successful.

With little to do besides stand by the door and check the bathroom, he was able to observe them for -- literally -- hours at a time. Much like with the portraits he drew, Greg tried to pay attention to every last detail. The way they talked, and walked, how they dressed and spoke, how they shook hands, and who they shook them with.

He also took note of how they responded to him.

In reality, Greg was powerless. He had no way of getting someone a table, let alone a comped meal or free glass of wine. He had no jobs to offer. He did not have a Rolodex full of big shot contacts to share with them. He had no tickets to a ballgame to slip their way. He was just a kid standing at the door. He held the keys to nothing.

And yet, there was no telling that to some guests. They perceived Greg to be the gatekeeper -- the sole arbiter deciding who walked right in The Club and who waited in the line winding down the street.

And the inevitable offers flowed because of it. There were sharply-dressed men who handed him business cards, and barely-dressed women who flashed flirtatious grins. One heavy hitter even went so far as to invite Greg out for an afternoon on his yacht.

Each time, he told the customers that he had no influence at Club (or anywhere else, for that matter) -- but they never seemed to believe him. In fact, the more Greg protested, the more convinced they seemed to be that the young doorman was exactly who they perceived him to be -- and the nicer they treated him as a result.

Of course, that's not to say all customers showed such courtesy to all employees. More than once, Greg saw a wealthy executive talking to a server or busboy like they were a parent scolding a small child. And then there was the guest who added an 'o' on the end of nouns ("Where is my car-o?") -- just to mock a valet parking attendant's difficulty with English.

Even when the customers meant well, some gave into stereotypes. One time, for example, a lady urged Greg to keep working hard and saving his money until he could afford college (assuming -- incorrectly -- that he must not have a degree if he was working as a doorman).

Make no mistake, the great majority of the patrons were good to the staff -- but these isolated instances impacted Greg a great deal.

Grandma was glad to hear it. She said his tenure at The Club had taught him an important lesson: "The only thing you should assume about a person based on their job...is that they have one."

One of Greg's most memorable experiences at The Club actually occurred when there were no customers around at all.

Most nights, after The Club closed, the staff saddled up to the bar themselves -- to have a glass of wine, swap stories, count tips, rest their feet, and just generally unwind a little before heading home.

It was an inclusive social atmosphere, but Greg was uncertain if he'd be welcome and initially skipped out on the gatherings. After all, he only worked there two nights a week, rarely interacted with his co-workers throughout the night (since he spent most of his shifts standing outside the door), was among the youngest on staff, and he personally never drank.

When he eventually did venture inside and pull up a chair, he realized his concerns had been unfounded. Nobody teased him about having juice instead of wine. They included him in conversations. They made an effort to ask about his civic projects. Some even asked to participate in a brunch. In short, he was treated like part of the team.

On a practical level, the after-work get-togethers served another purpose. Greg had been struggling so much with his sleepless nights, he'd been seeking out people by phone who worked midnight shifts -- a customer service rep for an airline, an ER doctor -- just so he could have someone -- *anyone* -- to talk to while the rest of the world slept soundly. As a result, he was rarely in a rush to leave The Club and oftentimes looked for a reason -- any reason -- to stick around even after he finished his juice.

As the one year anniversary of The Brunch Bunch approached, Greg sensed the end was near. He enjoyed what he'd been doing, but he was just plain exhausted. Up at 7 a.m. every morning during the week, in case he was called to teach. Working at schools most of those days until 3 or 4. Lifting weights after school. Spending most weeknights on the phone coordinating that weekend's brunch. Volunteering every Saturday afternoon at The Center. Working every Friday and Saturday night at The Club until around 2 a.m. Spending all day Sunday running the brunch. Not to mention, trying to help his father with finance work, visiting his Grandma regularly, working on his portraits, and attempting to have some semblance of a social life. And then, waking up Monday morning and doing it all over again. Every single week for a full year, without exception.

There was just no way he could keep up the pace any longer. Greg's mind was set. Week 52 of The Brunch Bunch would not just mark its One Year Anniversary. It would also mark the end of the program meeting on a weekly basis.

And so it was, one winter night after the customers had left The Club, and while his co-workers were socializing by the bar, Greg -- looking for any excuse to linger around a bit longer before heading home -- grabbed a pencil and piece of scrap paper from the host stand, and began to write a letter about the brunches -- a letter that thanked all those who had participated in making his vision a reality, and explained why it was the right time for him to take a break.

At least, that was his intention.

A half hour later, Greg had written a note emphasizing why it was so important to *continue*.

He later said, "It was as if my hand was listening to the words flowing from my heart instead of my head."

Right then and there at The Club, as Greg re-read the words he'd just written, his adrenaline now fully flowing, he changed his mind and vowed to press on with the weekly program. In the meantime,

The Brunch Bunch suddenly had its very own Mission Statement. What Greg scribbled down that night on that scrap paper would appear -- almost word for word -- on a new set of shirts given to everyone who came to one of the weekly brunches in the months that followed.

**

In June, Greg's *second* year as a substitute teacher came to an end, and he went on another series of job interviews -- and this time, he actually wanted to get hired.

He was still going to continue volunteering at The Center on Saturdays and hosting the brunches on Sundays -- but Charlie and the others from back home were now well on their way ascending the corporate ladder, and Greg was anxious to catch up.

It turned out there was just one little problem with his plan.

Nobody wanted to hire him.

Most interviewers said a "substitute teaching restaurant doorman" was not exactly what they were looking for. Others felt he was too concerned with helping people to focus on anything else -- let alone another job. In the end, for one reason or another, not one single company offered him a full-time position of any kind.

With his own personal dreams slipping away, Greg did what he always did -- distracted himself from thinking about it by focusing on his philanthropic efforts. He continued volunteering at The Center. The brunch program kept meeting — 70 straight weeks and counting. He even arranged for a company to donate the money and manpower needed to build an entire garden inside the empty atrium of a grade school in The Green.

It seemed like he was spending every waking moment on his civic efforts. In fact, he was just getting started.

One Sunday, during one of the weekly brunches, an elderly man who'd been sitting a couple tables over approached Greg and said, "I'd like to help if I can. Is your group a 501 *c* 3?"

Greg began to fidget uncertainly with his ears. He had no idea what that meant.

The man patted Greg on the shoulder and said that was unfortunate. He then wished the group well and went on his way.

As soon as Greg got home, he called Charlie.

"Hey, what's a 501 c 3?"

"They teach entire courses in business school about this. I can't --"

"Give me the short version."

"It's a type of not-for-profit organization."

"What's a not-for-profit organization?" Greg asked.

Charlie laughed, having known full well that his forever-curious friend would never be content with such an abbreviated answer.

"In general, if somebody wants to donate money, they're probably going to want a tax deduction for doing it. To get that, their donation has to be made to an organization formally designated as a not-for-profit organization," he explained patiently.

As Charlie's words sunk in, Greg's mind began racing with ideas.

He asked excitedly, "If I started a not-for-profit company and we were able to accept donations, could I use that money to help students in other ways besides taking them to brunch?"

"It'd depend on the group's official mission, but, in general, yes."

"Like, say, we could send kids to college?"

Charlie took a deep breath. He now knew exactly where his old pal was going with the questions. The kid rejected from every college he hoped to attend now wanted to help other students get there.

As much as he admired the idea, Charlie knew that Greg was only setting himself up for disappointment. The guy could barely substract without a calculator. There was just no way he could run a foundation.

As a friend, Charlie knew he had to jettison the idea before Greg got carried away and actually *pursued* it.

"Yes, a nonprofit organization could use donations to provide scholarships for college-bound students, but you are not qualified to run something like that. So, just stick with the brunches."

Greg could feel his heart beating rapidly. He knew Charlie was right -- he had no real clue what was involved with such an undertaking. And even if he did, he could always pursue it later in life after his own future was secure. He knew he should be using his extra time now to look for a job, not launch another civic project.

And yet, he just could not walk away.

Sure, in theory, it was a civic goal he could pursue later in life, but there were no assurances he'd be alive later to do it. The only way to guarantee something got done was to do it now. Yes, it was true he didn't know anything about running such an organization, but it was also true that he could learn. And, above all else, he'd be damned if Charlie could tell him what he was capable of achieving. His mind was made. He was taking the leap.

"I'm gonna do it!" Greg declared defiantly.

"Do what?"

"Start an organization, get donations, send students to college, and change the world!"

"You don't have any idea what you're getting yourself into."

"If the goal is to not make a profit," Greg replied, "I mean, to *not* make money? How hard could that be?"

**

People assumed the new group would be called The Brunch Bunch Foundation, but Greg quickly rejected the suggestion. He said his organization was going to do much more than just take kids to brunch. One day, he said, they would fund college scholarships -- and he wanted a name which reflected that broader vision. The name he ended up choosing was *The 11-10-02 Foundation.*

11-10-02 stood for Greg's 30th birthday, November 10, 2002, and his belief people thirty and under were as capable as anyone when it came to making a difference.

Greg explained, "People kept saying I was too young to be a philanthropist, and I really felt the exact opposite was true -- anybody at any age can be a philanthropist -- so I figured, instead of hiding my age, I'd put it out there for everyone to see."

The symbolism notwithstanding, the unusual name was cause for a lot of head-scratching and laughter.

"11-10-02 sounds like my locker combination," one kid cackled.

Despite the ridicule, Greg remained steadfast in his decision.

With the name chosen, his next step was to try and get a little bit of schooling in the finer art of finance. He begrudgingly asked his father for some help. To his pleasant surprise, Mark seemed happy to assist and set up a meeting for him with Edward Ansel.

A highly regarded accountant for nearly thirty years, Mr. Ansel was a certifiable expert and Greg knew it. What he *didn't* know is that Mr. Ansel had no real intention of teaching him a thing.

To the contrary, Mark had recruited Mr. Ansel to overwhelm his son with forms, facts and figures until the kid realized just how far in over his head he was, came to his senses, and scrapped the idea.

Unfortunately for Mark, things did not go quite as expected.

By the time the meeting was over, instead of Mr. Ansel persuading Greg to let go of this idea to start a nonprofit foundation, the wanna-be

philanthropist had somehow turned the tables and convinced him to
become its pro bono accountant.

As Mr. Ansel later told his partner, "The good news is we have a
new client. The bad news is that they're not going to pay us, and they
keep their files in a cereal box."

As Greg packed up his lunchbox briefcase and headed home from
the meeting, a top accountant now in the mix, he felt on top of the
world -- but the exhiliration would not last long.

Before The Foundation could begin, he needed to assemble a
Board of Directors. It seemed easy enough -- he only needed two
people to join him -- but he couldn't get anyone to do it.

Not Grandma, who didn't want the hassle. Not Ansel, who said
Mark was already upset at him for agreeing to help with the account-
ing. Not even Harvard Charlie, Greg's friend of nearly twenty years.

Charlie later admitted, "I thought his efforts were noble, but
frankly, I was just starting out in corporate America, and the last thing
I wanted on my resume was a position of formal leadership in an
organization that went belly up. And let's face it, the Foundation *was*
going to fail. Greg may have meant well, but he was clueless."

In the end, without anyone else willing to help, Greg reluctantly
turned to his parents to bail him out and fill the two spots until he
could find (convince) people to replace them.

They agreed to do it, but their motives were hardly altruistic.

Mark stated bluntly, "Our thinking was, the sooner he got two
people to serve on the Board, the sooner he could start. The sooner he
started, the sooner he failed. The sooner he failed, the sooner he gave
up and got a real job, or went to grad school."

Greg appreciated his parents' help, but he despised the seemingly
universal sentiment his failure was a foregone conclusion. Nobody
seemed to believe he could run something of this magnitude.

Nobody, that is, except Grandma.

"Don't get me wrong," she told him at the time. "When they say
you're gonna fall on your face, they're definitely right. But what they
don't realize is, when you do fall on your face, you're not gonna *quit*."

Simple as it sounded, Grandma's wisdom was the formula for
success -- just keep getting it wrong until you get it right. All Greg
had to do was follow that basic principle and eventually the Foundation would prosper.

Grandma said the only real question was if he'd be willing to set aside his own goals like law school and writing books and films long enough to do it. He looked her in the eye and said he was willing to spend as much time as it took to prove people wrong and build an organization that could change the world.

Grandma smiled and said, "In that case, there's just one more thing you need."

"What's that?"

"A place to sit."

"How come?" Greg asked.

"Because it is going to take *so* long that if you don't have a place to sit, your feet are going to hurt."

And with that, she gave him her rocking chair -- the very chair in which she rocked him more than twenty-five years earlier.

The gift from Grandma boosted Greg's confidence. His spirits were lifted even further when the Foundation received its first actual donation -- $100 from a couple from the Shore -- but it didn't take long before that excitement wore off and Greg realized 'not making a profit' wasn't so easy after all.

Between the papers to fill out and the decisions to make, the Foundation took up more time than he could have ever imagined -- and using his free time to get it all done wasn't an option because there simply wasn't any free time left.

The first step he took was a costly one -- quitting his part-time job as a doorman. He learned a lot from The Boss, liked his co-workers, and enjoyed the customers, but he just didn't have a choice.

He needed *time*.

The extra hours did help, but he still needed more time *during* the week when he could call people at work. He decided to use his lunch break to do it. He knew ten minutes a day wasn't much, but he figured it was ten minutes more than nothing. So, he searched around Blue Academy for a place to sit and make calls.

Finally, he found a room on the 4th floor. It wasn't very big -- the size of a large walk-in closet -- and half of it was taken up by a dishwashing bin -- but it had a phone and a desk, so Greg took it. He declared it to be his "first office" and even hung up his very own 'BOARDROOM' sign on the ledge.

It turned out there was just one small problem.

It was The Lunch Lady's desk and phone, that dishwashing bin was where she and her two co-workers cleaned the trays, and nobody else was supposed to enter that room without her permission -- let alone start putting things up on the ledge.

Everyone figured she would kick Greg out, but she never did -- letting him use her desk for five to ten minutes each day.

On the surface, Greg and The Lunch Lady seemed to be quite an odd couple -- different genders, ages, races, religions, cultures and backgrounds -- but they enjoyed each other's company. The Lunch Lady was amused by Greg's grand dreams and admired his desire to help others. In turn, he respected her work ethic, and her no-nonsense approach reminded him of his Grandma and The Bully.

He was particularly fascinated by the pride she took in the school lunchroom -- *because there wasn't one.* In its absence, for one hour each day, the tiny fourth floor hall was filled with tables and seats so the kids could sit down, a few classes at a time, and have a tray of food and drink some milk before heading back to class -- at which time, the tables and seats were put away and the hallway reverted back to its intended form.

At first glance, it could be a sad sight -- a school lacking the space and resources to provide something so basic that most kids at most schools take it for granted -- but there was no telling that to The Lunch Lady. In fact, she took as much pride in her makeshift lunchroom as The Boss took in his multi-million dollar Club.

And the more Greg watched her treat that hallway like a five-star restaurant, the more inspired he became.

The Lunch Lady was one of many memorable characters who became part of Greg's improbable collection of friends.

Guy was another.

A twenty-something free-lance photographer, Guy first met Greg when he showed up to take pictures of The Brunch Bunch for an article in a local paper. After he snapped his shots, Guy packed up his things and turned to leave the restaurant.

"Where ya going?" Greg asked between sips of his shake.

Guy shrugged uncertainly and said his work was done.

"Sit down and join us!" Greg insisted.

Guy reluctantly did so, unsure what exactly he could bring to the table -- but within seconds, those thoughts disappeared as he was bombarded by questions from the kids sitting around him.

"What's the most interesting thing you ever photographed?"

"How do you do it so the people don't get those red eyes?"

By the time the meal was done, Guy had gone from taking photos of the group to being a genuine part of it.

The article in the local paper about what Greg was doing helped bring in a few donations -- but the guy hoping to change the world was still raising little more than spare change. When even the most basic supplies seemed too expensive, Greg turned to his new friend, The Lunch Lady, for guidance.

"Just do what I do," she said.

"What's that?"

"Do the best you can with what you have."

The advice added up to less than ten words, but after she said it, he started treating everything in his apartment like it was *sacred*.

A lunchbox became a briefcase. Empty cereal boxes became filing cabinets. That brick he kept after the man beat up his car with it? It was now a paper weight.

Even his fridge was used to store files.

Greg next turned his attention to spreading the word about his fledgling group. He decided the internet was a good way to start.

Harvard Charlie offered to introduce him to someone who could create a website -- many of his friends were players in the dot-com rush -- but Greg said he'd do it on his own.

"Since when do you know about websites?" Charlie asked.

"I don't," Greg said matter-of-factly, "but I will."

Night after night, he sat at his computer, until finally he had taught himself how to create a website. The one he put together was not too intricate, but it was effective -- and more donations started trickling in.

Greg also began spreading the word to potential supporters through a periodic newsletter. In theory, it seemed to be a sound, logical step in the growth of a new Foundation -- but the correspondence itself struck many as confusing. In contrast to traditional nonprofit mailings which avidly solicit contributions, Greg's letters rarely asked for anything.

He took an equally unorthodox approach to another popular avenue of communication for nonprofit organizations -- holiday cards.

His ex-girlfriend Katie laughed, "He started sending them out in the summer. He said that every other nonprofit sent out holiday cards in December, and he didn't want his to get lost in the shuffle."

Despite the unusual methods (or, perhaps, because of them), more and more donations started to show up in the mail.

One of them was a check for *five thousand dollars* -- thanks to another family from the Shore. When Greg saw it, he started running in circles, waving the check in the air and hollering. It was the single biggest check he'd ever held in his life.

Knowing there were people who believed so strongly in what he was doing, Greg felt motivated to look for ways to raise even more money. Charlie explained that he could write 'grant request' letters to private foundations and civic-minded companies.

Greg gave it his best shot -- spending hours and hours filling out forms and writing proposals -- but every response was the same.

No.

As the rejections started piling up, he felt like a high school senior all over again. He wanted to tear up the letters into little pieces, but his Grandma insisted he should do the exact opposite.

"We've been through this," she huffed. "Rejection is something to be *proud* of. Don't throw out letters like that. *Frame* them."

Accepting rejection letters was one thing -- turning them into art seemed like quite another -- but Greg did as she advised. He literally framed a stack of the rejection letters and hung them on his wall.

It would not be the only time Grandma gave him advice that left him scratching his head.

When he continued to struggle in his efforts to raise the millions of dollars he hoped to raise, she said, "Instead of trying to change the whole world, just start with the world outside your window."

Greg was crushed. The way he figured, you don't tell someone to focus on small dreams unless you think they can't reach big ones.

A few days later, when he attended that Sunday's brunch, her words were still weighing on his mind. As he sulked in silence, the other people at the table realized something was wrong.

After he explained why he was upset, one of the kids (Josh) offered some interesting words of encouragement: "It sounds like your Grandma didn't say *stay* small. She just said *start* small. You know, like, you start small now, then one day, you get big."

Another student, Trace, provided another unique perspective.

He said, "Even if your efforts do stay small and you only end up helping your own little neighborhood, that's still good. I mean, even superheroes like Batman (Gotham) and Superman (Metropolis) focus their efforts on just one city, not the entire world."

The more Greg thought about what Trace and Josh said, the better he felt about his Grandma's advice. Instead of waiting until he raised enough money to fund the college scholarships he dreamed of, he decided he would use what little he'd raised so far to make a smaller but immediate difference to help his local community.

With an unobstructed view of The Green, Greg could see dozens of places where he could lend a hand when he looked out his window, but it took less than a minute for him to pinpoint precisely where he wanted to start: the place exactly four blocks due west whose front porch light kept him company each and every sleepless night.

In addition to its special place outside the window, Blue Academy also had a special place in Greg's heart. It was where he spent his first day as a sub, where those first two kids he took for shakes went to school, and where he shared an 'office' with the Lunch Lady.

Admittedly, Blue didn't look like much on the outside -- the bright paint had started to chip off long ago, and the windows were dark and worn down -- but Greg had moved far beyond that first impression.

There was no doubt in his mind. Blue Academy was the first place he wanted to help. And sooner than expected, he had a chance to do it.

One day, he asked the kind-hearted clerk, Ms. Boggs, if he could have a school t-shirt to wear around town. She smiled warmly and said she appreciated his school pride -- but there was no way she could give him one. Blue Academy had no school shirts.

"We can't afford them," she said with a shrug.

Greg couldn't believe his ears. How can kids be expected to take pride in their school if they can't wear shirts with its name across the front? He knew right away this was a perfect chance for his young organization to help make a small but lasting difference. He went home, designed new school t-shirts that met with Principal Brooks' approval, persuaded a shirt company to knock down the price, and then promptly ordered six hundred.

A few weeks later, Principal Brooks arranged a special all-school assembly where Greg could unveil the surprise -- though, it turned out the 'all-school assembly' speech was really anything but.

Blue Academy had no auditorium -- or even a gym -- so the 'event' had to take place in the dimly lit first floor hallway. And the hall was obviously too small to fit the whole student body, so only a few dozen kids got the chance to be there.

Some people even suggested it was more like an announcement

than a bonafide speech -- but Greg didn't seem to mind the modest
surroundings one bit. In fact, as he looked around at Blue Academy's
students and staff -- *his friends* -- he never seemed happier.

At the end of his speech, Greg unveiled the shirts. At first, the
kids started hollering and applauding. But then, he mentioned one
little caveat that dampened their mood a bit.

"I'm not donating these shirts to you," he said. "I'm donating them
to *your teachers*. When they feel you've behaved well enough to
represent Blue Academy the way it should be represented, then they'll
give you your shirt. Maybe that happens today. Maybe, it's next
month. It's entirely up to them."

The teachers almost instinctively sat up a little, just as Greg had
hoped. More often than not, they had an inadequate supply of books
and supplies, but as The Lunch Lady said, they just did the best they
could with what they had -- knowing that, just maybe, all you have *is*
all you need. Even on the long days, the teachers at Blue Academy did
their best to act as a support system for one another -- reinforcing the
sense "we're all in this together." To Greg, they were everything
educators should be -- and everything he was trying so hard to be.
And so, as much as he wanted his Foundation to do something for the
kids, he wanted to make sure it happened in a way that was reinforcing
the teachers' authority instead of usurping it.

In the days that followed, the Foundation began giving out grants
to other schools and other students.

Each grant was named after one of Greg's favorite old instructors
-- from his first grade teacher to his professors from college. He
appreciated them when he was one of their students, but he appreciated them even more now that he understood firsthand how hard it is
to be a good teacher.

Sometimes, the grants were distributed to schools or organizations
-- five hundred dollars for books, three hundred for art supplies.

Other grants were presented to individual students. In one case, a
grant for school supplies was given to a girl who worked at the local
grocery store every day after school, but never complained about the
long hours. In another instance, a grant for music supplies was
awarded to a student because she finished her piano solo during a
recital even though a baby started crying in the audience.

Such grants were small -- just fifty or a hundred dollars apiece --
but Greg insisted they made an impact because they reinforced impor-

tant qualities like work ethic and perseverance.

"And besides," he chimed in, "it was *something*. And something is better than nothing."

After the speech at Blue Academy, Greg began getting invited to speak at other schools about overcoming obstacles and helping others. Each time, he opted to speak from the heart instead of writing a speech or using notes.

His friends often joked that, given how much he rambled, he was asking for disaster -- but their concerns proved unfounded. One of Greg's favorite courses back in Louisiana had been Public Speaking, and apparently, he soaked up every word of advice the professor offered because, in front of a crowd, his rapid-fire style of talking gave way to a remarkably slow and deliberate approach, and he never went longer than the time allotted to him.

A teacher who attended a speech later wrote that Greg's words were "calm and surreal, and floated through the air."

Of all the invitations Greg received, the sweetest by far was the one extended by his old high school to speak at an all-school assembly. It was the triumphant return he'd envisioned for years.

At least, it was supposed to be.

**

As the gate in front of Mortimer Dowhill Crest Randolph opened and the car made its way down the tree-lined path winding through campus, Greg gazed with interest out the window. All things considered, the school looked much like he'd left it.

He was such a relatively recent graduate, in fact, that many of his old teachers were still there. And when he entered the Grand Hall a few moments before the assembly, they all happily approached to greet him. All of them, that is, except one.

Mr. Welton.

He walked straight to the far end of the Hall and took a seat without saying a single word to his former protege. And as if the silent treatment wasn't insult enough, Welton wouldn't even look at the podium -- positioning himself in such a way that he was staring out a window instead. Literally and figuratively, he gave the cold shoulder to the guest of honor.

Greg had brought The Letter with him to MDCR that day. He

wasn't really sure why -- maybe, if Welton apologized, he'd throw it out as a symbolic gesture of moving forward -- but he now had a much less conciliatory plan in mind. As he could feel his blood pressure starting to rise and a reserve of deeply buried anger bubbling back toward the surface, Greg's gut reaction was to pull The Letter out of his pocket, read it out loud in front of the audience, and start hurling obscenities at Welton until they turned off the microphone.

But he resisted the temptation.

Looking out at the smiling faces of all his other old teachers who had always been kind to him, looking out at the impressionable teenagers sitting beside them, he just couldn't do it. The school had asked him to send a positive message to those students, and no matter how upset he was, that's what he was going to do.

So instead of bringing up Mr. Welton and The Letter, Greg spoke instead about the many *good* things he remembered about the school and the teachers there who had such a positive influence on his life. And then, he talked to the kids about diversity and service -- using his brunch program and nonprofit organization as examples.

Greg hoped his mature response to Welton's silence would lead to something positive -- perhaps, an apology would finally come his way -- but after the speech, the man still did not say a word to him.

Not to admit he was wrong all those years ago. Not to congratulate Greg on his success in college. Not to commend him for making a difference in the community. Not to thank him for avoiding mention of The Letter during the speech. Not even to say hello. Not one word.

Greg headed back home feeling sick about the experience.

What happened to a positive attitude leading to positive results?

And then, just when he was *this close* to being convinced that his effort to stay positive was pointless, he found out about Clifford.

A sophomore on scholarship at Mortimer Dowhill, Cliff was mindful of the imposing college bills that he faced in the not too far off future. But after hearing Greg's speech, he came to an inspiring conclusion: He wanted to help other students get the financial aid they needed to realize *their* dreams of higher education, and he wanted to do it now instead of later.

In the days that followed, without telling anyone, Cliff started writing letters to companies all over the country -- asking them to help the Foundation send kids to college.

The boy's efforts did not succeed, but the mere fact that he tried led Greg to believe his appearance at MDCR was worth it after all.

And as fate would have it, Cliff's efforts inspired another student (Fitz) at another school to try and make a difference, too.

Fitz said, "This kid, Cliff, was a sophomore. I was a *junior.* So, when I heard about what he tried to do, I figured that if he was old enough to try and help, then I was, too."

Fitz decided he would help by assembling a jazz group and staging a concert with all the proceeds going to The 11-10-02 Foundation (and, in turn, the Foundation pledged to donate those proceeds to help another school's music program).

Over the next few months, Fitz and his pals practiced songs, passed out fliers and told everyone they knew about the show. They even got their principal to let them use the school auditorium.

As Greg sat in the audience, surrounded by people of different cultures, ages, races and backgrounds, and listened to the performance, he could not have been happier. Going back to his days in Louisiana, his goal had been to inspire others to make a difference. So, the efforts of Fitz and the band were -- literally -- music to his ears.

The kids not only helped the Foundation. As time went on, in their own unique ways, they helped the man who started it, too.

When Greg was upset someone had not treated him nicely, it was a student who put his feelings back in perspective with a note about a time when someone was *really* not treated nicely" -- when her cousin was murdered. (Greg was so struck by the note he kept it in his wallet for years afterward).

When *Good Morning America* announced they would be burying a Time Capsule that, among other things, chronicled Greg's streak of weekly brunches (now up to 100) and he showed up at school that day feeling a little too self-important, it was a kid who pointed out he was wearing two different shoes and instantly put him back in his place. (Grandma loved the story so much she ordered Greg to start wearing mismatched socks every day -- so that a single glance at his feet would remind him how quickly Mr. TV Star was humbled by a child.)

And those were just two examples of many.

Time and time again, Greg left school at the end of the day with a new lesson he learned from the kids he was supposedly helping.

**

The Foundation was beginning to blossom. Greg even managed to get actual business execs who never lived under the same roof to

ₛ parents on the Board of Directors. But that is not to say his
ₘₙ was getting any easier. The newest setback involved his feet.

One morning, Greg woke up to the sounds of thousands of people
running down the street beneath his window. It turned out to be The
City's annual marathon. From his view, Greg could see the parade of
runners curved around the neighborhood and into the distance. In that
moment, he couldn't help thinking of his Grandma's constant refrain
about life being more meaningful if it wasn't always straight lines.

Right then and there, he decided to start training for a marathon.

Things seemed to get off to a good start until, seemingly out of
nowhere, Greg was unable to walk without pain. According to the
doctor, the problem required surgery.

At first, while he was disappointed that he wouldn't get to take
part in the marathon, Greg viewed the news he'd need to spend a few
days off his feet as a vacation of sorts -- expecting a wheelchair to be
like the Big Wheel he rode as a boy. Against doctor's orders, he even
insisted on -- literally -- wheeling himself home from the hospital.

He was quite the sight to behold -- laughing and singing as he
inched his bandaged body down The City's busiest streets.

Once he finally made it home and the painkillers wore off, however, he quickly got a rude awakening. Three days in a wheelchair
proved to be a grounding experience in more ways than one. In the
process, he developed a newfound respect for the strength of people
who deal with physical obstacles every day of their lives.

He said, "At first, a wheelchair seems fun, but then every bump in
the sidewalk becomes a battle. Your thumbs hurt from all the wheeling. You can't go down steps. You can't reach stuff on the top shelf at
the grocery store. I've learned a lot about being in a wheelchair."

It would be several weeks until he was walking regularly again,
but his Grandma insisted that he see the positive side of things.

She said, "If you have to walk slower, it takes you longer to get
somewhere, and the longer it takes you to get somewhere, the more
you appreciate getting there once you finally do."

The operation didn't stop Greg's streak of brunches -- he had the
kids wheel him to the restaurant -- but it was a close call. And it
wasn't the only one. In the preceding months, he overcame every
obstacle and schedule conflict imaginable to keep The Streak alive.
There were blizzards, heat waves and the day his car broke down ten

minutes before a brunch. Not to mention, birthday parties, weddings, anniversaries, and sometimes, he was sick or just plain tired.

But in the end, nothing ever got in the way of his Streak -- leading to even more tension than usual between Greg and his father.

Mark said, "His priorities were way off. If a family function occurred on a weekend, he skipped it. After thirty years of marriage, Rose and I went to Las Vegas and renewed our wedding vows in front of friends and family, and he didn't even come. Said he had to stay in town to host the brunch. The bottom line -- he was bringing strangers together every weekend...at the expense of being with people he'd known all his life."

Even among those who saw great value in The Brunch Bunch, there were many who wondered why Greg felt so strongly about sacrificing so much just to keep his Ripkenesque streak in tact.

As one observer put it, "It was a wonderful program, but I really don't think anyone would've thought any less of it if he took a week off every now and then. I mean, the whole thing was done on a voluntary basis. It's not like he had to do it at all."

But, really, to Greg, that was the whole point.

He said, "The way I figured, if one guy could sacrifice so much of his time, every single week, without exception, without excuses, through bad weather and operations and everything else -- when obligated to spend none at all -- then how could you say you're too busy to give up a tiny fraction of yours?"

Jalen Harmony was among those who took notice.

Born into one of the wealthiest families in the country, Jalen had truly lived a life of luxury. She carried herself with humility -- she avoided name-dropping and detested when others did it -- but there was still no denying her lineage. Her last name alone opened doors.

And then, one day, Greg opened one for her.

As the story goes...Jalen and one of her friends were getting together for Sunday brunch -- at the very same restaurant Greg had chosen as the site of that week's Brunch Bunch outing. They happened to be arriving at the same time, and Greg -- despite having no idea who Jalen was -- held the door for her and her friend.

It was a small gesture -- one that had become second nature to Greg after all his nights doing the same for customers at The Club. But it was the type of small gesture from a stranger that Jalen appreci-ated, after years and years of people who did know who she was trying to impress her with such grand ones.

Over the course of brunch, she watched Greg and his group with interest -- this was clearly not the typical clientele at the restaurants she frequented -- before she called over a waiter to ask for details. She was touched by what she heard, introduced herself to Greg, gave him her number, and encouraged him to call.

He recognized the last name, of course -- but he thought nothing of it. Just as there are plenty of Kennedy's who have no ties to the famous political family, it simply didn't cross Greg's mind that Jalen Harmony was one of *those* Harmony's.

And even if it had, he probably wouldn't have cared. Between growing up in the Shore, going to school at Mortimer Dowhill and working at The Club, he had met more than his share of people with well-known names and big bank accounts.

Jalen seemed kind, and that was enough for him. And so began the start of an unlikely friendship between the two.

A couple months later, Greg had the same operation on the other foot -- and was back in a wheelchair for three more days. Within a week, he was on his feet again, but he no longer could run around as freely as he once did.

Grandma once again insisted he make the best out of it.

She said, "Just do things you can do sitting down -- like art."

He followed her advice and spent more time on his sketches, and sure enough, they actually seemed to improve. Before long, the kid who could barely draw a straight line had slowly but surely begun drawing portraits that were practically *lifelike*.

The drawings had gotten *so* good, in fact, that one day, a man literally broke into Greg's apartment just to see them.

"I wasn't going to take anything," the man insisted, when questioned later. "I'm a repairman, and I fixed his sink last month, and I just wanted to see if he'd drawn anything new since I was there."

The incident proved to be a traumatic one for Greg. It triggered a flashback of his run-in with a burglar nearly twenty years earlier -- and a fresh batch of sleepless nights soon followed.

Hoping to regain his sense of security, he decided to do the same thing that worked when he was a child -- get a dog.

At least, that was his plan. His building prohibited pets, so he settled for the closest alternative -- a life-sized clay dog.

Greg's girlfriend at the time, Erica, laughed, "He gave it a name and even got the thing a leash. A *leash*. It was a *clay dog*. You know, sometimes, they'd write about Greg in the paper like he was this young visionary, and I used to think, don't any of these people realize that he *talks to a clay dog*?!"

With his new canine companion to protect him, Greg was able to sleep a little easier -- but, more often than not, he stayed up late anyway working on his sketches. For as he drew them, he got carried away into the worlds of the people he was drawing -- imagining their friends, their families, their fate -- and lost all track of time.

For a guy who rarely wanted to sit still, let alone sit still *and silent*, art seemed to be just what the doctor ordered.

Rose joked, "I wouldn't say he had become an entirely patient person, but art definitely pushed him further in that direction."

He spent weeks on each drawing -- perfecting every hair, wrinkle and freckle --- before framing them and putting them up on his wall.

As it turned out, art did more than just flex the muscles of Greg's imagination and improve his patience. It also helped him develop some *perspective*.

He learned that when he was drawing a mouth, for example, he had to contemplate two things at once. Besides focusing on how the mouth looked, he also had to consider how that piece fit into the larger puzzle -- the face -- he was putting together. Over time, he realized the lesson applied to more than art. It also applied to life.

He explained, "Art and life both revolve around that same basic principle -- that there are always two processes at work. What you are doing at the moment and how that moment factors into the bigger picture. Lose sight of one, and you're bound to fail at both. A well-drawn mouth can still turn a portrait into a caricature if it is drawn next to a nose instead of beneath it."

One of Greg's most prized portraits was his drawing of Martin Luther King, Jr. He hung it on his wall right by his desk. And so, in an ironic way, more than seven years after Greg hatched his still-secret *Dream* in that dormitory hallway in Louisiana, he still felt like Dr. King was looking over his shoulder.

This time around, though, it was not just the late Reverend keeping an eye on Greg. From left to right, top to bottom, the wall was filled with his portraits of a variety of leaders throughout history like Harriet Tubman, John F. Kennedy and Gandhi.

Mixed in among these portraits of historical leaders were others featuring his favorite cinematic characters -- like Jack Stanton (*Primary Colors*) and Red Redding (*Shawshank Redemption*). And so it came to be that the wall had become yet another facet of Greg's life that blended fiction and reality.

And the more time he spent on his art, the more those lines seemed to blur. For while they were just sketches, of course -- pencil put to paper -- Greg eventually began to see them in a different light.

For, late at night, as he stared in silence at the row of faces on his wall, he came to believe they were looking back at him. And before long, just as happened with The Silhouette Man and Ladder Horse years earlier, Greg began to talk with Governor Stanton, President Kennedy, Dr. King and the others who were 'present'.

At first, he addressed his Wall of Advisors deferentially and spoke only of issues he deemed worthy of their time. These were iconic leaders, after all. But, as Greg became more accustomed to their presence, he could not help casting formalities aside. Before long, they were all on a first name basis and the topics became more personal.

Like The Silhouette Man and The Ladder Horse, the Advisors proved to be great listeners -- so much so, they never interjected a single time. Frankly, Greg would've loved to get their input on all kinds of things, but their mere presence was appreciated all the same. Just like when he was a boy, more than anything else, on lonely sleepless nights, Greg simply valued the company.

In between portraits, Greg worked on creating 11-10-02's logo. He'd been trying to come up with one ever since starting the organization. His friends suggested hiring an expert to do it, but Greg refused -- insisting he could get it done.

He said, "I already know what I want the logo to include. I can see the different parts in my head. The only problem is that they're all jumbled up. All I gotta do is unscramble them like pieces of a puzzle, and it doesn't take an expert to do that. It just takes time."

A year and a half later, he'd finally managed to do it.

Greg turned his sketched image over to an expert graphic designer, who turned it into a reality. Greg insisted the finished product was *perfect*, but others were not so sure. In fact, most of his friends openly laughed at the design.

"It's a jumbled mess. It looks like something a fifth grader would do!" Cresta howled.

She was only teasing him, but in a sense, the Logo *was* drawn by a 5th grader. Because, after all these years, Greg finally drew the picture he'd been trying to draw since he was a boy. A picture that represented the things he saw outside his childhood window. From top to bottom, the images in the Logo represented The Silhouette Man, The Ladder Horse, the three bushes and his puppy's grave (beneath the middle bush). The triangle that connected all the dots? It represented the tent Greg put up in the yard on the weekends.

Harvard Charlie could not believe his eyes when he saw it.

"You spend a year and a half on this thing, and *this* is what you come up with? Are you crazy? You weren't supposed to draw a picture of what you saw out your window when you were little. The logo was supposed to be an image that represents *the Foundation*."

Charlie was trying to help, but his words upset Greg greatly.

As kids, the two lived parallel lives -- the same schools, same camps and (it was expected) same prosperous future -- but somewhere along the way, their lives drifted in different directions. Charlie followed the path that was 'expected' -- Ivy Leagues, then corporate America, and now, business school. Greg, on the other hand, detoured off the 'fast track' and carved out a much less certain trail that included stops in Louisiana, The Club and The Green.

Charlie wore tailored suits, carried a briefcase, traveled the world and took his dates out to elegant restaurants. Greg wore mismatched socks, carried a lunchbox, rarely ventured beyond the world outside his window and took his dates to local diners with coupons clipped out of the paper.

Their philosophies were different, too.

Charlie did believe in philanthropy. He just didn't believe in doing it now. The way he saw it, you make money, and once you're older and successful, then you help others. Greg, on the other hand, believed the giving back *was* the success. From his point of view, you focus on helping others first, and then, once you've succeeded at doing that, you begin thinking about your own bank account.

(Somewhat ironically, it apparently never dawned on either man at the time that both ideas -- making money and making a difference -- could be pursued simultaneously).

Greg didn't care that their philosophies and paths veered in such different directions. Nor did he mind the fact that Charlie's road was so much more financially lucrative. As long as Charlie was happy, he was genuinely happy for him. It was just that Greg's father reminded him on a daily basis that Charlie was living the life he "could be and should be" living, and after a while, it began to upset him.

So, instead of taking Charlie's comment for what it was -- advice from a friend -- Greg saw it as the guy he was "supposed to be" telling him what he was "supposed to do" -- and he couldn't stand it.

Grandma had little patience for his whining.

"Stop comparing yourself to Charlie," she huffed. "Charlie is Charlie. Greg is Greg. If you're doing better than you were doing a year ago, then you're doing just fine."

In reality, the Logo was a lot more complex than Charlie or anyone else realized. Yes, its different parts were inspired by what Greg saw outside his childhood window, but that was just Phase One. Every part of the Logo had a *second* meaning revolving around the Foundation's mentoring program.

The Three Ovals did not just represent three bushes. They also were three glasses -- symbolizing the day Greg and two kids had the milkshakes that eventually led to the start of The Brunch Bunch.

The Tombstone represented the tombstone in Greg's old yard. It also represented the philosophy that he first learned from his brief friendship with the puppy who was buried there -- a philosophy reinforced when Bailey was killed years later. That being, seize the chance to get to know new friends today because there is no guarantee they will still be there tomorrow.

The Ladder represented The Ladder Horse in the backyard. It also represented what Greg hoped the kids were learning at brunch -- the ladder's five rungs symbolizing five steps to success: ethics, etiquette, effort, education and (positive) environment.

The Silhouette on top of the ladder represented The Silhouette

Man swingset in Greg's old yard. It also represented the idea that if a kid took the lessons taught at brunch to heart, then he or she climbs the ladder's five rungs and makes themselves, and the program, a success.

The Triangle represented the tent Greg used to put up in the backyard. It also represented a mountain, and the belief that making a mountain out of a molehill isn't always such a bad thing. That it was good to make a big deal out of something small if it's done for the right reason. And that's what had happened with The Brunch Bunch -- a couple shakes turned into a full-fledged program.

With the brunches in full swing and the Logo now in place, a real organization was beginning to take shape and Greg gave more and more thought to pursuing his original goal -- scholarships.

Charlie asked him how he planned to raise the necessary funds.

"I don't have a plan to raise the money," Greg replied matter-of-factly. "The money will show up on its own."

Charlie could not believe what he was hearing.

"Money doesn't just *show up*," he snapped. "You need a plan -- a business plan -- if you hope to generate revenue."

"Not in this case," Greg insisted. "Now that the Foundation is all set up, all I have to do is step back and get out of the way, and the money will come pouring in."

Charlie scratched his head, unsure exactly where to begin.

"How did you come up with this idea? Money just showing up. How'd you come up with this?" he asked, a bit exasperated.

Greg smiled and said, "*Field of Dreams*. It was a movie --"

Charlie cut him off mid-sentence. He had heard enough. Yes, there was a film about an Iowa farmer named Ray Kinsella who built a baseball diamond in his yard, and yes, people started showing up out of nowhere after he built it, but a rational person couldn't base his business model on such a precedent. *It was a movie.*

Greg begged to differ.

"Think what you want, Charlie, but that baseball field, it's *real*. People still go there all the time."

Charlie was at a total loss for words. It was true, the baseball field did exist, but it was constructed by a movie crew -- not by a fictitious farmer -- and left in tact as a tourist attraction after the film came out.

Despite Charlie's response, Greg remained undeterred.

And that's how it came to be that The 11-10-02 Foundation launched its first fundraising campaign by doing....*nothing.*

As Greg's feet healed and he waited for the checks to start showing up out of thin air, he continued trying to help others whenever he could -- whether it was hosting the weekly brunches (now on the verge of their three year anniversary), bringing more friends with him to volunteer at The Center (more than a hundred had now joined him), surprising a hard-working music teacher with a grant for more instruments, or dressing up as Santa Claus on Christmas Eve and delivering gifts to a church in The Green.

None of these efforts were global in their magnitude -- in fact, they were decidedly small -- but that was the point. Greg believed even such small efforts would have a uniquely positive *ripple effect* -- inspiring other people to believe they could make a difference, too. Each person contributing to society in their own small way.

And that's exactly what happened.

In some cases, people were inspired to support Greg's goals. They signed up for a brunch, volunteered at The Center, or made donations to The 11-10-02 Foundation. Some were Greg's friends -- one of his old camp counselors sent him a brand new desk. Some were strangers -- a woman in Oklahoma sent a brand new fax machine, another from Florida sent five hundred dollars.

In other cases, people heard about Greg's efforts and were inspired to set new goals of their own. More than once, he got a note from someone who said his story inspired them to become a teacher.

As the weeks passed, Greg's story continued to spread in unexpected -- and increasingly remarkable -- ways.

Shortly before Christmas, he served as Honorary Principal at Blue Academy. At the start of the new year, a suburban English teacher assigned Greg's story to her students as part of a unit on intolerance and diversity, along with *Schindler's List* directed by Steven Spielberg and *Night* by Holocaust survivor Elie Wiesel. A month after that, another school brought Greg and Wiesel -- the substitute teacher and the Nobel Peace Prize honoree -- to speak on the same day. Two months after that, Greg and Grandma graced the cover of *Senior News.* And then, a New York fashion magazine did an article *about what Greg wore* -- including a close-up picture of his mismatched socks.

The President of the United States even got in on the act.

When The Brunch Bunch reached its three year anniversary, he sent a letter encouraging them to continue their efforts.

"How did the President even know?" Charlie asked.

"You wouldn't believe me if I told you," Greg replied.

He wasn't kidding.

It seems that a few months earlier, a White House staffer was filing some letters sent to the President when she came across a note about The Brunch Bunch, and was taken by its mission. The staffer also was struck by the identity of the group's founder. After all, she hadn't seen Greg in nearly ten years, when he left Louisiana to spend his junior year in England, then never came back.

The White House staffer was Galloway Roarke.

**

Despite all the unusual twists and turns, Greg was determined to stay focused -- and grounded. With that in mind, he returned to his hometown to speak at his old middle school and announce a special grant in honor of one of the teachers who tried especially hard to help him when he was a boy. Then, he accepted an invitation to visit Bailey's town to speak at *his* old school and announce a grant from the Foundation that would help the students there.

For weeks, Greg had been anticipating the latter. He had never been to Bailey's school before -- or, for that matter, the town where it was located -- and he had a heartfelt surprise up his sleeve for the students and staff who would be in attendance.

When the day arrived, it soon became clear Greg was not the only one anticipating the event. Upon stepping inside the auditorium, he discovered a group of Bailey's old friends, teachers and coaches already waiting there to greet him.

"I thought I'd just be speaking to the student body and faculty," Greg whispered to the school rep who had escorted him inside.

She smiled and said, "News of the event spread around town, and we began getting calls from people who knew Bailey and wanted to be here. He was a special young man, you know."

One by one, the visitors began introducing themselves to Greg -- approaching him with hugs and handshakes, not to mention an array of photos and old clippings from the paper.

"Here," said one of Bailey's old coaches, handing Greg some articles, "I made you copies. I know how much he meant to you."

Greg was genuinely touched to see these people cared so deeply about Bailey, and he comforted them with smiles that were truly sincere -- but deep down, he felt sick. Literally. Ten minutes before the speech, he dashed off to the bathroom and threw up.

Over the years, to Greg, Bailey had come to represent a belief -- make an effort to get to know others now since there's no guarantee they'll be here later. He referred to Bailey as a 'friend' -- or, at times, even a 'good friend' -- when people asked because he genuinely had considered him one (and tended to use such words to describe every-one he met). Besides, it seemed awkward to say his 'acquaintance' died. But the reality was that he hardly knew the guy.

Whereas, these people did. They knew Bailey, and they loved him, To these people, Bailey was much more than just an inspiring symbol. He had been a living, breathing *friend*. And talking to them before the speech, it hit Greg like a ton of bricks that there's a huge difference.

In the future, he'd make an increasingly conscious effort to refer to Bailey as just a 'new friend' or 'someone he knew'.

In the meantime, he had a speech to give -- and an audience eager to hear it.

Despite the knots in his stomach, the event seemed to go fine. In addition to announcing the grant for the school, Greg revealed the surprise -- an essay contest with the winning student receiving a grant from the Foundation as well. He named both grants after Bailey.

A couple hours after he arrived, Greg pulled out of the school parking lot, feeling that he had accomplished something meaningful.

In the past, when he forgot that a journey of any kind is not complete until you get back to where you started -- when he began to celebrate success prematurely -- he somehow got derailed.

As fate would have it, this time was no different.

Less than ten minutes into the drive home, Greg's car died.

While he waited for assistance, the eternally impatient young man tried to come up with something to do to pass the time. All he had with him was the packet of articles about Bailey he'd been given before the speech, but he had only accepted them to be polite and had no intention of actually reading them -- still preferring to learn nothing new about his old peer's life or tragic death.

But as the minutes passed, and he sat there waiting, with nothing else to do and a packet full of answers to decade-old questions sitting by his side, he found it impossible to ignore them any longer. Finally, he opened the packet.

It turned out to be a mixed blessing.

He later recalled, "I wish I could say it gave me some sense of closure to know some of the details of his death, but it didn't. He was an innocent victim of a drive-by shooting. Knowing the details didn't make that any better."

On the bright side, the articles did provide Greg a greater sense of Bailey's amazing *life* -- the things he achieved, the people he touched, the future he was planning. The guy really had been everything he seemed to be in the short time they knew each other.

Greg decided to name his Foundation's first college scholarship in Bailey's memory, too.

He later explained, "My reasons for wanting to help other kids get to college had a lot more to do with Mr. Welton than Bailey, but I wanted to use the platform I now had to focus on somebody whose impact was a *positive* one -- and that was what Bailey was all about."

The money to fund the scholarship was given to the Foundation by an anonymous donor who showed up seemingly out of the blue.

It was obviously just a fortuitous coincidence that this man was looking to do something generous and happened to learn about The Foundation around the same time -- but Greg gleefully insisted otherwise when sharing the news with Charlie.

"I told you! The *Field of Dreams* business model works! Lay the groundwork, and the money will show up out of the thin air!"

With the funding in place, all Greg had to do now was decide which student received the scholarship. To help narrow the field, he contacted eleven local schools and let them each nominate two seniors. To avoid any chance that a student's opportunity got lost in the shuffle -- or, worse yet, was subjected to someone's Weltonesque agenda -- he also personally drove to each school, met with each representative (usually, the college counselor) and made clear what he expected from them during the nomination process.

To their credit, most of the counselors -- already overworked as it is -- took the chance seriously, found some extra time (or, more accurately, stayed at work a little longer) and nominated some solid candidates as promised.

And the ones who didn't, as warned, were notified they would not get the opportunity again -- courtesy of a blistering letter. All these years after Welton let Greg down, the thought of someone failing to go the extra mile to get their students all the help possible remained his Achilles Heel.

Once selected, the nominees were asked to prepare applications.

To pick the winner, Greg asked a dozen of his friends to serve as judges. They agreed to do it, but they quickly realized it was no easy task. It was so hard, in fact, that they could not choose between two of the finalists.

Fortunately, before Greg had to think of a way to break the deadlock, an unlikely supporter solved the problem for him.

Bo Farnesworth was successful in business, considerate to his neighbors, drove responsibly, dressed immaculately, and tipped well.

And none of it seemed to matter.

He was a black man living in a mostly white community, and he seemed to be reminded of this distinction in some offensive way, large or small, on a regular basis.

As time went on, Bo became increasingly convinced there was no escaping the stereotypical slights. Eventually, he stopped trying.

And so it was, with that background in mind, that Bo noticed The Brunch Bunch one afternoon and hastily dismissed the group as little more than a feel-good, accomplish-nothing waste of time.

"They could have a brunch every week for a century, and people will still make presumptions," he muttered to himself.

A few days later, he sent an e-mail through the organization's website to express that belief. Bo doubted he would hear anything back, but Greg responded personally -- and forcefully.

"You don't like being judged. Don't judge us."

Over the next few weeks, the two men shared a frank exchange about stereotypes, the extent to which such things could be changed, and the value -- if any -- in trying to be the one who changed them. The dialogue did little to change Bo's mind about the impact of the weekly brunches -- but he did, at least, become convinced that the program's founder had good (albeit naive) intentions at heart.

In the weeks that followed, Bo even paid the bill for an entire brunch -- on one slightly amusing condition. Greg was not allowed to reveal the identity of the generous benefactor to anyone present.

Bo noted sarcastically, "If people around here found out I did something nice, it would ruin my reputation."

Later on, Bo agreed to be one of the judges on the Scholarship Board. And, after finding out two nominees had tied for first place, he started making calls and came up with the money to fund a second scholarship.

The Foundation not only had its first ever Scholar. It now had *two*.

This was something Greg pictured for years, and it definitely called for a celebration. He chose a popular local restaurant to be the site of the party. The Brunch Bunch had eaten there a number of times over the past couple years. The food was always amazing, and the staff always treated the group like royalty. Given that they also had a separate banquet room to handle private events, the Restaurant seemed to be a perfect fit.

Well, almost.

There was just *one little* snag. The fledgling Foundation could not promise full payment. Sure, if all the tickets sold, the bill would be paid. In the meantime, the Restaurant would have to take an I.O.U. (and a non-guaranteed one, at that), or there could be no event.

For the Restaurant, there seemed to be little incentive to go along with the plan. They already had plenty of clients. They didn't need to take a risk on something like this. And make no mistake, this was certainly a risk. By any logical standard, The 11-10-02 Foundation's event would not sell out.

It was a tiny organization run by a substitute teacher with a lunchbox for a briefcase. Its leader had never previously hosted a banquet, let alone a successful one. They had lined up zero corporate sponsors for the proposed event, and they weren't even going to be able to afford invitations to promote it.

Charlie chuckled, "Let me repeat that so it really sinks in. He wanted to ask a very popular place, in no need of his business, to take a non-guaranteed I.O.U. predicated upon ticket sales *and there weren't going to be any invitations.*"

The idea did seem preposterous. In fact, nobody else but Greg seemed to think it was even worth proposing. And yet, after hearing the sales pitch, the head of the Restaurant smiled warmly and said, "Let's take a look at the calendar and see what's available."

"You mean it?!" Greg said excitedly.

"Yes, I do," he said, with a smile. "I believe in you and what you're doing for those kids. And I'm sure you'll sell those tickets."

It was a gesture that Greg would never forget -- someone going out on a real limb to support one of his dreams.

After the space was booked, the Restaurant's event planner called Greg to plan the menu, but to her surprise, he asked her to do it.

He said, "It wasn't that I didn't care. It's just that everything they serve is good, so I really wasn't worried about what was on the menu. And, frankly, I was too busy thinking about what was going to happen *after* dinner to think about the actual meal."

Twenty years after peeking inside the projectionist's booth at the movie theater, seven years after he passed up the chance to study film in Europe, and four years after his brief trip to California, Greg still yearned for the chance to tell stories that impacted people's lives -- and the Gala was going to be his chance to do that. It was not just going to be a *program*. It was going to be a *show*.

His neighbor, Arthur, said, "In the overall scheme of things, it was really just going to be your standard awards banquet -- people go up to a podium, get a trophy, give a speech, sit down, that kind of thing -- but there was no telling Greg that. He talked about the thing like it was going to be a performance on Broadway."

And he wasted little time getting started with its production.

The first decision was easy -- the musical entertainment. Without even considering the possibility they were too young to handle such a big responsibility, Greg invited Fitz and his pals to be the evening's band -- out of appreciation for the concert they put together earlier.

With that out of the way, he began to focus on the trophies.

Some of Greg's friends couldn't understand why it mattered -- trophies are trophies, they said, the scholarship winners will just be happy to get one -- but he insisted it was an important decision.

He said, "Every great story has a *symbol*. Willy Wonka had those golden tickets. Forrest Gump, he had shrimp. I gotta have one, too."

He spent hours pouring through catalogs looking for a design that was unique, but none of them caught his eye. Until finally, he decided to just design his own...*using unwashed milkshake glasses.*

Greg's friends thought he was nuts when he told them about the idea, but he swore it was perfect.

"For one thing," he told them, "the glasses can symbolize the day I took the kids for shakes that led to all this. But more importantly, we're trying to show that everything and everyone has value -- and what better way is there to prove that than by turning moldy, dirty milkshake glasses into trophies?!"

After getting Mr. Goldberg the Trophy Maker to agree to make the trophies (despite the horrible smell), Greg turned his attention to selling tickets. He knew he had little time to waste.

Since there was no budget for invitations, he resorted to standing outside and approaching passers-by. Suffice it to say, not too many were impressed by the 'Gala' he was promoting.

After hearing Greg's curbside sales pitch, one observer said, "It seemed like a cute event, and I suppose he could call it whatever he wanted, but it wasn't actually a real *Gala*. A *Gala* is a fancy affair on a Saturday night at a big hotel. This was going to take place *on a Sunday...at a restaurant* -- with no sponsors, no invitations, and the band was a bunch of kids. Sorry, but that's no Gala."

Of course, even if it was a legitimate Gala, the street corner was not exactly the ideal place to try and sell the tickets to it. Convincing people walking down the street to drop fifty cents for a cup of lemonade they can drink right then and there is one thing. Getting someone to stop and shell out fifty dollars for a dinner that isn't taking place for a month is another.

Greg sold a whopping half-dozen tickets out on the street that first week, but he just stubbornly continued with his efforts.

As much as the Gala weighed on Greg's mind, it was not the only one he was thinking a bout. Around the same time, Jalen Harmony asked him to be her date at an annual charity function she was hosting in the massive ballroom of one of The City's most exquisite hotels.

Greg happily accepted the invitation. Jalen was fun to be around, and it seemed like the event at The Big Hotel would be an ideal chance to get a glimpse of what occurs at a Gala -- to ensure he was not overlooking anything as he planned his own.

As the night drew near, though, the substitute teacher became increasingly nervous. He was the guest of the evening's high-profile host, and he knew people were going to notice. He didn't want to let Jalen down or embarrass himself by saying the wrong thing.

Greg turned to Grandma for some advice.

She huffed, "Afraid of saying something stupid? Then, don't say nothing. Just shut up and listen. You got big ears. Use 'em."

Greg did as instructed -- spending most of the evening with his mouth closed and his ears open, listening intently and smiling politely as those around him talked about international travel, their political affiliations and blue-chip investments.

Things seemed to be going well, but as the evening went on, Greg could not stand to stay silent any longer. He desperately wanted to demonstrate he *belonged*. He wanted to prove he could be *one of them*. When there was a momentary lull, he decided to seize the opportunity.

"My Foundation is having a Gala this summer," he declared proudly to the table. "It's going to be just like this one."

As always, he should've just listened to Grandma. The attempt to impress the others sparked a series of well-intended questions -- all of which made him feel like crawling under the table.

"Which hotel is hosting it?" asked one guest politely.

"Well, actually, we're having it at a restaurant," he replied.

"Who's sponsoring it?" asked another.

"There are no sponsors," he said, a bit defeated.

"You'll have to send me an invitation," said a third, supportively.

"We don't have any," he uttered in a voice barely above a whisper.

Thanks to his own big mouth, the event had become a humiliating affair for Greg -- but it was hardly his only source of frustration. As spring became summer, he became increasingly upset by something else -- the media.

At first glance, there didn't seem to be much for him to gripe about -- the articles about him in the paper and the reports on TV always praised his efforts -- but it wasn't the way they described *him* that he found so offensive. It was the way they described the kids he helped. More often than not, the reporters used labels like *underprivileged* and *disadvantaged*, and it frustrated Greg to no end.

He said to Charlie, "I know those kids personally and some of them have explained why they don't like those labels --"

Charlie interrupted, "Aren't they being a little overly sensitive? It's not like *underprivileged* is a racial slur or something."

Greg nodded, "I thought the exact same thing, that this wasn't a big deal, but the more I thought about it, I realized they're right. For one thing, why does the media get to decide what a privilege is? And, when someone in the media says a kid is *less privileged*, tell me this -- *less privileged than who?*"

Charlie acknowledged the questions were good ones, but he still wasn't convinced there was a double standard.

"It's the media," he said, "they pass judgment on everyone."

"Oh, yeah? Okay, then tell me this. How often do you see an article with a headline like *Overprivileged kid wins spelling bee?*"

Charlie had no answer for that one.

The situation upset Greg so much he started giving reporters a list of words they had to promise not to use or he wouldn't do the interview, but a few broke their pledge as quickly as they made it.

"Did you hear that?" Greg screamed at the TV as the reporter used the term *disadvantaged*. "They promised not to do that! I just don't get it! Why run a story praising my efforts to fight stereotypes if you're just gonna turn around and use those very labels in the process?"

He continued to complain about the press on a daily basis until, finally, Grandma intervened.

"You're giving me a headache," she griped. "If you've got something to say about the media, just do what they do -- write it down. And don't ramble. You always ramble."

He did as she told him -- writing down his feelings, then condensing them to a single, ramble-free page. When he was done, he submitted the essay to the local paper as a guest column.

It was rejected.

"Now what?" he asked Grandma.

"*Now what???* How many times I gotta tell you this? If you got a good idea, never think about whether it will *succeed* or *fail*. Just think about whether it will succeed *now* or succeed *later*. So...if you like the column you wrote, then fix it up and submit it again."

Greg did as Grandma instructed -- adjusting the column a bit and then submitting it to the paper a second time. When it was rejected again, he stubbornly submitted it a third time. When it was rejected a third time, he showed up at a party where the head of the paper was slated to be and presented him the column in person.

The fourth time finally proved to be the charm.

Greg knew his column in and of itself certainly wouldn't solve the problem of labels and stereotypes, but it was, at least, *something*.

Of all the lines he wrote, he was most proud of the one that echoed what he'd been saying to students again and again.

The most important word in the world is your name.

And it was with that sentiment in mind that the column's byline incorporated something that had not seen the light of day very often since Greg was a child. His *full* name -- middle name, Forbes, included. Having spent so much time telling kids to take pride in *their* names, he decided it was time to finally embrace his own.

**

Greg had evolved from a shy child into a young man bursting with confidence. Even socially, he was finally coming into his own. The boy who stuttered when he saw the pretty girl with blue eyes was now being featured in magazines as one of The City's most eligible men.

"Hot! Hot! Hot!" declared one headline.

Despite his slightly atypical responses in the interviews (according to one profile, his 'ideal woman' had, among other things, the "courage of Harriet Tubman and wisdom of my Grandma"), he started receiving dozens of letters from single women.

Greg knew it was all silly, but given the teasing he took as a kid, it did not take long for the affection to go to his head. And just like always, it took even less time for him to be humbled back to reality.

When being primped and prepped for one of the magazine photo shoots, Mister Eligible suddenly noticed some black dust in the air.

"What's that?" he asked the hair stylist.

"Just powder," she replied. "to cover up the shine."

He didn't understand what she meant, so she picked up a mirror and showed him. When he saw what she was pointing at, his heart sank to his stomach. A clump of Greg's hair was missing.

Charlie said, "It was just a patch of hair -- certainly not the end of the world -- but you still had to feel bad for the guy. He was such a scrawny kid for so long, and here he was, after all those years in the gym, just when he started to feel comfortable about the way he looked, a patch of his hair suddenly falls out. There was always something."

Fortunately, not all the news was bad news.

Around that same time, Greg received a special award for public service and was flown to D.C. to attend a ceremony that summer.

The trip -- which marked the first time Greg had left home in nearly three years -- turned out to be one of the most memorable experiences of his life. He attended a reception with Senators, a dinner with the likes of former astronaut John Glenn and a ceremony in the Supreme Court with Justice Sandra Day O'Connor.

He also found time to visit the White House and say hello to his old college friend, Galloway. While he was there, he got to take the President's dog for a walk around the West Wing -- and ended up running into the President and the head of Argentina in the process.

Galloway rolled her eyes and chuckled, "Don't even ask."

Despite being in town for just three days, Greg's run-in with the Commander-in-Chief (and First Dog) was just one of several adventures he had in the nation's capital. Later that same night, at a reception, Greg took a wrong turn down a hallway and interrupted a reporter doing a broadcast for the nightly news. The next day, he strolled into the train station, unaware that a major movie was in the process of being filmed.   In yet another instance, he misread his itinerary and showed up to a suit-and-tie breakfast *in pajamas.*

"I thought when it said *breakfast: suit and tie,* it meant for me to go to breakfast, *then* put on a suit and tie," he pleaded.

Not that he seemed *too* concerned. While a hundred well-heeled guests watched with amusement, Greg sat down in his pajamas and ate two plates of pancakes before going back to his room to change.

As much fun as it was for Greg to 'rub elbows' with Senators, the President and a Supreme Court Justice, some of the other honorees in attendance -- 'ordinary' people who had made a difference in their respective communities. They were the ones who impacted him most. *They* were the ones he felt defined what public service was really all about. They were living proof of what Greg believed ever since he was a child reading about Harriet Tubman -- that anyone anywhere at any age can make a difference.

Of them all, Greg was most inspired by one of the four student honorees -- an eleven year old boy from Kentucky named Jarrett. The fact he was even alive was a miracle -- having spent his life battling cancer, already losing his hair and one leg in the process. And yet, instead of dwelling on his own problems, the boy started an organization to brighten up the lives of other kids facing obstacles.

Greg marveled at the boy's attitude. Little Jarrett had so much *inner* strength, even as his physical condition deteriorated. It was a humbling reminder there's more to life than how much weight you can lift and whether there's a shiny reflection off the top of your head.

The trip to D.C. inspired Greg to think about what he could do to expand his civic efforts. It didn't take long to come up with an idea.

As soon as he got home, he looked up the number of the university that Bailey had planned to attend had he lived. He then called and asked for the President's office. When an assistant answered, Greg politely introduced himself and explained why he was calling.

"About a decade ago, there was a guy who was going to attend your school on scholarship, but he was killed before he got the chance. And it dawned on me, since he never got to go to college back then, the money you would've used to fund his scholarship, it's probably just sitting in the bank, so I was thinking, maybe we could use that money to send a student to college *now.*"

Convinced it was a prank phone call, the assistant hung up.

Undeterred, Greg called right back.

"I think we were disconnected," he said politely.

The President's assistant didn't really know what to say. The man on the other end of the line was, apparently, serious.

"Okay, just so I understand this," she said, "you -- a complete stranger who's never contacted us before -- want us to create a scholarship in honor of someone who never actually went here, and you want us to provide the money to fund it."

"That pretty much sums it up," Greg said.

"Is that all?" she asked with a chuckle.

"Oooh," he said. "I'm glad you asked. There is one other thing. I'd really appreciate if you could get it done in the next two weeks so it can be announced at the Gala we're having."

The Assistant waited for the man on the other end of the line to laugh, but he never did. Greg really was serious.

Hopelessly, blissfully, obliviously, serious.

When Charlie heard about the call, he chastised his old pal.

"Do you like when people laugh at you? Is that why you do these things?" he asked.

"Don't you have some merger to worry about?"

"Even if they *could* do it," Charlie replied, "why did you think they would care about doing a favor for you? *They don't know you!*"

"Because," Greg said, "it makes sense, and I asked nicely."

For better or worse, he took the same idealistic, glass is half-full approach to ticket sales. No matter how many people turned him down, he still insisted the Gala would sell out.

His ex-girlfriend, Jenny said, "He'd get 49 rejections for every one yes -- but he didn't see it as '*one yes out of fifty*'. He just saw it as '*one yes*'. And, if you take that approach, and you stick with it, then eventually, the yes's add up and the tickets get sold."

Everywhere he went, those tickets were the first and last topic of conversation. One afternoon, his car died (again). The rental car service sent out a driver to pick him up. By the time she got Greg back to the facility, the driver had already written a check for two tickets to the Gala.

Jenny said, "It wasn't just about raising money for the Foundation. I think Greg desperately wanted to justify the faith that the head of the Restaurant showed in him. He wanted to pay that bill."

And when all was said and done, he was able to do just that.

Despite having no sponsors to help purchase blocks of tickets, despite having no Planning Committee to help spread the word, despite not even having any invitations... somehow, some way, one or two seats at a time, the event sold out.

The morning of the Gala

With a 'full house' expected for the big show, Greg wanted to check and double-check all the details, but it was a luxury he just didn't have. Gala or no Gala, it was Sunday, and that meant it was time for brunch. And this one was going to be special.

The 172nd brunch in a row was going to be Greg's very last one.

He had promised his parents he'd go to law school or get a high-paying job once he fulfilled his goal of sending a kid to college. If he chose a school or job out of state, the streak of brunches was bound to end. Rather than drag it out, he decided to just bring everything to an end on one, grand unforgettable day.

And this was going to be that day.

For the final outing of The Brunch Bunch, Greg thought about organizing a reunion of the hundreds of people who'd come to at least one brunch over the years. But as the day drew near, he had a change of heart -- deciding it would be more fitting to end the streak of brunches the exact same unassuming way it started.

One man, two kids and three milkshakes.

So just past noon, without any media or fanfare, Greg and two students -- Trace and Josh -- made the short walk to go get a bite to eat, gulp down some shakes and bring the streak of brunches to a simple and quiet end.

At least, that was the plan.

When they arrived, the restaurant refused to let Greg in.

Not that he should've been surprised. After all, he had not arbitrarily chosen any restaurant. This was Dorethy Keyser's Place.

Two years earlier, when Greg first started bringing The Brunch Bunch to different spots around the city, the restaurant community supported the program with open arms -- offering wonderful meals, impeccable service and significant discounts. With one exception. Dorethy Keyser's Place (known around town as DKP's).

Dorethy's granddaughter, the third generation of the family to run the place, told Greg she could provide The Bunch a great meal and great service, but she would not be able to hold a table for such a big group or offer them a discount.

Keyser had every right to make that decision, of course, but there was no telling Greg that. Rather than accept the possibility DKP's could not afford to give a discount, or that they already supported their fill of worthy causes, or that they simply didn't like to support any, or that they just weren't set up to accommodate groups of that size on busy weekend mornings, Greg took it *personally* -- convinced that the lady was trying to undermine the success of the program he spent more than three years building from the ground up.

It was the same apparent persecution complex Greg displayed over and over since the Welton debacle. If someone -- especially someone in a position of authority -- didn't fully support his plan, he became convinced that they were actively trying to sabotage it. And he almost always responded the same way -- lashing out with long, rambling notes oozing with self-righteous anger.

Rose said, "The letters weren't going to accomplish a thing, other than upsetting the people who received them, but he insisted on writing them. He had kept his mouth shut when he was victimized by Welton. He just wasn't going to stay quiet again. If he saw someone interfering with his dreams -- or anyone's dreams for that matter -- he felt it was his personal responsibility to say something."

Others warned him there would eventually be a price to pay.

A business-wise friend, Abby, said, "People have long memories, and sooner or later, you're going to cross paths with one of these people, and they're still going to be upset about some dumb letter you wrote a few years earlier."

And, sure enough, that's exactly what happened with DKP's.

After they were unwilling to discount the brunches, Greg wrote a note ripping Keyser's management. Two years later, they had not forgotten the sting of his words.

So much so, they not only wouldn't give him a discount or hold him a table -- now, apparently, they wouldn't even serve him.

Unaware of the history, Josh and Trace were stunned by how Greg was treated, but they were even more surprised by his response. The same man who protested even the smallest injustice walked away from this one with a relative whimper -- putting up a half-hearted protest at best before taking the boys to a different restaurant a few doors down and acting like nothing happened.

Trace said, "I didn't know what to make of it. I thought maybe, with this being the last brunch in such a long streak, he just wanted to end things on a positive note. At least, that was my best guess because once we got to the other restaurant, he never discussed it."

Three hours later

The Gala was scheduled to start at exactly twenty-five minutes after six, but it got off to a bumpy start.

Charlie noted, "Six-fifteen rolls around, Greg is nowhere to be found -- and nobody had any idea where they were supposed to sit."

The man with the mismatched socks did finally show up just before dinner was served, but it wasn't exactly like he saved the day.

He forgot to bring the seating chart.

Greg apologized repeatedly for his tardiness and the oversight, but in truth, his 'missteps' were as calculated as could be.

He later confessed, "In the weeks leading up to the event, people kept insisting I had to make a pre-arranged seating chart, so the guests could sit with their friends -- but I wanted the Gala to be like the brunches. Step out of your comfort zone, diversify your life a little, eat with strangers, meet a few people."

In the end, he came up with a nifty solution. He played along and agreed to make a seating chart, and then used his (well-deserved) image as an easily distracted fool to his advantage -- pretending he lost track of time and forgot the diagram in his rush to get there.

The seating free-for-all was just one of many reasons Greg had to feel good as the Gala got underway.

A student named Rockefeller was another.

In contrast to all the other guests sporting suits and dresses, the kid with the memorable name was decked out in a tuxedo.

"What's up with the tux?" Greg asked.

The boy replied, "If it's a Gala to you, then it's a Gala to me."

Greg smiled warmly at the remark.

From the first time they met, Rockefeller ("Rocky" to friends) had been one of his favorite students -- hard-working in and out of class, working full-time to help pay his family's bills, always polite to teachers and other students, plus he had the fancy-sounding kind of name a guy with the middle name Forbes could appreciate.

Once Rocky and the other guests chose their seats, they ate to their hearts' content as the sound of Fitz's jazz band filled the air.

When the delicious meal was done, everyone looked at Greg, assuming he would be first to speak, but they were in for a surprise. Josh and Trace -- the students he brunched with earlier in the day -- approached the microphone and announced *they* would be hosting the show. And that's really what it was going to be. *A show.*

Greg had scripted out the entire program right down to the smallest detail. And he didn't just script the award presenters' lines. He even scripted out their *movements.* It actually said things in the script like 'Look stage left and cough'.

The program began with three tributes to the person after whom Greg named the Foundation's first scholarships.

The three tributes were intended to represent three of the many facets of Bailey's life -- family, sports and school.

First, one of Bailey's relatives gave a speech about him. Then, a representative of the football camp where Greg and Bailey met a decade earlier went on stage and announced a plaque was being put up in the locker room in their honor -- a plaque that talked about athletics and life being about more than just winning games.

Then, it was time for the third of the three tributes.

A representative of the college Bailey planned to attend had he lived went on stage and announced that the school had in fact decided to grant Greg's wish and create a one-time, four year scholarship named after someone they'd never met and who never attended their school, *and fund the entire thing on their own.*

Somewhat amusingly, Greg was the only person in the room who did not seem absolutely astounded that this had happened -- let alone that it had occurred in a span of just a few weeks.

The audience, having assumed the university rep was done with his announcement, began to applaud loudly in support of it. But, as it turned out, the man had yet another twist to share.

"We also decided," the man said from his spot at the podium, "that even though we're funding this ourselves, and even though we've never met Greg a single time, we're going to let him decide who gets the four year scholarship."

It was an almost incomprehensible leap of faith -- Charlie nearly choked on a piece of bread when the announcement was made -- but it would be just one of many surprises to come throughout the evening.

After the crowd settled down, Trace said it was time to pay tribute to the supporters who helped make the Foundation a success. Everyone expected a bunch of wealthy donors to get called up on stage -- that was how such things usually worked at a Gala -- but Greg had insisted the moment also be used to shine a light on people whose contributions usually get overlooked in public. And so, the award recipients included people like the accountant who helped with the financial work, and the lady who printed the Foundation's business cards.

After some more awards and grants were handed out, it was revealed the next surprise was for Elliott, the long-time Brunch Bunch Kid who caught the foul ball at his first pro baseball game.

The principal of a highly selective high school -- a school that turned Elliott down when he applied two years earlier -- approached the microphone and told the audience Greg had recently been a guest speaker at their school.

"In the weeks that followed," she explained to the audience, "a number of our students joined The Brunch Bunch, and as a result, they met Elliott. And one by one, they returned to campus and said the same thing -- the school would be an even better place with him in it."

The principal paused, smiled and said, "And we agree."

Two years after Elliott was rejected, the high school not only let him in -- they gave him a scholarship to boot.

As Elliott leapt on stage and hugged the principal, Greg watched on with pride. It was a moment that showed the true potential of the network he created. Make no mistake, there was nothing unique about people using their connections to help a friend. It occurs every day. What *was* unique was that, in this case, the people doing it were teenagers and the friend they were helping was from a different racial, cultural and economic background.

It was the same game. Just changing who gets to play.

After Elliott sat down, the co-hosts returned to the podium and said it was time to do what everyone was waiting for -- give out the Foundation's first ever scholarships.

Suddenly, the doors to the banquet room opened and three students walked in, each one holding a Milkshake Trophy.

Greg's ex-girlfriend, Alyssa, laughed, "The doors open, like it's this big, dramatic moment -- and remember, most people had not seen the trophies -- so when they see these ugly, moldy, dirty milkshake glasses for the first time -- the looks on their faces, it was classic."

While most guests were distracted by the appearance (and smell) of the eccentric trophies, the people who served as scholarship judges were puzzled by the *number* of them. There were only scheduled to be *two* scholarships, but there were *three* trophies.

Charlie leaned over to his date and whispered, "I don't know what's up Greg's sleeve, but some kid here is in for a *big* surprise."

He was right. There was a major surprise coming, and after the first two scholars were honored, Rockefeller went on stage to unveil it.

As the audience watched on, the kid in the tux peeled the sticker off the front of the third and final trophy and discovered the surprise Scholar was someone he had known all his life.

Himself.

According to the co-hosts' copy of the script, that was the grand finale. So, while Rocky's mom sobbed with joy, Trace and Josh approached the podium to thank everyone for coming and say goodnight. When suddenly, Greg rose from his seat and headed toward the stage to say something for the first time all night.

"Sorry to interrupt," he said, "but I think the hosts' scripts are missing a page or two -- because we're just getting started."

He paused, then added, "First up is the live auction. People kept telling me every *real* Gala has one, so we're gonna have one, too."

The audience leaned forward in their seats. What valuable item was going to be auctioned off to raise money? An exotic trip, perhaps? Uh, not exactly. The "valuable item" turned out to be an autographed copy of *Senior News* -- the issue with Greg and Grandma on the cover.

The audience started laughing, but Greg insisted it was no joke.

In a voice that would've made P.T. Barnum proud, he declared, "This isn't just any magazine cover, folks. This one is signed by the world's greatest Grandma! And if the world's greatest athlete's auto-graph is valuable, then the world's greatest Grandma's is valuable, too! We start the bidding at *fiiive thouuusand dollllars!*"

Charlie later recalled, "I know that already seems nuts as it is, but I'd like to point out that his Grandma *didn't even sign her name*. Just the word *Grandma*. It's like auctioning off a bat signed by Babe Ruth, except that instead of signing his name, he signed the word *Athlete*."

Greg waited in silence for someone to make the opening bid of five thousand dollars, but nobody even offered a buck. The joy and the excitement building all night had come to a sudden and awkward halt, but Greg refused to budge.

It seemed like the silence was going to last forever, when suddenly, a complete stranger in the back of the room ran up to the podium, said he felt inspired by the night, wanted the autograph, and was willing to bid $5,000 just to have it.

[The backstory on how the generous bidder ended up at the Gala was a memorable one. About seven months earlier, Greg agreed to watch a friend's dog for a few days. When the dog went to the bathroom all over his apartment, Greg hired a carpet cleaner to get out the stains. The workers did a great job, so he took the time to call the company's main office to express his appreciation. The man who answered the phone happened to be the owner of the company. Curious about the customer who took the time to call just to pay a compliment, the owner looked up Greg online and was touched by what he read about the young man's civic efforts. When the Gala at the Restaurant was announced, the guy ordered a couple of tickets. Now, here he was buying Grandma's autograph.]

Thanks to the man's generosity, the Foundation had received one of its largest donations ever. And it had not been the product of an elaborate fundraising campaign, a slickly-produced mailing, or a detailed grant proposal. It was, simply enough, part of the ripple effect of a young person agreeing to watch a friend's dog.

The audience was shocked by the $5,000 bid -- including Grandma, who hollered that the carpet cleaning man was "crazier than Greg!" Little did she know, she hadn't seen anything yet. Her grandkid was just getting started.

As soon as things calmed down, without the slightest warning, Greg turned to his right and surprised Josh, the co-host, with a five thousand dollar scholarship. And before anyone could catch their breath, he turned to his left and surprised Trace with one, too!

The audience leapt to their feet to give a standing ovation.

The scholarships for the co-hosts seemed like an incredible twist -- one that nobody saw coming. It also seemed to be the perfect ending, but Greg declared he still had one more announcement to make. He said it had to do with his "immediate future."

He took a deep breath, then told everyone how he promised his parents that he'd move on after he sent a kid to college.

It seemed like he was giving a farewell speech, until he began to segue into what appeared to be an oddly-timed tangent -- telling the crowd how he'd been denied access to a restaurant earlier in the day.

He took another breath, looked at his parents, shrugged his shoulders and said, "So, I'm sorry, but what happened today proves there's still just too much work to be done. I just can't walk away."

The brunches would continue. The Foundation would, too.

An entire room of eyes upon her, Rose tried her best to maintain her composure. Mark, on the other hand, did little to conceal his anger. The blood vessels were practically popping out of his forehead.

And yet, Greg was not done.

When the room quieted down, he asked the students who were *not* there to get scholarships to rise. There turned out to be fifteen in all.

He told them he was setting up criteria based on attendance, GPA, conduct and civic service, and that each of the fifteen who could meet the criteria would get $5,000 for college. In the meantime, he said, he'd begin the process of raising the $75,000 needed to cover the pledge in case they all met the criteria.

Then, and only then, Greg said the show was over.

As the crowd headed toward the exits still reeling from all the twists and turns, Charlie approached his old pal to get some answers.

"Okay. First things first. You were denied access to a restaurant? What restaurant?" he asked suspiciously, convinced there was a catch.

"Dorethy Keyser's Place," Greg said matter-of-factly.

It was just as Charlie figured.

He wagged his finger and said,"You know what I think? I think you didn't want to walk away from this, and you felt like you needed an excuse if your parents gave you flak about it, so this morning, you purposely went to the one restaurant where you knew you might get a hard time just so you could show up tonight and tell everyone you've got to keep fighting the good fight. Getting turned away from Keyser's -- that wasn't a change in the script. It was *part* of it."

Greg smiled but said nothing.

As the two men made their way to the door, Charlie said he had another question.

"How'd you come up with the cash for those scholarships? The ones for the co-hosts and the one for the kid in the tux, where did you come up with all that extra money?"

"Remember how I was going to finally take a salary for running the Foundation?"

"Yeah," said Charlie.

Greg shrugged, "I decided not to take it."

His longtime friend was speechless.

By his own admission, for better or worse, Charlie's *self-worth* was tied inextricably to his *net worth*. Everything he was, everything he hoped to be, revolved around his rapidly accumulating wealth -- what it represented, what it could buy, the doors it could open. And so, the idea that a guy would walk away from an entire salary for the sake of helping others was something Charlie just could not grasp.

And yet, in reality, the modest salary Greg had just passed up in order to help a few more kids was small potatoes compared to what he had already sacrificed financially since finishing college.

One observer reasoned, "Greg graduated up at the top of his class from Froehmann Whitfield, and before that, up at the top of his class from Mortimer Dowhill. With that kind of academic pedigree, if he goes corporate straight out of college, and then you factor in bonuses and raises over the next four years, plus interest on what he puts in the bank, not to mention what he'd pull in from investments, then by even the most conservative estimates, as of the Gala, he'd walked away from a half-million dollars -- *at least.*"

Greg's willingness to sacrifice so much income seemed to stand in stark contrast to his penny-pinching approach to daily life -- a trait upon which a few of his ex-girlfriends were all too happy to reflect.

Said one, "We went for sushi on Valentine's. Everything was great until the bill came. *He tried paying with a coupon. On Valentine's.*"

Said another, "Whenever we were leaving a restaurant that had paper napkins, he would get extras and take them with, just so he never had to buy any. Cheapest guy I ever met. Nice guy, but cheap."

Greg acknowledged such anecdotes were true -- he actually seemed proud of them -- but he bristled at the conclusion.

"I'm not cheap," he snapped. "I'm *frugal.* And there's a big difference. Cheap people buy stuff all the time, but it's crappy stuff. Frugal people buy nice things. We just don't do it that often."

Laugh as his friends and ex-girlfriends might, Greg knew it was the same conservative financial philosophy that had allowed his nonprofit organization's bank account to just keep gradually growing, despite still never having accepted a single five-figure donation.

Grandma -- who enjoyed coupon-clipping so much that she actually considered it to be a *hobby* -- concurred, "You don't pay them any attention. How much you make means far less than how much you don't spend."

Of course, on this night, at the Gala, Greg had not pledged to *save* money. He had pledged to *raise some*. $75,000, to be specific.

And Charlie wanted to know how he was going to do it.

He said, "How is a substitute teacher gonna come up with 75 K?"

Despite Charlie's condescending tone, the question caused Greg to smile. This was the question he'd been waiting for. Like any director, he wanted to leave the audience with at least one unanswered question. A plot twist -- *a cliffhanger* -- that would make them think. And this was that question. The question nobody could answer. Not even his Ivy League pal.

And how could Greg be so sure that nobody knew the answer?

Simple. *Because there wasn't one yet.*

Truth be told, as Greg headed for the exit, he had absolutely no idea how he was going to come up with the money.

"You have no plan?!" Charlie yelled. "It's *seventy-five grand*!"

Greg replied, "Give me a break for one night, will ya? Those fifteen kids won't be graduating for a year or two, so I have at least a few months to come up with an idea."

Little did he know it would only take him a few *hours*.

**

When Greg arrived home from the Gala, he was so tired that he headed straight to bed without even changing out of his suit.

At least, he *tried* to go to bed.

He had so many thoughts running through his mind that he was simply unable to sleep. Instead of continuing to toss and turn, he decided to put his shoes back on, go for a walk and get a milkshake.

Three blocks down the road, he found a place that was still open, but they didn't have shakes on the menu.

As he turned to leave, a customer suddenly called after him.

"Hey," the man said, "My name is Louis. I'm a doctor. I go to the gym where you take those kids every Sunday. Come meet my friend, Maddie, and tell her what you do. She'd really be inspired."

Greg was tired, but he agreed to do as Louis asked (in return for a grilled cheese sandwich). After hearing the story, Maddie said she was *so* inspired that she wanted them to go with Greg for the shake right then and right there. When a waitress, Sugar, heard what was going on, she took off her apron and said she wanted to clock out and go with Greg for a shake, too.

Off they went, in the middle of the night, a doctor, an artist, a waitress and a substitute teacher in search of some milkshakes.

A few blocks down the road, they came upon a popular twenty-four hour restaurant called The Tempo Cafe and headed inside.

For the next thirty minutes, the four sat at a table trading stories and enjoying their shakes. As they did, Greg decided he wanted to keep some souvenirs from the night -- so he went over to the manager on duty and asked if he could keep the glasses they were using.

The manager was in no mood to deal with a goofy customer so he turned down Greg's request and told him to go back to his seat. While Greg tried to change his mind, a man walked in the Cafe's front door and immediately thought Greg looked familiar. When he overheard the conversation about milkshake glasses, he suddenly put it all together.

"Milkshakes?!" he hollered. "That's why I know you! You and your friends take kids for shakes! I read about it in the paper!"

The man was *so* excited that he ran over to the table, sat in Greg's seat and *finished Greg's shake*.

Sitting around the table in the middle of the night at a twenty-four hour cafe, Louis, Maddie, Sugar and the Complete Stranger laughed and joked and gulped down the rest of the shakes without giving a single second's thought to the fact that they were from different races, cultures and backgrounds.

After watching with pride from his perch near the register, Greg pulled up a chair and joined in the fun -- until, shortly after four a.m., the five new friends called it a night and went their separate ways.

As he walked back to his apartment, four glasses dripping a trail of vanilla behind him, Greg was smiling from ear to ear. And not just because the day was one of the most incredible of his life (though it was). Or even because the manager at the Cafe changed his mind and let him keep the glasses (though he did). No, he was smiling because he'd just come up with the idea that would help him raise all that money he'd just pledged to raise at the end of the Gala. And this wasn't just any old idea cooking in Greg's head. He was absolutely certain it was the *world's greatest idea -- ever.*

And what was it?

Greg decided that if people were that excited to have a milkshake with him, then he could *charge people five thousand dollars to do it.*

(In reality, his plan was to sit down for a shake with anyone who donated $5,000, as a way to celebrate the new scholarship they'd be funding -- but there was no telling Greg that. He kept insisting his plan was to 'sell' the world's most expensive milkshakes.)

He figured it was a sure-fire way to come up with the money to fund the scholarships, but as word began to spread, most people thought his *foolproof idea* was simply *proof he was a fool*.

Even Grandma had her doubts.

She cracked, "I wouldn't pay five grand to have a shake with Steve Spielberg. And let me tell you something about Greg. The kid sure ain't no Steve Spielberg."

Shortly before Greg revealed the milkshake idea publicly, he attended a meeting with representatives from the esteemed consulting firm, Sharp, Witt & Tacque.

An SW&T rep explained, "We read about Greg and his nonprofit organization in the paper. He clearly had come up with creative ideas to help the community. The only problem was that he lacked the business savvy to take them to the next level. We wanted to help on a pro bono basis. It was a way for us to give back, and to give our young associates a chance to develop hands-on experience at the same time."

Not surprisingly, the Ivy League reject bristled at the slightly condescending tone, but he agreed to meet. And so, there he was, in a backward baseball cap and flip-flops, sitting at a table in a 44th floor conference room, across from three young men -- all decked out in the nicest suits last year's holiday bonuses could buy.

"They're like three little frickin' Charlie's," Greg thought to himself, his leg shaking anxiously underneath the table.

For the next ten minutes, the trio led their guest through a detailed power point presentation they had prepared in advance of the meeting.

The plan was impressive -- certainly sophisticated -- but Greg couldn't help noticing it lacked one key essential component.

Client input.

Sharp, Witt & Tacque had come up with ways to implement the 'next phase' of the The 11-10-02 Foundation's vision -- without first asking the head of the Foundation what exactly it was he envisioned.

Greg did his best to tell them politely that their ideas, while interesting, had no relevance to what he had in mind.

One of the three reps smiled politely and said, "Well, okay, why don't you tell us what you're thinking."

Greg leaned forward in his seat and proceeded to tell them all about his dream of 'selling' milkshakes for $5,000 each and using the unwashed glasses as scholarship trophies.

To his dismay, SW&T's reps did not share his enthusiasm.

In fact, they abruptly ended the meeting. The milkshake idea was, in their view, so unconventional, ridiculous and destined-to-fail that they didn't want to take even the slightest chance it was mistakenly attributed to them -- for fear it would damage their credibility with actual clients.

He would never hear from them again.

Greg resented all the pessimism, but as the days passed, even he had to admit this was one time that the critics seemed to be right. No matter how hard he tried, he couldn't 'sell' a single $5,000 shake.

To add to Greg's troubles, something else *was* sold -- the building where he lived. He was reluctant to pack up and move, but he soon began to see a silver lining. He spent nearly four years trying to change the world outside his window. Perhaps, a new apartment with a new window would give him a chance to take on new challenges.

A few months later, when he moved in his new place a few blocks away, before even unpacking his bags, he put Grandma's rocking chair by the window and began exploring his new view.

To the left, he could see The Green -- the community where he spent much of his time teaching over the past several years. To the right, he could see The Big Hotel -- the site of the event he attended with Jalen Harmony. There was less than a mile between the two, but Greg knew there might as well be a thousand. The world of The Green and the world of The Big Hotel rarely if ever merged together.

Almost instantly, he knew what he could do to change his new view for the better. Just as he built a bridge between his campus and the community in Louisiana, just as he built a bridge between adults and students from different backgrounds through the brunches, and just as he built a bridge between people of different generations through the visits to The Center, he now dreamed of building one between The Green and The Big Hotel. To connect the dots on his left and on his right. To create an opportunity for the two worlds to *co-exist together* instead of just *side-by-side*.

Greg stayed up night after night plotting ways to make it happen, but it wasn't the only reason his new view kept him up late.

As fate would have it, just as with his old view, of the hundreds of places he could see outside his window, there was one light that remained visible late into the night, each and every night. In his old view, it was the front porch light of Blue Academy. In his new view, it was the neon sign outside the local movie theater. If the former was a painful reminder of the new job he was struggling to master, the latter was an equally agonizing reminder of the lifelong dream he was sacrificing in the process.

Night after night, the glow of that neon sign filled his head with thoughts of what might have been -- and the chances he gave up to pursue it. Like the chance to study film in England while in college, and the chance he had to live in California after he graduated. There was a part of him that yearned to go back and chase that filmmaking dream. He was human, after all, and he did have his own dreams, too -- and he knew that with each passing day of each passing year, those dreams were drifting further away.

"If you miss it so much," his friends always asked, "why don't you just go to California?"

"Maybe some day," Greg always replied, his voice trailing off -- knowing full well that day wasn't coming any time soon.

Simply put, he just couldn't walk away.

When he first started helping people during and after his college years, his primary motive may well have been to "undo" what he felt had been done to him -- or, at the very least, distract himself from thinking about it -- but over the years, he had genuinely come to care for the students and the teachers helped by the Foundation. In the process, he invested much more than his organization's money into their future. He'd invested his life.

Fortunately for Greg, there was one piece of news to keep his spirits high. He 'sold' his first $5,000 shake -- and to a professional hockey star, no less.

[The backstory: One night, Greg went to a bar with a friend. Since Greg was wearing flip-flops (dress shoes hurt his forever sore feet), the bar refused to let them in. Searching for an alternative, Greg suggested they go to The Club. It was an upscale place, but he obviously knew the people there, and he thought they might be understanding about his feet. As it turned out, they were -- welcoming him warmly on his first ever visit as a customer.

After just a few minutes inside, a guest walked up to Greg and said he recognized him as the former doorman. The man said he recently read a newspaper article about Greg's civic efforts, and he was intrigued to see a young guy doing something so positive. The man said he represented some well-known pro athletes and thought, perhaps, there might be a way for one of his clients (the hockey star) to help out by donating $5,000. Greg smiled broadly and told the man that was *perfect* because that's how much his new milkshakes cost. The man chuckled and said it was a sweet idea -- pun intended -- but they just wanted to make a donation, no milkshake needed. Knowing that a pro athlete drinking the very first shake was a one-of-a-kind chance to generate the press needed to launch his latest idea, Greg was adamant -- "If your client won't meet me for a shake, then we won't accept the donation." At that point, more than a few folks might have taken their generous offer elsewhere, but this man understood marketing, and was a good sport, so he agreed to go along with it. Greg and the hockey legend met for shakes a few weeks later -- drinking them on the 10th hole at the latter's annual charity golf outing.]

Just like clockwork, a celebrated pro athlete drinking a $5,000 shake on a golf course made headlines in a bunch of papers.

And the next thing you know, the Ripple Effect had begun. Other people started contacting Greg to order a $5,000 milkshake of their own.   A law firm ordered one for their founder. A banker ordered a strawberry one for his wife for Valentine's. And on and on it went.

Greg's shakes became so popular that the carpet cleaning company (whose owner bought Grandma's autograph at auction) even used Greg and Grandma in an ad. (According to the tongue-in-cheek spot, Grandma hired the company because Greg "won't sit at the table when he drinks his shakes and keeps spilling on my carpet.")

After a few months, Greg raised the 'price' up to $7,500 per shake -- adding whipped cream to justify the increase.

"Do you see that?" he shrieked to his unamused father. "Supply and demand! Just like you always talked about!"

He seemed to be pushing his luck, but the 'orders' kept coming.

Each time Greg met one of the 'buyers' for a shake, he saved their used, unwashed glass so it could be turned into a trophy to go along with the scholarship that would be named after the person who 'bought' it (or the company they represented, or one of their relatives if they drank the shake in someone's honor or memory).

As unlikely as it might've seemed when he first came up with the idea, so many people sponsored one of Greg's shakes that he was able to cover the scholarships he pledged to fund if any of the still-eligible kids met the criteria he'd announced at the Gala -- and there was *still* money to spare. And he knew exactly how he wanted to use the rest.

In the fall, the Foundation gave a college scholarship to Cliff (the kid from his old high school who launched a letter-writing campaign to try and help raise money to fund scholarships) and one to Fitz (the student who staged a jazz concert for the same purpose).

While Greg's organization was succeeding beyond anyone's expectations, his own path continued to be as up and down as ever.

One day, he received a call from someone working at Vernon Froehmann Whitfield University. She said they were impressed by everything he had accomplished in the community and wanted to recognize him in a public way for his efforts.

Greg was genuinely moved by the news.

Despite his success in school and since, the University had never made a real effort to embrace him as one of their own. Perhaps they wanted nothing to do with a kid who made a mockery of their strict application process by showing up unannounced and walking in off the street. Perhaps they resented the premise that a student rejected by the Ivy's had aced their classes. Perhaps they harbored a grudge over the letters he wrote, questioning the competence and/or intentions of school officials. Perhaps they objected to a student graduating with Highest Distinction and then no-showing Commencement.

Whatever the reason, one thing was clear. They wanted nothing to do with the guy. Even when Greg said *he* would help *them* -- offering to help current students find jobs or internships -- administrators never even bothered replying.

It didn't matter he was a graduate. His efforts in the community had not seemed to matter, either. They wanted nothing to do with him.

Until, apparently, now.

"I really think this is Froehmann Whitfield's way of extending an olive branch to me," Greg said excitedly to his mom.

Rose had her doubts, but her idealistic son seemed certain -- his impression further reinforced when he was invited to speak on campus to a group of current students interested in community service.

For Greg, it felt like a tremendous weight lifted off his shoulders. After all these years, he was finally going to be *one of them.*

Or so he thought.

Some time later, a VFWU rep informed him they were not going to recognize his efforts after all.

When Greg asked what happened, another VWFU official -- in a voice notably devoid of any compassion -- said: "We concluded it would not be appropriate to acknowledge you went here."

The comment by the school official -- that it wouldn't be appropriate to acknowledge he was one of their graduates -- devastated Greg. After how hard he studied and the grades he got as a student, and after everything he'd done in the community since graduating, he still wasn't good enough to be seen as one of them.

His ex-girlfriend, Katie, recalled, "It just crushed him."

To make matters worse, the event on campus where Greg was slated to speak -- which turned out to be an entirely unrelated student-run affair -- was scheduled for the very next night.

In light of the painful remark just made to him on the phone, he was tempted to cancel -- but Grandma would not have it.

"You said you'd show up," she stammered. "You show up!"

Greg agreed to honor his commitment -- but, in truth, he did so only after he'd come up with what he considered an even better way to retaliate -- use the speech as an opportunity to vent about the mistreatment he felt he had endured over and over again from school administrators.

But, just as happened at the Mortimer Dowhill event, when push came to shove, he couldn't bring himself to say a bad word about anyone. Looking out at the students, he knew they had shown up at the event to hear about volunteerism and philanthropy -- not a former student's long list of gripes with the administration. And so, in the end, he stuck with the positive topics he was asked to address.

After the speech, a VFWU professor, aware of what had transpired the day before, sent Greg a note commending him for 'taking the higher road' -- and Greg did feel good about doing that.

But that comment made by the school rep -- that it was concluded it would not be appropriate for the university to acknowledge he was *one of them* -- still hurt deeply. And it would continue to hurt him for a long time to come.

Between the demands on his time and these occasional frustrations he encountered along the way, Greg was sleeping less and less, which meant he had less energy, which meant he was exercising less. Plus, his hair continued to fall out in clumps -- until, finally, he just shaved off what was left.

He was horrified by what he saw in the mirror -- and not just because his ears stuck out more than ever. As odd as this sounds, his skull seemed to have a number of bumps and dents.

"It looks like my head was used for batting practice," he wailed.

He turned to Grandma to console him, but she didn't seem too concerned. In fact, she actually appeared to be *amused*.

"You spent half your life running into walls. What did you expect your head to look like?" she chuckled. "Besides, you oughtta just be glad you can see your head at all. Some people got no eyes."

Greg tried his best to stay positive as Grandma instructed, but it was much easier said than done. A year after being featured in magazines as a young, strong, healthy bachelor, he was bald, weak and exhausted.

Things soon progressed from bad to worse.

Greg's ex-girlfriend, Lissa, said, "He didn't want to see himself, so he stopped using his lights."

From sundown to sunrise, his apartment was virtually pitch black. Just the glow from his computer screen, and some residual light from the movie theater's neon sign and the other lights out his window. Even in his bathroom, Greg kept the lights off -- brushing his teeth and taking showers entirely in the dark.

Lissa said, "It was totally depressing to be around."

Then, one day, as Greg entered the dark bathroom, thanks to a bit of light sneaking in from the window in the other room, he caught an unexpected glimpse of his shadowy reflection in the mirror.

The Silhouette Man had returned once more.

Upon seeing his childhood friend, Greg immediately thought back to their other unexpected reunions over the years -- and how those sightings had compelled him to refocus his thoughts and energy back to things that mattered most. This time was no different.

Determined to snap out of the funk he was in, Greg announced plans to revive his dream to run in a marathon -- collecting donations for each mile he ran, just as he collected them for each book he read when he was a boy.

He said, "It was a way to get back in good shape and raise money for The Foundation at the same time."

His friends admired his goal, but they doubted he could do it.

"You've had two operations on your feet and never run in a marathon," said Arthur, a friend and an experienced runner. "What makes you think you can do this?"

The answer was one that those who knew Greg probably should have seen coming.

"If Forrest Gump can run non-stop for a couple years," Greg explained, "I think I can handle running a couple miles one time."

Obviously, it made no sense to think it was possible to complete a marathon without any training just because a made-up character ran non-stop for several years, and Arthur was going to try and explain that to Greg -- but the issue turned out to be moot.

A few weeks after pledging to make the 26.2 mile run, Greg had to have two more operations on his feet.

On the bright side, somewhere between the anesthesia and the incisions, he somehow convinced his new foot doctor to make a donation to The Foundation. On the not-so-good side, the operations put Greg back in a wheelchair for a few more days.

He inched his way around town as needed -- he wasn't about to let the setback keep him from brunch -- but he spent the lion's share of his free time, up in his room, retreating further from those around him.

The combustible mix of pain, darkness, solitude and depression caused Greg to endure another round of long sleepless nights.

Grandma urged him to devote the extra time to his art.

He did as she instructed -- distracting himself from the numbers on the clock that never seemed to move a single second closer to sunrise by focusing on one portrait after the next.

Slowly but surely, he filled another 8.5 x 11 inch space on his wall with another framed portrait in much the same way that an imprisoned man covers his arms and back with one tattoo at a time.

When he wasn't working on his portraits, Greg spent more time focusing on his Logo.

Back when he first drew it, people thought the Logo was too simple. What they did not know at the time was that the Logo had more than one meaning -- and even more than two. According to Greg, there was a *third* meaning. And, he decided, this was the perfect time to unveil it -- so that, once again, he could distract himself from the pain in his own life by helping other people improve theirs.

In Version One, the Logo represented the things Greg saw outside his childhood window. In Version Two, it represented the different parts of the mentoring program. Version Three was going to be all about scholarships -- *new* scholarships, to be exact.

In Version Three, *The Ladder* symbolized Greg's belief you should never underestimate the strength of those who help themselves up the ladder of success. With that belief in mind, the new Ladder Scholarship was going to assist students who were so busy working to, for instance, help their family pay the bills that their grades suffered a bit because of it. It would also help students who moved to America when they were teens -- their overall GPA not reflecting their true ability because it was weighed down by those early semesters when they were still trying to learn a new language. The students only had B or C grade point averages, but they had a straight A work ethic.

The Tombstone represented Greg's philosophy that the only thing that lives forever is a legacy -- and that in order to leave one, you first must create one. With that in mind, The Legacy Scholarship was going to go to a student who was carrying on Greg's legacy: breaking barriers, building bridges and making a difference at a young age.

The Three Ovals once again depicted three milkshake glasses. But this time, instead of representing the day Greg took two kids for shakes and the woman sitting next to them moved her purse, they symbolized the Milkshake Glass Trophies that were going to be given to the new Scholars.

Greg intended to get to work creating the other two pieces of the puzzle -- the scholarships based on *The Triangle* and *The Silhouette Man* images in the logo -- but his schedule was so packed that it was difficult to find the time to do it.

And then, September 11th happened.

That Friday, anxious to get away from the relentless TV coverage of the terrorist attacks he watched all week long, Greg accepted an invitation to attend a special service promoting peace and harmony. Afterwards, he went for dinner with five of the other people there -- four of whom he'd never met.

Ironically, it turned out that three of the five went to college in Louisiana and the other two graduated from Froehmann Whitfield.

As a result, they managed to make it all the way through their salads exchanging stories about school, but it was just a matter of time until the talk turned back to 9-11. It really was an impossible subject to avoid. The entire nation was talking about it.

The difference -- what made this conversation unlike so many of the others -- is that instead of dwelling on what happened, these five young people were talking about what could be done *in response*.

One of the five, a young building developer named Jonathan, was thinking about it from a real estate perspective. What could be built on that space where the Trade Centers stood to prove the nation was still standing? Greg, on the other hand, was thinking about the kids. What could be done to show them that you can turn anything -- even something *this* negative -- into something positive?

By the time the bill came, the two young men who had never before met decided to try and find a way to combine their two ideas. The plan they came up with was a contest where high school students would create designs to rebuild the space where the Trade Centers stood, then write essays explaining how their designs captured the strength people in New York were showing in the aftermath of 9-11.

The idea was well-received.

A teacher named Mr. Mack said, "I tell students that a building can tell a powerful story. This was a chance for them to do exactly that -- design buildings that tell powerful stories."

It was also a chance for them to go to college.

The students who won the contest were going to receive The 11-10-02 Foundation Mountain Scholarships -- named after the mountain in the Logo and representative of the idea that it is good to build something big and positive out of something negative.

**

Following 9-11, a number of schools invited Greg to speak to students about intolerance, diversity and dealing with tragedy.

One invitation brought him to Kentucky.

He looked forward to his first ever visit to the Bluegrass State, but under the circumstances, he wasn't too sure what kind of a response to expect. In the wake of such a horrible terrorist act, it would be very understandable if even the kindest of people were a little reluctant to roll out the welcome wagon. And yet, the people of Kentucky were as hospitable as could be.

When Greg got lost in his rental car, a woman didn't just give him instructions -- she gave him her map. That night, when he asked a local resident where he should eat, she not only suggested a place -- she went there with him so he wouldn't eat by himself. The next day, when he strolled into the local courthouse and asked if he could check his e-mail there, a man instantly rose from his seat and offered up his desk. (It was only as Greg was leaving that he discovered the man *was the judge.*)

The way everyone welcomed a complete stranger with open arms would have made Greg feel good at any time, but to see them do it just days after 9-11 really was astounding.

In a nation suddenly (and understandably) consumed with home-land security, the citizens of Kentucky Greg met had refused to change their good-natured ways.

As Greg wrote in a guest column for the paper at the end of his trip, "After the last three days, I've reached a conclusion. The world would be a better place if everyone was a little more Kentucky."

While he was there, he also got the chance to spend time with Little Jarrett and his family.

Once again, the child with cancer put Greg's own problems into perspective. How could he complain about the pain in his feet when Jarrett only had one leg? How could he complain about being bald at the age of 28 when Jarrett looked that way since he was ten?

Greg also paid a visit to the hospital in Kentucky where Jarrett's organization brought toys to other sick kids. Seeing the program the boy put together in spite of all his obstacles, Greg was reminded yet again that a person's *true* strength has little if anything to do with how big and strong they seem on the outside.

That reminder helped give him the idea for the final scholarship.

In Version Three, *The Silhouette Man* stood for the idea you should never measure a person's strength by the shape of their shadow, or silhouette. With that in mind, the Silhouette Scholarship was going to help a student who achieved great things despite having to deal with physical obstacles along the way -- their true strength found within.

**

The boy from Kentucky was not the only student helping out the community at a young age. Clifford -- the student from Greg's old high school -- was trying to make a difference, too.

On his very first day of college, Cliff went for a walk and found a local grade school where he could volunteer. Over the next few months, he returned to the grade school on a regular basis and began bringing his new college classmates with him.

If Cliff's efforts seemed to parallel those made by Greg when he was a college freshman a decade earlier, it was no coincidence.

Cliff acknowledged, "I was trying to trace his civic footsteps from when he was my age."

Before long, university officials found out about what Cliff was doing, and it was just a short time later that they invited Greg to come speak on their campus -- hoping he would inspire more of their students to become more engaged in the community.

The speech at Cliff's college was scheduled for November 8. That night, Greg shared his story with the assembled students, expressed his admiration for the efforts Cliff made to follow in his footsteps, and encouraged the others in attendance to realize they too could and should make a difference while they were young.

Greg could have flown home the next day -- the 9th -- but as a way of showing Cliff that he was proud of his volunteer efforts, he decided to stay through the weekend and hold that week's brunch there -- the first time it had ever been held out of town.

And so, on Greg's 29th birthday, 11-10-01, a beautiful autumn day, Greg, Cliff and the others met up for brunch.

The other 'adults' included people who worked at Cliff's university and some of Greg's friends who lived in the area. The 'kids' were a handful of the ones Cliff tutored at that local grade school.

At first glance, it appeared to be like all the previous brunches. Adults and students eating a great meal at a great restaurant, while talking about college and careers, learning about diverse cultures and backgrounds. But it was clearly no ordinary brunch. For instead of turning to the adults and asking them questions, Cliff was now *answering* questions that the kids were asking *him*.

Right before Greg's eyes, a student became a teacher.

In the process, by passing on the kindness, Cliff had brought the whole experience full circle. And, it turned out, that was all Greg was waiting to see. He declared that, after 243 weeks in a row, his streak of weekly brunches had reached a simple and sudden end.

If the end of The Streak was a fitting way to celebrate Greg's birthday, then the events of that night were icing on the cake.

Inspired by Greg's speech, Cliff's roommate (Perry) decided he wanted to bring people of different cultures and backgrounds together, too -- and he wanted to do it immediately.

He decided Greg's 29th birthday was the perfect excuse to start. So while the brunch was taking place that afternoon, Perry was calling all over town asking people to come together that very night.

He admitted, "It was pretty short notice, so I was hoping for, maybe, five or six people to RSVP."

The response surpassed anything he could've anticipated. That night, *forty complete strangers* gathered together for the dinner party.

Greg was overwhelmed by their efforts, and particularly touched by the restaurant that was chosen -- a place called John Harvard's.

"We thought about taking him to the actual university," Perry later said with a grin, "but that was a little bit out of our budget."

For two hours, forty people set aside their differences and made new friends. They ate and laughed and joked and sang *Happy Birth-day* to a guy they didn't know.

And then, at the end of the night, they presented Greg with a special gift. *A menu.*

That's all it really was -- just a menu -- but there was no telling that to the birthday boy. As everyone went their separate ways, he clutched that menu with the word *Harvard's* across the front like it was as important as an actual diploma bearing the same name.

And that's because, to him, it was.

**

As word spread that The Brunch Bunch Streak ended, people began to tally up the statistics -- such as the fact that over 700 people from dozens of states and six different continents had attended at least one of the brunches.

One of Greg's friends, Cresta, observed, "It was such a gradual thing, you know, one week at a time, that you never really noticed how big it had gotten until, in the end, you step back and realize, wow, that thing started with one guy, two kids and three milkshakes."

More than any other measuring stick, it was the sheer *length* of The Streak that caught people's eye. Greg was *twenty-four years old* the day he took the two kids for shakes and *twenty-nine* when he finally took a break 243 weeks later. It was a commitment of time that was impossible to deny -- and, for many, impossible to even imagine.

As one kid, Trace, pointed out, "I graduated from middle school, went to high school, graduated high school and went to college, and the man had *still* never missed a single week of brunch."

When Greg first started the program, some thought it was little more than a platform from which he would eventually run for office. At the very least, there were many who assumed his ever-wandering mind would lead him to move on quickly to another idea -- the brunches falling by the wayside in the process. But, when weeks turned into months, and months turned into years, and Greg had still never taken a single week off, even the most pessimistic doubters had to admit his focus had not waned and his dedication to the program had transcended a convenient 'photo op'.

Ms. Franklin, an Assistant Principal who was initially ambivalent about the brunches, said, "One week, two weeks, maybe even three, and a skeptic wants to say he only did it for his resume? Fine. I'll be the first to admit that ran through my mind when it first started, because I've seen that kind of thing many times. But *243* weeks? *In a row?* That's a genuine commitment."

Annie, a local parent who'd supported the idea since its inception, proudly added, "And keep in mind, it wasn't like Greg was just *showing up* at those brunches. He was negotiating discounts with restaurants, lining up the students, getting permission from their parents, then rounding up an equal number of adults to attend the brunch and agree to pay for it. *You* try that some time. Just once, even. Let alone every single week *for nearly five years.* And remember, it's not like it was Greg's job to do this. He was also giving speeches, substitute teaching, running the Foundation, and on and on. Putting the brunches together, coming up with the money to pay for it, and personally attending each outing, for 243 straight weeks...this was what he did in his *free time*."

The pats on the back were well-deserved, but the more compliments Greg received for maintaining The Streak for such a long time despite all the obstacles in his path, the more he began to believe he could overcome *any* obstacle without *any* help from *anyone*.

It didn't take long before he was humbled back to reality.

Greg and one of his friends, Guy the Photographer, went to see Elliott play basketball at his new school. After the game, Greg went to take a picture with Elliott, but the camera wouldn't work.

"Want some help?" asked Guy.

"I can do it," Greg said snidely. "It's photography, not physics."

Guy watched with amusement as Greg shook the camera, pushed its buttons, checked the lens, then shook it again -- until, finally, he gave up and declared the camera unfixable.

Guy chuckled softly, casually yanked the aluminum flip-top off of Greg's soda can, inserted it in just the right place in the camera and said, "Say cheese."

Greg laughed him off, insisting that could not *possibly* do the trick. But, sure enough - FLASH - it worked like a charm.

Guy later explained, "It turned out the piece of the camera that covers the batteries had fallen off and there simply needed to be a substitute of some kind to hold the batteries firmly in place and act as a conductor of the current."

In the process of finding that substitute and inserting it in just the right place, Guy not only solved the problem -- he reinforced an important lesson Greg tended to forget from time to time: Life is a

challenge, but it's not an exam. It is okay to ask for help from someone who knows more than you.

People thought the end of The Streak meant Greg might finally
take a vacation, but now that schools were nominating students for the
new scholarships, he wanted to get right to work lining up the judges.
So, he spent his first brunch-free weekend in nearly five years with his
Grandma, but then it was right back to volunteering.

The Legacy Scholarship Judging Panel was the easiest one to
assemble. Given the personal nature of the scholarship -- the fact that
it was going to be given to a student who was carrying on the legacy
Greg was trying to leave -- he decided to select the winner himself.
For the other three kinds of scholarships (The Ladder, The Mountain
and The Silhouette), he decided to line up thirty judges -- ten for each
panel -- to pick the winners.

At first, he planned on asking some friends to volunteer to do it,
but one phone call from Lambert Grover Wakefield changed all that.

Some time earlier, Greg read an article in which the very well-
known CEO described himself as a man who remained modest despite
his great success. He also insisted that he always made time to help
others (or as, he called them, the 'little people').

Having learned his lesson from Guy the Photographer about not
asking for advice, Greg eagerly looked up Wakefield's office number
to set up a meeting.

"What is this regarding?" Wakefield's assistant asked.

"I read the article about how he likes to teach young people what
he knows about business. I'd love to talk to him and learn from him."

The assistant quickly (but politely) dismissed Greg -- and did so
again each time he called thereafter -- saying her boss was in a meeting, out of town, or just plain not available. Until, finally, one time
Greg called, the assistant said his timing was perfect.

"Stay by the phone, and he'll call you in two minutes," she said.

Greg excitedly paced back and forth, rehearsing every question he
wanted to ask. Right on cue, the phone rang -- but before Greg could
ask a single question, the CEO made a statement of his own.

"You should've taken the hint. I don't talk to people your age."

Greg tried to respond, but it was too late.

Mr. Wakefield had already hung up.

The man had literally called just to hang up.

Upon hearing the news, Grandma had little sympathy.

She said, "That's why you never make a hero out of someone you do not know. You can admire certain qualities they got. But never make 'em out to be a hero if you don't know 'em."

The Wakefield encounter was a humiliating experience for Greg, but it was hardly the only one over the past few years. There were phone calls not returned, letters ignored, e-mails unanswered, meetings postponed or just altogether cancelled -- not to mention, a never-ending stream of rejections and letdowns from those who did show up and did respond.

In one memorable case, Greg contacted the head of a well-known nonprofit organization to ask for a meeting.

"If someone like him could give me some advice or guidance, I think it would really help," he said humbly to the man's assistant.

To his delight, the meeting was granted. Greg was so determined to make the most of the opportunity that he -- literally -- prepared a list of typewritten questions. But, as it turned out, the man had not set aside time to answer Greg's questions. He set aside time to *ask* one.

"Would you consider closing your Foundation and turning over all its assets to our organization?" he wanted to know.

Instead of offering words of advice to help a young person and his little nonprofit endeavor continue to grow, this man had agreed to meet so he could try and convince Greg to give up everything he had built and turn over everything he had raised.

In another instance, shortly after the Foundation's creation, a man named Michael J. Cachette called out of the blue, said he read an article about Greg, and wanted to meet for lunch. (For his part, Greg had no idea Cachette represented a philanthropic organization worth billions. Just the prospect of a 'free lunch' was enough to entice him to accept the invitation.)

"We think your efforts can become something special," Cachette said, over sandwiches. "Our only concern is your foray into the nonprofit sector might be a temporary stop en route to law school or corporate America or politics. So, what I want to do, I want to give you my card, and when you feel you've proven this thing's got legs, you call me, and I think you'll find us there to support you."

To some, the situation might have seemed suspect -- a complete stranger offering an unspecified amount of nonguaranteed financial support at an undetermined point some day down the road. But to others who were familiar with the deep pockets Cachette represented, the offer presented a very real, much-needed lifeline.

Charlie said, "Greg had no real office, no real anything. And this guy, Cachette, his organization handed out six figure donations the way most people give out sticks of gum."

And yet, as weeks turned into months, Greg still had not taken up Cachette's offer and dialed the number. If and when he did call, he wanted to be certain beyond any shadow of a doubt that he had proven this was no flash in the pan. If that meant a few more months of struggling in the meantime, so be it.

Finally, after three long years, Greg felt the moment had arrived and picked up the phone. Cachette responded warmly to the call -- expressing admiration for what Greg had achieved and the patience he had demonstrated in waiting so long to call him -- and suggested the two meet again.

When they met, Cachette gave every indication support for Greg's Foundation would be forthcoming. He even took the young man on a tour of his organization's offices and introduced him to 'some of the people you'll be working with after the grant is approved'.

Before they parted ways, Cachette asked Greg to submit a request for funding -- a mere formality, he insisted. Greg promptly did as asked and then ran to the mailbox each day, awaiting the arrival of what was going to be the largest check he'd ever held.

A check that never would arrive.

As it turned out, the windfall contribution he had envisioned all these years was little more than a mirage. In its place, he received an all-too-familiar, single-paged form letter of rejection.

When Greg contacted Cachette to find out what happened, he got a response so ironic that it bordered on near cruelty.

Cachette said matter-of-factly, "You did such a fine job without our assistance that we concluded you don't need any."

When she heard about the disappointing turn of events, Grandma insisted to Greg that it was a blessing in disguise.

She said, "How many times have I told you? The reward for hard work isn't supposed to be a big fat check. The reward for hard work is more hard work. If this guy had lived up to his promise and your organization got the big grant, your life would've been easier. What kind of reward is that? Quit crying and get back to work."

From time to time, Greg responded to such setbacks by firing off a long, rambling letter. In one or two cases, the sense of disappointment was so profound that it even landed him in the ER with chest pain.

But, more often than not, with Grandma's advice in mind, Greg took the rejection in stride -- or, at least, funneled the anger toward more hard work on something positive.

And *that* is exactly what he set out to do in the case of Lamburt G. Wakefield -- the CEO who called back just to hang up.

In the days that followed, Greg vowed he would prove Wakefield was the exception and not the rule -- that most big-time executives *were* willing to lend their time and wisdom to support the efforts of young people. Greg said he would look up the names of very success-ful people, track down their phone numbers and work hard to convince them to serve on one of his new Scholarship Boards.

Greg's friends understood why he was upset, but they insisted he was only setting himself up for more disappointment. They said most powerful executives would never take his call, let alone agree to give their time to help out a tiny Foundation run by a substitute teacher they had never met.

Greg always replied the same way.

"Apparently, you've never heard of Brantley Foster."

A decade or so earlier, Brantley Foster was an ambitious college graduate from the Midwest who moved to New York with wide-eyed dreams of conquering Wall Street. Determined to get his foot in the door, he accepted a spot sorting packages in a company's mailroom.

The firm's culture dictated mailroom staffers were not even supposed to say 'Hello' to The Suits, let alone seek a promotion to join their ranks -- but Brantley refused to play by these rules. He sought out some of the Big Apple's heaviest hitters, and convinced them to listen to his ideas. With their support, he eventually took over the major corporation whose mail he had been sorting.

To Greg, it was an inspiring precedent.

Of course, there was just one little problem -- Brantley Foster didn't actually exist and neither did the big-shots who supported his ideas. They were all just characters in a movie. But, as always, that mattered little to Greg. If Brantley could win over the top executives around town, then he figured he could, too.

And so, despite the doubters, Greg moved forward with his plan.

As expected, some of the business leaders he called turned him down and others never replied at all -- but he took the rejections in stride and kept dialing more numbers. Until, finally, he managed to actually get through to an executive or two.

At first, he was overcome with joy -- they took his calls! -- but he quickly discovered that "Yes, I'm willing to listen" and "Yes, I'm on board" meant two distinctly different things.

Having heard a thousand pitches a thousand times from a thousand people, these men and women were not the type to sign on to every proposal that came their way (or, for that matter, every tenth or every hundredth). They had questions -- lots of questions -- and unfortunately for Greg, he didn't have many good answers.

"How many years have you been giving out scholarships?"
"Worldwide? Historically? Counting last year? Uh, one."
"Who else has signed up to be on this Board so far?"
"Including the ones who signed up last week? Um, nobody."
"I can hardly hear you. What's that noise in the background?"
"Oh, um, that's, uh, the Lunch Lady's radio."

When it became clear just how small an operation this was, many of the big-time executives politely declined the offer.

In turn, Greg just kept making more calls and answering more questions. Until, eventually, *finally*, the persistence paid off.

A couple of prominent leaders agreed to serve on the Scholarship Board. And once they did, the ripple effect started to take place, and the dominoes began to fall. Within a day, after word got out that they'd signed on, another two said yes. And then, a few more after that.

The head of a major toy company, Mr. MacMillan, was among those who agreed to be part of it. He said, "Was it the largest charity on Earth? Of course not. But as a guy who started from nothing, I didn't care about how old Greg was or how big his project was. He had work ethic and passion, so he had my respect."

When all was said and done, the young substitute teacher had quite improbably assembled a group of thirty of America's most accomplished men and women to join his team.

Even Greg's father took notice.

Mark conceded, "This wasn't a group of imaginary friends. These were people who ran companies with a collective net worth in the billions of dollars. I have no idea how he pulled it off."

(Amusing side note: As much as he appreciated his father's

begrudging approval, Greg seemed much more enthused by the article in a local magazine that compared what he had done to the achievements of none other than...Brantley Foster.)

Once the execs were on board, Greg divided them into three groups of ten -- one to select the Ladder Scholars, one to choose the Mountain Scholars and one to pick the Silhouette Scholar.

The meetings, which were scheduled for three consecutive Thursdays, were not going to take place for several months -- but Greg wasted no time at all getting started with their planning.

The decision to do that was understandable -- these were going to be three very important meetings -- but what he really needed to do with the extra time was take a vacation. He was *exhausted* -- to the point that he was having sudden sleeping spells. Sometimes, it was a cause for humor -- on one date, Greg fell asleep headfirst into her soup -- but it was usually more serious -- one night, he collapsed in the shower, hitting his head and cutting it open.

And it wasn't just his body showing signs of wear and tear. The rocking chair was, too. In fact, Greg spent so many hours rocking in the chair that he *rocked a hole right through it* -- the splinters of the seat falling to the ground.

He was reluctant to tell Grandma what happened to her chair, but she actually smiled when he broke the news. She called the chair's splinters a "symbol of his work ethic" and a "reminder that the reward for hard work is more hard work" and said to save them.

She said, "Next time somebody says you're not smart enough to do something, or not experienced enough, or whatever, you look at those splinters and remember that what makes you special is that you're willing to spend as much time as it takes to make up for what you don't have -- and that you'll keep at it until you get it right."

Greg was relieved by her reaction and did as she instructed -- framing the splinters on his wall, along with a handwritten note that read: *"Work Ethic: To be willing to work so hard for so long that you rock a hole through your chair."*

Greg did feel good about that message, but he missed the chair.

He had come to care for it as if it were an extension of the beloved Grandma who gave it to him. To him, it was much more than *just* a place to sit. Much like The Silhouette Man and The Ladder Horse from his childhood, The Chair had become Greg's *friend*. A devoted supporter who was always willing to stay up late and keep him company. A constant companion who never teased him. A loyal friend who never betrayed him. A patient listener who always lent him an ear. And now, she was gone.

Unfortunately, Greg didn't have much time to mourn.

With all four scholarships created (The Legacy, The Mountain, The Ladder and The Silhouette) and the judges' meetings coming up, it was time to plan another party where the winners would be honored.

Given the success of the first Gala, Greg's friends said he should bring everyone back to the same Restaurant for the second one -- but, to their surprise, he had another place in mind. *The Big Hotel.*

He loved everything about that first event, but a number of people still teased him every time he referred to it as a *Gala.*

"It was a banquet," they insisted. "Restaurants host banquets. Hotels host Galas."

Greg knew he should pay them no attention, but he just couldn't help himself. He wanted to prove he could put on a *real* Gala like Jalen Harmony and other sophisticated socialites do. He wanted to prove he could be *one of them.* And he was certain that a successful event for 500 people in the 10,000 square foot Regal Ballroom at The Big Hotel would silence all the doubters for good.

And what's more, just like he dreamed when he first moved into his new apartment, he wanted to build a bridge between The Green on his left and The Big Hotel on his right -- and this seemed like the perfect chance to do it.

His grand plans were admirable, but a bonafide Gala at The Big Hotel seemed like an awfully big step for the substitute teacher with the tiny Foundation.

Greg insisted he was up to the challenge and wasted no time trying to prove it. In just a matter of days, he set up a new website to promote the night, lined up a big company as the evening's title sponsor and persuaded a business magazine to run a pro bono ad to publicize it.

[The ad was slated to feature Greg -- holding a milkshake glass, of course -- surrounded by some of the prominent execs who had agreed to serve on the Scholarship Boards. It was great exposure for the Foundation -- but, in truth, there was only one set of eyes to which Greg gave much thought. His father's. When Greg was young, Mark used to point to the CEOs featured inside such magazines, and say, "I want to see you in here some day, son. Side by side with men like these." All these years later, he had fulfilled his father's wishes -- but he'd done it on his own terms. And he just couldn't help laughing at the thought of Mark nearly spitting out his coffee when he opened the magazine and saw his goofy son staring back at him.]

As for the event itself, to make sure it ran smoothly, Greg created a Planning Committee comprised of a dozen friends willing to volunteer their time. With their help, he was certain the event would be a piece of cake to pull off, but it soon became clear he had gone from one extreme -- refusing to ask a friend (the photographer) for help -- to another -- demanding his friends (on the Planning Committee) devote every waking minute to doing so.

No matter what his friends on the Committee did, Greg wanted them to do more. No matter how much time they spent, he told them to spend more. And he didn't ask nicely, either. Day after day, he sent them angry notes and barked orders at them through the phone. He was so determined to reach his goal that he lost sight of the feelings of the people who were helping him do it.

Not surprisingly, his approach left volunteers feeling disrespected and unappreciated -- until, one by one, they started to quit. After just a few weeks, most of the Committee had disappeared.

Knowing the event was too big to put together on his own, Greg turned to another outlet for assistance -- interns. It seemed like a perfect solution. The students could get some meaningful experience, and he could get some free help to fill the huge void left by the now-defunct Planning Committee.

Among the first to be interviewed was a local co-ed named Kat.

She recalled, "I was really nervous before the interview, but then Greg walked in the conference room, and he was wearing a backwards hat and flip-flops. Definitely not what I was expecting."

The interview itself took her by surprise, too.

"I was all prepared for a serious interview, but his first question was: 'Which one of the *Rocky* movies is your favorite?"

(Amusing side note: Having never heard of the legendary boxer, Kat said her favorite *Rocky* film was "the one with Bullwinkle.")

While Greg and his interns focused their attention on the Gala, others focused their attention on him.

In the summer, Zeta Beta Tau honored him as its Man of Distinction. In the winter, he received a special honor given to just one person in the nation each day. A few months later, The First Lady of the U.S. even chimed in -- writing that Greg and The 11-10-02 Foundation had changed the way we as a society view success...and milkshakes.

The White House-as-return address notwithstanding, it was a different note -- from a community college -- that touched him most.

In the spring, officials at a community college called PSC invited Greg to be their next Commencement Speaker -- making him the youngest person ever asked. At the event, the school also planned to give him an honorary degree -- making him the youngest person in the school's history to ever receive one.

Greg proudly accepted the offer and eagerly shared the news with his family. Six years after he no-showed his own graduation, he was finally going to have his long-awaited chance to wear a cap and gown.

He was *so* excited he decided to treat the event like it actually *was* his graduation. When PSC officials told him the speaker always wears a special set of colors around the neck to recognize where he or she went to college, Greg decided he would not wear any colors at all.

"Just the cap and gown like my fellow graduates," he insisted.

Mark rolled his eyes with contempt as he listened to his son go on and on about an honorary degree from a community college as if it meant as much as a real one from an Ivy League-level school.

Despite his father's grumblings, Greg continued to treat the upcoming event like it was going to be his actual college graduation -- requesting tickets so he could have supporters in the audience cheering him on just like the 'other graduates' were going to have.

The school granted the request -- but his parents refused to attend, his sister was unable to go and his Grandma said she was too ill to make the trip. Determined to still put the tickets to good use, Greg invited some of his Foundation's Scholars to take their place.

The event at PSC was going to be a special one, but it was not the only one on Greg's mind. During that same period, he received an invitation to speak at Distinguished Day -- the prestigious annual event which brings hundreds of VFWU graduates back to campus (many decked out in their school colors, no less) to hear a handful of "distinguished" alums and professors speak about various topics.

For any number of reasons, the invitation extended to Greg came as a shock. He was much younger than those typically asked to speak at the event, and regardless of what he had achieved, he'd be the first to admit that his resume paled in comparison to those on the typical list of invited speakers -- such as the Four Star General or Pulitzer Prize winner. Throw in his rocky history with school officials when he was a student -- plus, the recent incident where they announced plans to recognize his civic efforts, then changed their mind because they'd concluded it "would not be appropriate" to acknowledge he was a graduate -- and the invitation was truly stunning.

In fact, Greg seemed to be the only one who took it at face value. The way he saw it, the invitation made perfect sense.

He said at the time, with a heavy dose of it's-about-time self-righteousness, "It shows that the people in charge at my alma mater finally realize I am one of them and worthy of *respect.* This is their way of trying to make amends for everything they've done to me."

Others were not quite as quick to share that view.

His mom, Rose, predicted, "There was *no way* the invitation was what it appeared to be. There *had* to be a catch."

Unfortunately, she was right.

VFWU was a large school with many people on staff. Some rarely if ever crossed paths, let alone spoke to each other on a regular basis. And this annual event, however significant, was planned by just a handful of them. As a result, the VFWU reps who invited Greg to be one of the 'distinguished' speakers were, apparently, not even aware of the relationship (or lack thereof) between him and his alma mater -- let alone trying to heal its wounds.

The invitation, while certainly still an honor, did not reflect any desire by the school's top administrators to embrace Greg as one of their own. The powers-that-be didn't even know he'd been asked.

Rose shook her head with sadness as she recalled the moment.

She sighed, "He wanted so badly to be treated like he was a part of the team by everyone who worked there. And, in fairness, he had every right to want that. He had earned that. He was a graduate. A graduate with Highest Distinction. But it just wasn't going to happen. At least not in the way he envisioned -- with some big, grand effort to bring back him back into the fold. This wasn't some movie, where everything gets tied together with a nice little bow in the end. This was real life. And in real life, he just wasn't that important to them."

Greg's first instinct was to back out of the commitment to speak at the event. His second idea was to keep the booking and simply never show up -- leaving organizers in a lurch in front of the alums whose deep pockets they coveted. Ultimately, he settled on the same spite-filled option he had considered the other time he was asked to speak at VFWU: show up as promised, then use the live microphone to excoriate the school's administration.

"And this time," he vowed, "I'm really gonna do it!"

Except that, like always, in the end, he didn't. Looking out at an audience of men and women in their fifties and sixties who still knew (and sang) the school's fight song, he just didn't have the heart to tarnish an annual day they cherished. Instead, with the advice of Grandma echoing in his head ("You get more with honey than with vinegar"), he was polite to one and all, gave a positive speech about the value of making a difference and left campus as quietly and uneventfully as he had arrived.

Graduation Day - PSC

While the five 11-10-02 Foundation Scholars took their seats in the auditorium's back row, Greg took his seat up on stage. Decked out in his cap and gown (with mismatched socks peeking out the bottom), he looked out at the sea of people seated before him and smiled.

Row after row of graduates. Thousands of parents, grandparents, siblings and friends. It was *exactly* as he'd always dreamed.

Halfway through the ceremony, PSC's President went up to the podium to introduce Greg. It was a traditional introduction -- talking about the graduation speaker's accomplishments and the awards he had received -- until he mentioned something that took the audience by surprise: This was the first college graduation Greg ever attended.

It seemed hard to believe, but it was true. The man trying so hard to help kids get to college had never witnessed let alone taken part in a college commencement.

He not only skipped his own -- *he'd never been to anyone's.*

When the introduction was over, Greg took a deep breath, rose from his seat, approached the microphone and began his speech. He didn't have a single note to guide him, but he didn't need any. This was a moment he pictured since he was a boy.

He began by telling his 'fellow graduates' about his lifelong effort to draw, and what his Grandma told him about straight lines when he was little. And then, he reflected on some of the obstacles he faced to get to this moment and this stage -- how it turned out his life had not been much of a straight line, either.

"But," he concluded, "the thing is, knowing what I know now, I don't regret it, because my Grandma was right. A straight line might be the shortest distance between two points, but it's definitely *not* the most rewarding."

He paused for a moment to let his words sink in.

As they did, he asked The 11-10-02 Foundation Scholars in attendance to stand. As 2,000 people turned around to look at the five students in the back of the auditorium, Greg told them how proud he was to have them there and how important it was that they "cross a stage just like this one" some day down the road.

And then, he turned his attention back to the graduates sitting up front -- men and women who worked so hard to reach this moment. He said he hoped they were as proud of the obstacles they overcame as they were proud of the goals they achieved -- and as proud to be a part of the graduating class as he was.

He concluded his remarks by saying, "When you get up here to get your degree, I hope you'll pause for just a second, so that you can see what I now see as I stand here, because take my word for it, I walked uphill both ways to reach the top of this mountain, but no matter how long it took, it was worth the climb to see this view."

He paused, looked out at the thousands of graduates, faculty and guests seated before him, let out a breath nearly three decades in the making, smiled broadly, nodded his head for emphasis, and as his eyes filled with tears of joy, repeated those final words one last time.

"It was worth the climb to see this view."

The audience rose en masse to applaud his remarks.

PSC's President later said it was the first standing ovation he'd ever seen for a graduation speaker during his tenure.

Normally, with the speech complete, the honorary degree presentation would come next. Before the event, though, Greg begged school officials to make an exception and let him line up with his 'fellow graduates' so he could do what he'd never done -- cross the stage at a college commencement.

The event planners granted Greg's unusual request, but they didn't want to mess up the alphabetical order of the graduates, so they told him to just file in at the back of the line.

One by one, the students crossed the stage as Greg moved closer and closer to achieving his goal. After all these years, and so many ups and downs, he was now just minutes away from holding a college degree for the first time.

As the line moved forward one graduate at a time, Greg watched the smiles on the faces of those ahead of him as their friends and family hooted and hollered and beamed with pride. After meeting so many students over the past six years and learning about their struggles in and out of school, he really was honored to be associated with a group that included so many adult learners, first generation graduates and students working outside of class so they could pay their own way.

Moment by moment, Greg inched ever closer, until finally, every name was called but his. Every graduate had crossed the stage but him. After 29 years, 6 months and 7 days, his coveted diploma was now just a few precious feet away.

All he had to do was take those last few steps.

As the audience cheered him on and his name echoed through the rafters, Greg crossed the stage and accepted his degree.

As he did, he noticed an irony too sweet for words: The guy who had spent his entire life trying to learn how to draw -- the guy whose Grandma taught him not to worry if his path wasn't always marked by straight lines -- had just been given an Honorary Degree in the *Arts*.

He smiled, hoisted it in the air and screamed with joy.

Long ago, he expected to be an Ivy League valedictorian. Now, he was a thin, frail, limping, tired, bald man graduating last in his class with an honorary degree from a community college.

And he'd never been happier in his entire life.

**

Greg deeply apreciated the reception he received at PSC, but it paled in comparison to the importance he placed on the opinion of his Grandma. He still lived and breathed for her approval.

So, after the event, Greg took the photos to her apartment. As soon as he arrived, he began excitedly flipping through the stack -- giving Grandma a play-by-play description of each picture as he did.

"This is me in my cap and gown before I went on stage! And this is me giving my speech! And this is me getting the degree!"

It was *such* a perfect moment that Greg wished it could go on forever -- these were the pictures he'd been looking forward to giving her for *years* -- but he knew that, eventually, it had to end. After all, the first of the three Scholarship Boards had their meeting in a few days. And as with everything else, there had been a bump in the road.

The problem in this case was that the prominent executives who agreed to serve on the Scholarship Boards were *so* busy that it soon became clear there was just no way their schedules would allow them time to review all the nominees' applications.

It seemed to be a genuine dilemma, until Greg came up with a perfect solution. He decided to create a *Junior* Scholarship Board responsible for going through the nominees and selecting the finalists. That way, when the three *Senior* Scholarship Boards met, they would only have to review ten nominees apiece.

Everyone liked the idea -- until Greg announced the Junior Board would be *a bunch of teenagers.*

The decision to give young people this opportunity struck many as a big mistake -- "You can't trust a bunch of kids with something like this!" one skeptic said -- but Greg disagreed. As far as he was concerned, the idea was not only consistent with his goals -- it *was* his goal. To prove young people can make a difference, too.

"And besides," Greg added, "who can appreciate the college process better than the people currently going through it? They'll make great judges. I'm sure of it."

And so, despite the critics, he moved forward with the plan -- rounding up a dozen students to serve on the Junior Board. Two teens from Greg's hometown -- a girl named Claire and a boy named Alex -- were put in charge.

When the time came, the Junior Board met in a back room at a local restaurant and began reviewing the applications. Despite the doubters, the group took its role seriously. In fact, they took it so seriously that their meeting lasted well past midnight.

With the finalists selected, it was time for the Senior Boards to meet.   The Ladder Board went first.

At precisely ten minutes past six, Greg walked into the spacious conference room where the ten executives were gathered, took his seat at the head of the table and said in the most confident of voices, "Ladies and gentlemen, it's time for us to get down to business."

Decked out in a perfectly-pressed suit, a handful of America's most successful leaders sitting along either side, for one fleeting moment, the substitute teacher looked and felt like a *real* CEO.

But after crossing the stage with the students of PSC, it no longer mattered to him quite so much if anyone else agreed.

He no longer wanted to be *one of them.*

He wanted them to be *one of us.*

And it was right about then that everyone noticed something quite unusual hanging up on the wall. It was Greg's BOARDROOM sign -- the very same one he hung up years earlier in the Lunch Lady's room at Blue Academy. He brought it to the meeting and put it up on the wall before the Board Members arrived.

"I wasn't stepping into their world. They were stepping into ours," Greg said with pride, when asked why he brought the sign.

As for the meeting itself, the execs were impressed by the relevance of the criteria by which they were asked to assess the finalists.

Mr. MacMillan said, "Greg told us to ask ourselves one basic question -- which one of these kids would we hire? When you're asked to do that, you don't worry about ticky-tack things. You worry about work ethic and attendance and other things that actually matter in the context of the real world. Will the kid show up on time? Will he or she work hard? I loved it."

Seven days later, the Mountain Scholarship Board met. To everyone's delight, the entrants had come up with truly creative ideas.

In one instance, a finalist proposed rebuilding the two towers as they were -- and then building a third, even bigger building in between them with 10th floor walkways connecting the three.

The student said, "The building in the middle, that would be like the two towers' mom, and the walkways, that's the mom holding her children's hands to help keep them safe in the future."

The architecture, real estate and engineering executives on the judging panel spent two hours scrutinizing the designs, and discussing them with the same level of attention and consideration given to the multi-million dollar projects they usually worked on each day.

Another seven days later, the Silhouette Scholarship Board took its turn. The last of the judging panels had a particularly difficult task. They had to evaluate what the nominees had overcome, relative to what they had achieved. It was not an easy thing to do, but after two hours of debate, they managed to do it.

As the meeting came to an end, Greg tucked his BOARDROOM sign underneath one arm and his lunchbox briefcase under another, and walked out the door with a feeling of exhiliration.

With the applications reviewed and judges' votes cast, the next step in the process was one of Greg's favorites. In the morning, he placed a call to Mr. Goldberg: "We've got some more Scholars, so make some room in your trophy factory because I've got a box full of stinky, smelly, unwashed milkshake glasses to bring you!"

On the verge of fulfilling the third version of the Logo, Greg started thinking more than ever about Grandma. He knew he never would have been able to get so far without her support. She was the one who gave him The Chair and made him believe a substitute teaching restaurant doorman could build a Foundation from scratch. She was the one who taught him how to deal with rejection. The one who urged him to work twice as much as kids who seemed twice as smart. The one who convinced him it was okay if he couldn't draw straight lines.

Day after day, for nearly three decades, Grandma had been there for him. It might have been *tough love*, but it was love all the same. Unequivocal, unwavering, *unconditional* love.

In return, Greg repeatedly tried to show his appreciation. He called almost every day. He visited as often as he could. And over the years, he arranged everything from a surprise party for her birthday to autographs from her favorite TV stars. And yet, Greg always felt like he still had not done enough to thank her. He wanted her to understand she was the World's Greatest Grandma.

Whenever he told her that, she wagged her finger and said, "That's what *you* think. You ask other kids, and you'll get other answers."

Greg nodded politely, but her words did little to sway him. He knew there were millions of *really great* grandmothers, but *his* Grandma was truly in a league all her own -- and no matter what it took, he wanted to convince her of that.

So much so, when he heard of a national contest looking to honor an outstanding grandmother, he eagerly set aside everything else on his agenda to take the time to nominate her.

He figured she would be the obvious choice, but the judges ultimately did not agree and selected another nominee.

Not surprisingly, Greg was incensed, but he refused to let a little setback get in his way. He began trying to come up with another way to prove his Grandma was the greatest. Finally, a few days after the Scholarship Board meetings, Greg came up with the perfect plan.

His plan was to enter Grandma into an 'international search' for the Worlds Greatest Grandma via WorldsGreatestGrandma.com.

Charlie wasn't so sure the idea made much sense. If Greg's Grandma wasn't picked in a nationwide competition, the odds of her being chosen in a worldwide one didn't seem particularly good.

Until, that is, Greg revealed he had aquired the website hosting the competition, and there would be just one judge on the panel -- *him*.

The contest was obviously a farce, but Greg insisted otherwise. He vowed to be a 'fair' judge and proceeded with the plan. He submitted an essay to nominate Grandma -- then declared the 'competition' closed. A few minutes later, the judging panel (himself) read the (only) nomination and selected the winning Grandma (his own).

When Charlie heard the news, he could not stop laughing.

"How was that *possibly* fair?" he chuckled.

"The Panel considered every essay," Greg shot back defiantly.

Charlie started pointing out the obvious -- *there was only one essay and it was the one and only member of the judging panel who submitted it* -- but Greg was too excited to care. In fact, he was so proud of himself that he thought he was going to *burst*.

He *could not wait* to see the look on Grandma's face when he told her that whether she liked it or not, she was, *officially*, the *WorldsGreatestGrandma*!

But he never got the chance.

A few hours later, that very same day, just as he was heading out the door to make the drive to Grandma's apartment, the phone began to ring. He decided to step back inside and answer it.

"Greg?" the voice on the other end of the line asked softly.

"Yes?"

"Your Grandma just passed away."

Greg had never felt anything so painful in his life. He knew she was old -- her ability to walk, talk, see, hear all fading away -- but he'd never prepared himself for the day she would actually be *gone*.

The timing made the tragedy that much worse.

Charlie said, "Every time Greg was about to celebrate reaching a goal, something went wrong. It happened to him so often that, at some point, it seemed to become part of who he was. Even he was able to laugh about it at some point. But this one -- his Grandma passing away just moments before he left to go tell her about the new website created in her honor -- this one was just brutal."

By the end of the week, Greg's sadness and grief caused by the loss of Grandma and its timing became literally all-consuming.

Hoping to clear some of the thoughts from his head, he sent an open letter to his friends and wrote a guest column about her for *Senior News*. He was just trying to vent his feelings about her loss, but as fate would have it, by taking the time to do it, the single most negative experience of his life gave birth to something positive.

In the days that followed, people all over the country began responding to what Greg wrote about Grandma. Some of those responses included donations to the Foundation in her honor.

When Greg took a moment to add up all the checks, he suddenly realized there was enough to help another student go to college.

A few days later, he met with Grandma's caretaker on a bench behind the building where she had lived happily for the past decade. For twenty minutes, the two sat quietly, gulping down shakes and toasting the creation of this new and unexpected scholarship.

**

When Greg first ventured inside The Center with those spare bagels years earlier, he never could've imagined the day would come that one of those seemingly fragile, elderly residents would be among his greatest sources of strength during the darkest period of his life.

And yet, as soon as Grandma passed away, Greg knew The Bully was the person to turn to for support.

Over the previous few years, The Bully had become like family to Greg -- and, it seemed, vice versa. He still visited her on a weekly basis, and he had been among those invited to attend her 80th birthday party (ever the prankster, she made sure his name tag read: TWERP). As time went on, The Bully and Greg used to say good-naturedly that she had become his 'backup' Grandma -- just in case one was ever needed. And now, one was.

Greg stopped by The Center to tell her what happened, but before he'd even spoken, she sensed something was wrong.

"What is it?" she asked.

"My Grandma passed away."

The Bully smiled compassionately, touched his hand, and said, "You're stuck with me...like glue."

Make no mistake, there was no truly replacing Grandma. Greg would feel the pain of her death for years to come, but in the short term, The Bully's unwavering friendship helped as much as anything could. Her wisdom helped, too.

She said, "I know you miss your Grandma, but you can't sit still thinking about it, or it will eat you up inside. You gotta keep moving, focus on something. Do what we do here -- let the blood flow."

Instinctively, he knew her advice made sense. It was the same coping mechanism he had used much of his life -- distracting himself from pain by focusing on something that would benefit others.

In this case, mercifully, he didn't have to look far to find that benevolent distraction. The Gala at The Big Hotel was shaping up to be a night to remember and needed his full attention.

Four tables worth of items had been lined up for the night's silent auction. A bunch of great companies had signed on as sponsors. There were even going to be invitations this time around -- *thousands* of them.

Ironically, all the invitations created a new problem. Somebody had to stuff, seal and stamp all the envelopes.

Fortunately for Greg, a bunch of students volunteered to do it. He appreciated all of them lending a hand, but one kid in particular clearly stuck out from the others. His name was A.C. Lucas.

A couple months earlier, A.C. had been nominated for one of the Ladder Scholarships, but the Board did not pick him. A middle linebacker who looked the part, A.C. hardly seemed the type to take defeat with a gracious smile, and yet, here he was -- offering to help with the invitations for the party honoring the students who were picked for the scholarships instead of him.

Knowing firsthand how hard it was to cope with rejection as a high school senior, Greg wanted to do something to recognize A.C.'s maturity -- so he gave him two free tickets to the Gala.

Some runners-up would have said 'thanks but no thanks' when offered the chance to watch someone honored in their place, but A.C. was so grateful for the tickets that he said he'd get there early.

A.C. was not the only student looking forward to the big event.

A week before it took place, Elliott presented his former substitute teacher with a gift -- the foul ball.

Greg smiled, "That was, like, five years ago when you caught it."

"I know," Elliott replied, "and I've kept it all this time, and now I want you to have it. It'll bring you luck next week."

The kids may have been excited about the Gala, but Greg was not. For him, planning the event had long since become a *chore*. An obligation that he made so it must therefore be kept.

In much the same way that Greg ultimately realized Froehmann Whitfield -- despite all its noted attributes -- could not replace the joys he left behind in Louisiana, he had discovered that, for all the great things The Big Hotel was, there was one thing it wasn't and never could be.

It could never be the Restaurant.

He missed the head of the Restaurant, who had entrusted him with that IOU, and their event planner, who treated him more like a friend than a client. He missed the generous helpings of food, the personal touch of the service, the intimacy of the Banquet Room, and the fact that he got away without creating an assigned seating chart. The Big Hotel was spectacular. It just wasn't the right fit in this case.

And so it was that he could not escape the irony that, yet again, he had chosen a great place for the wrong reason. And yet again, in the process, he had given up something he loved.

After years of dreaming and months of planning, the big night at The Big Hotel finally arrived. At a quarter to six, hundreds of people began parading inside the Regal Ballroom to find their seats.

Just as Greg hoped, the event was bringing people from different backgrounds together. Corporate executives, young professionals, teachers, kids, families from The Green -- they were all there. For one night, they were all coming together under a single roof. For one night, *everything* seemed to be coming together just right.

Well, almost everything.

As the guests began arriving at the luxurious hotel, they noticed Greg milling about...*in pajama pants and a t-shirt.*

"I came here early to check on last-minute details, and I lost all track of time," he said apologetically to each guest he encountered.

In reality, just as at the first Gala, his apparent disarray was by design. He could not stand the fact that he had to prepare a seating chart for The Big Hotel Gala. So, he stubbornly (and purposely) created one that was virtually impossible to decipher -- in the hope that guests would eventually give up trying to make sense of it and just find an open seat. And he didn't want to be present when it happened, to avoid being asked to sort out the confusion -- hence, the pajamas giving him an excuse to go change outfits as the guests were arriving.

While Greg went and put on his suit, the nearly 500 guests in attendance found their seats and enjoyed a three course meal. As they looked around the massive Regal Ballroom, the supporters who had been around since the beginning could not believe how much the Foundation had grown. But if they were concerned things would change as they grew, those concerns quickly went away.

Charlie said, "Greg lined up security guards -- big guys in dark suits and dark glasses -- to keep an eye on the trophies. I'll admit, at first glance, it added to the sense this was a prestigious event. But then, you remember the trophies are *used milkshake glasses.* This was still the same goofy guy doing things in the same goofy way."

Almost to the point of defiance, Greg insisted a change of scenery would not lead to a change in philosophy.

He said, "It was no longer about becoming *one of them.* It was about *them* becoming *one of us.*"

Above all else, no matter how sophisticated the backdrop, the night at The Big Hotel would still be a chance for the *kids* to shine. Greg once again booked Fitz and his friends to play the music. Instead of using elaborate objects as table centerpieces, he opted to use milkshake glasses handpainted by Blue Academy students. And instead of bringing in some celebrity, Greg chose Rocky -- the 'kid in the tux' at the first Gala -- to be the guest speaker at this one.

[Funny side note: In the weeks leading up to the event, Greg had been promoting a special appearance by 'an elected leader'. Given the increasingly high profile of the Foundation, some were expecting it to be a Senator or a Governor. Needless to say, those in attendance were quite amused when the 'elected leader' invited to speak during the event turned out to be Rocky -- who had been voted into Student Government during his freshman year of college.]

Just like at the first Gala, the Gala co-hosts were teens, too. This time, it was Cliff and two girls, Brandie and Hannah.

Entrusting the last of those three with such a prominent role seemed particularly surprising. In contrast to Cliff and Brandie (both of whom were long-time Brunch Bunch members), Hannah had never even met Greg. Still, he insisted she was perfect for the part, and she eagerly accepted the offer to serve as one of the big night's co-hosts.

She said, "I had no idea why I was asked, but I was excited!"

Greg made it back to The Big Hotel just as the plates were being cleared. With dinner over and the 'director' back on the 'set', it was time for the show to begin.

It started with the presentation of awards to a few of the Foundation's supporters. Once again, the honorees were not your typical cast of characters. Greg stubbornly insisted on the awards going to some more of the supporters who traditionally get overlooked (like Mr. Goldberg the Trophy Maker).   There was also an honor lined up for The Lunch Lady and her two co-workers -- dinner for three at one of the nicest restaurants in the entire country.

The scholarships were next.

The first was the one created and funded in memory of Bailey by the university he was going to attend had he lived. Greg spent two years looking for the right student to receive it -- determined to validate the trust he'd been given. In the end, he couldn't choose between two students, and luckily for them, the school decided Greg didn't have to pick -- agreeing to give scholarships to both of them!

And the good news just kept coming.

A few moments later, it was announced the Foundation was so proud of how A.C. handled rejection -- offering to stuff invitations for the Gala -- that a brand new scholarship was created just for him.

Even better, it was announced that the college A.C. was going to attend had agreed to *quadruple* match the scholarship!

It was then Rocky's turn to be surprised (again). In the middle of his keynote address, the 'elected leader' in the tux noticed the head of the university he attended walking toward the stage. She said the school was so impressed by Rocky's freshman year that they were going to match the scholarship given to him by the Foundation!

With those surprises out of the way, it was time to give scholarships to the kids who met that criteria Greg laid out at the first Gala.

The challenge had been a success in more ways than one. Of the fifteen students, three of them received jobs from people they met through the process. Another three received internships. Two got computers, and another eight received grants from the Foundation. To top it off, three of them managed to meet the challenge itself and earn $5,000 for college.

The parade of surprises and scholarships brought smiles to the faces of everyone -- everyone except Greg. The man who pictured this night for years -- and scripted it all out right down to the final word on the final page -- was still anxiously pacing in the back of the room. Like any director, he wasn't going to relax until the final curtain fell.

Back on stage, the co-hosts announced it was time for the Foundation to raise some money. The live auction was next.

This time around, the packages were ones *nobody* laughed at -- a stay in France, a Total-Traveler cruise and a diamond to name a few.

Once the bids were in and the auction was complete, it was time to give out the last set of scholarships -- the ones representing the four symbols in Version Three of the logo. One by one, the scholarship winners were all called on stage.

The Legacy Scholarship was first. It went to Elliott. The Foul Ball Kid was well on his way to becoming a College Man.

The Ladder Scholars were honored next -- students who were more accurately measured by their work ethic than their GPA.

When they were done, the Mountain Scholars took their turn on stage -- their post-9/11 designs on display for all to see.

As the honorees returned to their seats, Charlie noticed a mother taking her daughter's trophy, showing it off around the table and then starting to cry. The young businessman was at a loss for words.

He said, "It wasn't gold. *It was a used, unwashed milkshake glass.* Was I the only one who could see that? The whole thing was surreal."

With the Legacy, Ladder and Mountain Scholars honored, there was just one thing left to do -- give out The Silhouette Scholarships and reveal who was standing on top of the mountain in this third version of the Logo.

The first Silhouette Scholarship was named after Little Jarrett. The boy from Kentucky was living proof a person's strength couldn't be measured by their size or shape. The scholarship went to a young man named Dennis, who graduated high school with all A's despite being confined to a wheelchair.

The second Silhouette Scholarship was named after Greg's Grandma. Despite being unable to walk or see in her final days, she had remained as strong as ever. The scholarship went to a young man named Dan. Despite a horrible accident that shortened his arms and forced him to spend his life on crutches, he managed to graduate high school at the top of his class.

Dennis and Dan were exactly what Greg envisioned when he created the Silhouette Scholarship. The two boys had a level of confidence and strength that shattered any stereotype about so-called *handicapped* kids. And as the two boys basked in the glow of their inspiring acceptance speeches, the audience rose to their feet and gave them a standing ovation.

The Silhouette Scholars had been honored. The picture was now complete. Or so it seemed.

As Hannah, the co-host, stepped forward for the show's conclusion, a young man suddenly ran on stage with a Milkshake Trophy and declared there was a third Silhouette Scholarship to give out.

As if in slow motion, Hannah peeled off the sticker covering the trophy's base. Sure enough, it was *her* name engraved on the front.

She wasn't merely a co-host. She was one of the night's honorees.

Her hands and legs began to shake, as she approached the microphone and tried to compose herself.

"I, uh, oh my gosh, wow, I just can't...I just don't...I, uh...."

The surprise had left her -- literally -- speechless.

The audience was clearly touched, but they were also confused. This last set of scholarships was *supposed to be* for students who dealt with physical obstacles. Given her tall thin frame, Hannah looked more like a cheerleader than a Silhouette Scholar.

But *that* was the point.

Hannah looked fine because her obstacle was an *internal* one. As a young girl, she had an operation on her heart that forced her to spend much of high school studying from home. So, her obstacle might have been hard to see, but it was certainly real. And just like Dennis and Dan, Hannah had not let her obstacles impede her success -- graduating near the top of her class despite what she endured.

As Hannah's mother watched her daughter surprised on stage, tears began to flow -- and she made no effort to wipe them away.

She later said, "Ever had a moment when you're so happy that you don't care you're crying, your makeup is running, and people are watching? Seeing Hannah up there, that was one of those moments."

The image of the Silhouette was yet another irony in a story filled with them. In Version Three of the Logo, the man standing on top of the mountain with his arms raised in victory turned out to represent three people instead of one. And, as fate would have it, one -- Dennis -- couldn't stand. The second -- Dan -- couldn't raise his arms. And the third -- Hannah -- wasn't a man at all.

In the back of the room, the boy everybody once laughed at because of his wide-eyed dreams could now be found laughing loudest of all. It may have taken nearly three decades, but as Dennis, Dan and Hannah stood on stage, Greg had done what people always said was impossible. *He had just made The Silhouette Man come to life.*

Perhaps even more ironic was the identity of the people who raised the money to fund the scholarship for Hannah.

Unlike most scholarships funded by corporations, or at least by wealthy individuals, Hannah's scholarship was made possible by *a bunch of teenagers.*

The civic-minded students worked diligently for months -- doing everything from baby-sitting to car-washing until they came up with enough money to fund two scholarships. The first was given to one of the Mountain Scholars earlier in the night. The second was the one given to Hannah.

To many in the crowd, the teens' efforts were a well-timed reminder why Greg started down this path in the first place.

As his neighbor, Arthur, put it, "The Foundation had support from people of all ages -- personally, I'm forty-two -- but, at the end of the day, the name -- 11-10-02 -- represented the belief that people thirty and under could make a difference, too. Knowing that a bunch of teenagers funded this final scholarship reminded us all of that. It brought the entire thing full circle. It was just very, very cool."

Even more cool, perhaps, was the fact that the teenagers who did it were led by Alex. After serving on the Junior Scholarship Board and reading about the nominees, he wanted to do more than just cast a vote -- hence, the decision to mobilize some friends and raise the money.

A native of the same town where Greg and Charlie were raised, Alex appeared at first glance to be cut from the same mold -- the same schools, the same camps, the same grand dreams -- but upon closer inspection, he was different.

On the one hand, Alex had already been accepted to the Ivy Leagues, was headed there in the fall, fully expected to land a high-paying job four years down the road -- and made no apologies for any of it. And yet, he was as anxious to make a difference as he was to make a fortune -- and hoped to inspire his classmates to do the same.

Alex was not solely following Charlie's path toward corporate America and material success -- nor had he completely walked away from that lucrative future to devote all his energy to working in the community as Greg had done. Instead, he was carving out his own unique path somewhere in the middle.

In the process, Alex became living proof that you don't have to choose between chasing your dreams and helping others reach theirs. If you want to conquer the world, you don't need to be 100% Charlie. If you want to change the world, you don't need to be 100% Greg. There is a middle ground. And Alex had found it.

With all the scholarships given out, Cliff approached the podium to thank everyone for coming and to remind them to drive safely on the way home. As he did, he suddenly noticed Greg making his way toward the stage for the first time all night.

History was about to repeat itself.

When he got to the podium, Greg said the hosts were missing the last page or two of the script. It was time for another live auction.

"The cruise, the trip and the diamond auctioned earlier were great," he said, "but I saved the most valuable item of all for last."

The audience was abuzz with excitement. What could be more valuable than a cruise, a trip and a diamond? *A new car? A new house?* Uh, not exactly. It turned out to be the stitches of Elliott's foul ball.

Greg's ex-girlfriend, Sloane, cracked, "Greg didn't even frame the ball -- just some of the red, stringy stuff."

Despite all the funny looks he was getting from the crowd, Greg insisted this was no gag. He said the story behind the foul ball symbolized believing in yourself and seizing opportunities. He said this was *art,* and he insisted, it was worth more than the cruise, the trip and the diamond *combined.* He said he felt so strongly about this that he was going to *start* the bidding at $5,000.

The ballroom rocked with laughter, but Greg did not care. He knew all he needed was one person to believe in his vision -- and he wasn't going to move an inch until one person did.

His neighbor, Arthur, said, "Two minutes passed -- literally -- and he just kept standing there, waiting for someone to bid. And I think a lot of us wanted to. We believed in him, but I mean, five grand is a ton of money, and I don't care what he said. It was string."

Thanks to the bright lights, sweat began to form atop Greg's shiny, bald head, but still, he refused to give up. He was going to stand there for as long as it took until somebody stood up with him.

And sure enough, it worked. Whether out of inspiration or sympathy, a complete stranger suddenly bid five thousand dollars.

The room was in shock. Five grand for some red string? From someone Greg had never even met? It seemed too good to be true.

And yet, it turned out to be little more than an Opening Act.

"That was a good start," Greg declared from the podium. "Now this next item, don't hold back, folks. It's our last item up for auction this evening -- and it's an *outstanding* one!"

Outstanding? Um, *ridiculous* might be a better way to put it.

The second item was a *framed scrap of aluminum.*

Guy, the photographer, laughed, "It was the flip-top from his soda can I used to get that camera to work -- *he had saved it and framed it!*"

Again, the audience laughed -- the thing was *literally* garbage --
and again, Greg was unfazed by the reaction. He knew one man's
garbage was another man's art, and he knew all he needed was one
person out of 500 to agree with him to prove it. And sure enough,
after another excruciatingly long period of silence, one person did.

From the back of the room, one of the very first executives to join
the Scholarship Board called out, "Five thousand."

The audience was stunned by the man's generous offer.

And yet, to Greg, it was apparently not quite generous enough.

"Five thousand dollars? My Grandma's autograph went for five
thousand dollars!" he replied from the stage, with a straight face. "A
piece of red string went for five grand! This is *aluminum!*"

The audience spun around to see the bidder's reaction -- many
assuming he'd storm out in anger that his incredible offer had been
mocked -- but he never did. To the contrary, the easy-going executive
was so supportive and *such* a good sport that he *outbid himself by
another three thousand dollars.*

In the process, the scrap of aluminum not only went for more
money than the cruise, trip and diamond *combined* -- it was the largest
one-time donation the Foundation had ever accepted.

It seemed to be a perfect finale -- a reminder that people really will
support your dreams if you believe in them enough -- but Greg was
still not done. With the auction's success, his confidence was soaring.
He knew it was time to make *the* announcement. The *really* big
announcement. The one he'd been waiting over a decade to make.

Greg took a deep breath, then declared, "I have a dream!"

The audience couldn't help giggling at the sound of four words
synonymous with one of history's most serious moments, coming out
of the mouth of a man who had been mingling outside the ballroom in
his pajamas a couple hours earlier. But Greg didn't laugh with them.
He had not chosen the words by accident. After all, this was not just
any dream he was about to unveil. This was *The Dream*. The one
hatched inside his mind when he was sitting on a mattress in a dormitory hallway in Louisiana, with the Dr. King poster over his shoulder.
A dream he considered so special that he'd kept it secret for nearly a
dozen years.

The crowd hushed silent with anticipation as Greg continued.

"My *Dream*," he said, "is much like Dr. King's Dream. A world of
people of different ages, races and cultures coming together and
finding common ground."

Except for one little twist.

In Greg's Dream, everyone was drinking milkshakes.

The audience began to laugh even louder than before, but again, Greg did not laugh with them. He insisted he was serious.

The crowd politely regained its composure -- though most of them were still unsure what Greg's oddball dream had to do with them.

They were about to find out.

"The way I figure," he said, "if my *Dream* is going to come true, it has to start some day and somewhere, and what better day than today? What better where than right here?"

Hannah, the Silhouette Scholar, recalled, "He wanted everybody to get up and leave the hotel right then and right there and go with him for milkshakes. It was the craziest thing I'd ever heard."

Indeed, the idea seemed ludicrous -- an entire ballroom of people in tailored suits and designer dresses going out together for shakes.

And yet, he meant it.

And when he asked those people in those expensive suits and fancy dresses to rise from their seats, *they did.*

Beaming from ear to ear, Greg told the audience now standing before him that there was just one last thing to be said before they embarked on this unusually 'sweet' journey together.

"As we make the walk, please don't only talk to the people you came here with tonight. I want you to talk to new people, too -- people you do not know. I want you to make new friends while we cross the street and go get shakes."

With that said, he skipped off the podium and headed toward the door. And people followed. Charlie, Kat the Intern, Hannah, Rocky, the other Scholars, their families, Mr. MacMillan and other heavy hitters from the Scholarship Boards, Guy the Photographer, Mr. Brooks and Ms. Boggs and The Lunch Lady and the others from Blue Academy, Mr. Ansel the Accountant, Bo Farnesworth, Fitz and the Band, Mr. Goldberg the Trophy Maker.

One by one, two by two, people of different races and ages, single moms and CEOs, they followed the substitute teacher with the mismatched socks and lunchbox briefcase out of the Regal Ballroom, down the hall, out the door of The Big Hotel and across the street to the little milkshake shop.

And as they made their way across the street that unforgettable summer night, they talked to the people walking on their left and on their right, whether they knew each other or not. Hundreds of people

...cending racial, cultural, generational, religious and economic barriers -- co-existing together instead of just side by side. So many people, in fact, that when they arrived, they filled up every inch of the milkshake shop, with an overflow crowd spilling out into the street.

And there they sat (or stood), in suits and dresses, laughing and joking, making new friends and gulping down shakes. It was *exactly* as Greg had dreamed all those years earlier.

When the night came to an end and people finally began to make their way home, Charlie walked up to his friend of twenty-five years, smiled warmly and said humbly, "It's not exactly how they taught us to do it in business school, but I do have to admit...you had a vision and you made it come to life. For what it's worth, I'm proud of you."

Greg reciprocated with a smile of his own. He always respected Charlie's path, but never thought the feeling was mutual. So, to hear his oldest friend acknowledge his way of doing things had value, too -- it meant a lot to the kid with no corner office.

But before Greg could say thanks, his old pal spoke again.

"There is one thing I don't get. If the shakes were so important, why didn't you just have them delivered to us at the hotel?"

"Because it wasn't about milkshakes."

"But I thought you said your dream was--"

"It was about the walk, Charlie."

And that, indeed, was the moral of Greg's story -- the moral it took him nearly thirty years to understand himself.

Whether you're trying to build a company, earn a college degree or just get a milkshake, it's the process of getting where you want to go that matters most. *That's* when you learn things -- on your way to getting where you want to go. It's not about *where* you go or what you get when you arrive that is of greatest importance.

It's the walk -- always the walk -- that matters most.

**

Now that Greg brought the streak of brunches full circle, helped thirty students get to college and even began pursuing *The Dream*, some people suggested he use what little time was left until his thirtieth birthday to *finally* take a much-deserved vacation.

Greg appreciated the thought, but he had a much different idea in mind. Instead of coasting to the finish line, he wanted to use the weeks that remained to test the limits of everything he learned over the previous twenty-nine years and eight months of his life.

And he knew exactly how he wanted to do it.

Over and over again, Greg was told the most important parts of his life were not real. His backyard friends were not real. Many of the people he admired in books and films were fictitious. The thirty dreams on his Idea List were unrealistic. He was just a 'special' student at Froehmann Whitfield. At one point, the skeptics accused him of having muscles that were artificial. He wasn't a real teacher. His part-time gig at The Club was not a real job. His room with the Lunch Lady was not an actual office. His first big speech -- the one at Blue Academy -- was not a legitimate one because it took place in a hallway. His pet dog was made out of clay. His milkshake glasses weren't real trophies. The 'Gala' at the Restaurant was not a bonafide Gala. The things he auctioned off were not genuine art. The degree from PSC was just honorary. Even the competition that declared his Grandma to be the world's greatest was called a farce.

Over and over and over again, for nearly thirty years, he heard the doubters say these things -- questioning the authenticity of the people, places and things he cherished most. And over and over and over again, he tried to prove them wrong.

Now, he wanted to do the opposite. Instead of convincing people something had value -- that it was *real* -- could he convince them to believe in something that even he admitted was *not*? Could he convince people to see the value in something that *really* didn't exist? Could he convince them to literally see value in *nothing*?

To find out the answer, he said he was going to create a film premiere from scratch. He was going to line up a caterer and get posters made, and there'd be newspaper ads and a billboard, too -- he could already picture all of it in his head -- and he vowed to get all the companies that would be involved to do their part *for free*.

It was a difficult task under the best of circumstances, but there was an added wrinkle that made it seemingly impossible.

There would not actually be a film.

Charlie insisted his old friend had finally gone off the deep end. No company in its right mind would support the premiere of a film that did not actually exist.

Greg strongly disagreed. He said experience taught him that it didn't matter if there was a film. He said if a person believed in something strongly enough, then others would believe in it, too -- even if they knew it didn't exist. So, despite the doubts, he started calling companies to ask for their support.

"Wait a second," said one CEO. "You want my company to help promote the premiere of a film that doesn't exist?"

"That's right," Greg said proudly. "There's no film. Not even a short one. There's zilch, nada, *nothing*! So whaddya say?"

The CEO turned down the idea, and he wasn't the only one. But each time, Greg just shrugged off the rejection and kept making more calls. And, sure enough, within a few days, he accomplished exactly what he set out to do -- and then some.

A photographer named Vincent and a graphic designer named Maria agreed to help make the posters. Kinko's agreed to print hundreds of copies once they were done. The local paper agreed to run ads in the movie section to promote the event, and a company even agreed to put up a billboard right in the middle of town.

And that was just the marketing side of things.

For the event itself, Greg lined up food and sodas for the hundreds of guests who would be attending. For dessert, there would be a special, giant cheesecake (in the shape of a milkshake, of course).

Greg's friends were stunned by what he put together, but they were positively speechless after discovering where the event would take place. *The movie theater.*

In a surreptitious meeting nearly a year earlier, Greg had somehow convinced the powers-that-be to have its theater host the premiere of a film that did not exist.

[The backstory was another memorable one. As the story goes...one day shortly after 9-11, Greg went to a local deli for lunch. One table over, there was a woman eating by herself, with some luggage by her side. Curious about what it was like to fly so soon after the terrorist attacks, Greg asked the woman about the heightened security at the airport. The question and its answer mushroomed into an hour-long conversation, as the two eventually scooted closer and finished their meal together.

The woman was just passing through town (hence, the luggage). In fact, in the years that followed, the two would never see each other again. But three months after their one fateful meeting, out of the blue, Greg received a packet from the movie theater company. The packet included a bunch of movie passes to be given out to students. (It turned out the woman with the luggage had written to them and encouraged the company to support his civic efforts.) Upon getting the packet, Greg immediately contacted the rep who had signed the kind note included with the passes and requested a meeting -- offering only the vague promise it would be "worth your time."

Despite it being the holidays, the request was granted, and the meeting took place three days later -- at which time, Greg revealed his idea about the premiere of a movie that did not exist.

While he was clearly enthusiastic, he proved to be hopelessly short on details. He had settled on a specific date (11-10-02) and a specific location (their theater outside his window), but that was it.

He also had nothing concrete to show in support of his idea. No preview of the movie (since, of course, there wasn't one), no list of sponsors (since, at that point, none had been approached let alone secured), not a single detail on paper at all.

In fact, the only piece of paper Greg *did* bring to the meeting was a decade old -- the letter announcing his acceptance to study film in England. He showed it to the rep of the movie theater company sitting across the desk, took a deep breath, and said, "My godfather was the projectionist at the local theater when I was a kid. I have loved movies ever since. I was supposed to go to England to study film when I was in college -- that's what this letter is about -- but I never got on the plane. And then, I gave up the chance to be in California and get into the movie business after college -- because I wanted to come back here to work in the schools. I can't go back in time and change any of that. And, now, I don't even know that I would. But it would mean so much to have one night -- the night I turn thirty -- where the dream did come true. Even if it's just for one night. Even if it's the premiere of a film that doesn't actually exist. It would mean so much. And the ticket sales could benefit the Foundation and we could help more kids. It would all be so perfect. Please help me make this dream come true."

The woman hearing Greg's plea had never met him before the meeting, but she was certainly no stranger to big dreams. After all, she dealt with people in the film industry for a living. And so, despite having no previous ties to Greg or his work, despite his anything-but-ordinary idea, despite the conspicuous absence of specifics in his proposal, and despite the fact there was no particular rush to commit to something not taking place for a full year, she agreed right then and there to come on board. The theater would host the premiere of a film they knew did not exist, and waive all costs in the process.]

"That was the thing," Greg's neighbor, Arthur, later observed. "Every time you want to dismiss him as a goof who wanders around aimlessly and happens upon opportunities through sheer luck, you discover he had the meeting with the movie theater rep a whole year earlier to lay the groundwork for the event on 11-10-02, and he never told a soul about it. He has this image -- the socks, the lunchbox, getting lost all the time, the nutty ideas, and all the serendipitous encounters that seem to lead to such incredible things -- it was like the Scarecrow with no brain -- but, in reality, he was more like the Wizard -- sitting in that little room of his, orchestrating the grandest of plans, mapping out the details months in advance. I don't care what his image was. Nothing he accomplished was by accident."

In a speech before several hundred supporters, Greg revealed the plans for his long-awaited thirtieth birthday.

"We're going to have a film premiere!" he shrieked.

Those in attendance seemed genuinely excited about the event -- until Greg revealed the twist: *there was no film.*

The audience was amused and confused all at once.

Elliott said, "The reception with the stars sounded cool, except that, well, if there's no actual movie, then who are the stars?"

A reception with movie stars -- that has no movie stars -- didn't sound too impressive, but Greg seemed to think otherwise. He said it was, in fact, *so* great that tickets were going to cost $125 apiece!

Arthur laughed, "Most of us thought he was *nuts.* This was the premiere of a film that did not exist. He would've been lucky if people agreed to show up *for free.* To charge people $125 to go?? Just nuts."

Arthur wasn't the only one who felt that way, but Greg didn't care one bit. He knew that if he kept believing in his idea strongly enough, then eventually other people would, too. And, sure enough, they did. Slowly but surely, as ridiculous as it seemed, people started filling out forms to buy tickets. Some bought as many as ten.

Annie, a local parent who had always told Greg to keep chasing his dreams, was loving every second of it.

"It wasn't like he tricked anyone," she boasted. "They all knew there was no movie. And yet, they were *still* ordering tickets."

It seemed like Greg had reached his latest goal well ahead of schedule -- but he was actually just getting warmed up. Having convinced all these companies to back the event, having persuaded the theater to host it, and now, having convinced hundreds of people to attend it, the stage was set for Greg to do what he had always dreamed. He was going to prove that something imaginary could become real. He was going to make *nothing* come to life.

"What do you mean?" Charlie asked his old pal.

"I'm making a movie!"

**

The idea seemed to be Greg's nuttiest yet. He had just one hundred days to learn how to make a film, come up with the equipment, assemble a cast, shoot the footage, edit it all together and have it ready to play on the night of 11-10-02.

It seemed impossible, especially with everything else already on his plate. But Greg assured his friends that it would all work out -- noting that Roy Hobbs didn't try out for pro baseball until he was much older, and he still became a champion.

"Who?" Charlie asked.

"Roy Hobbs. The guy in the film, *The Natural*. He was going to be a pro ballplayer, but he got sidetracked. By the time he finally had the chance to chase his dream, he was older and only had a small window of opportunity -- but he took a leap and went for it -- and his team won. Just like me and making movies. I was going to do it when I was younger, but I got sidetracked. And I only have a small window of opportunity to pursue now what I sacrificed then, but I'm gonna do it -- and I'm gonna come out on top, too."

And so it was, with a make-believe baseball player as his inspiration, Greg embarked on the project of a lifetime -- learning how to make a movie and then actually making it -- in a hundred days.

His first decision as a filmmaker was made with ease -- the topic.

To avoid wasting precious time researching a new subject, Greg decided the film would tell part of a story he already knew by heart -- his own. Specifically, it would chronicle the creation and subsequent growth of The 11-10-02 Foundation.

The title was an easy choice, too -- *11-10-02.com* -- a reference to both the topic and to the one and only night it would be shown.

"Wait a second," Charlie said, "it'll only be seen once?"

Greg confirmed his buddy's ears worked just fine. He said that one day, perhaps, he would tell the story of the first thirty years of his life, and maybe that would be read or watched around the world, but the film he was about to spend a hundred days and nights trying to make -- if he did get it done -- was only going to be a rough draft. It was only going to depict part of the story. And, it was only going to be seen one time -- the night of 11-10-02.

"Who spends a hundred days and nights making something, only to turn around and throw it away?" Charlie asked, exasperated.

Greg patted his millionaire friend on the back and replied, "Somebody who believes it's the walk that matters most."

In the days that followed, despite his inexperience, Greg actually got off to an impressive start. He got two friends to agree to help with the editing. He also managed to line up some film and cameras and even cold-called his way into access to a studio where real productions were filmed.

As Charlie watched Greg tripping over cables and trying to figure out how to turn on the camera, he became convinced his friend had pulled off his greatest coup ever when he talked his way into a studio.

Charlie said, "Calling up some production place where actual shows are filmed and saying, *'Hi, we've never met, but I'd like to use your studio for a while, starting immediately, and you're not gonna get paid. I have no experience, but don't worry, I won't break any of your really expensive equipment. And, remember, you can trust me because I'm a complete stranger.'* How does that work? I just don't get it."

"Well, that's not how I said it," Greg replied, slightly irritated.

"What part did I leave out?" Charlie demanded to know.

"The part where I said *Please*."

In the weeks leading up to the event, Greg did some media to hype the premiere. He even created a trailer to provide a sense of what could be expected on 11-10-02. Well, sort of.

The 'trailer' was a home video, which had been filmed just days before Grandma passed away, with her staring into the camera and saying matter-of-factly, "The story's a nice story, but the guy in charge, he ain't no Steve Spielberg."

While the trailer did not impress the critics, the movie poster did. The photographer, the graphic designer and Kinko's took Greg's idea -- a man and two students walking past the train tracks that separated The Green from The Big Hotel and the rest of The City -- and turned it into a poster that looked straight out of Hollywood.

At least, at first glance it did.

As with virtually all movie posters, the one for *11-10-02.com* listed credits at the bottom. On Greg's poster, however, most of those cited *did not actually exist*.

His ex-girlfriend, Sloane, said, "The clay dog he got after the repairman broke in his apartment? Apparently that clay dog was now a film producer named Raquel Dogg. He also insisted on listing his Grandma in the credits like she helped make the film. *Senior advisor,* it said. A nice gesture, except that, and I don't mean to be crass, but s*he had already passed away.*"

The review quotes featured on the poster were just as circumspect.

Noting that every 'real' movie poster had a review or two from critics, Greg set out to line up a couple of his own. And despite the fact there was no actual film to preview, he somehow persuaded three prominent reporters to provide them.

As one cleverly put it: "*A film like nothing I've ever seen.*"

Charlie concluded, "The credits, the critics, it was just goofy."

For his part, Greg was loving every second of it. On Friday nights, he'd go to the theater out his window, get popcorn and stand in the lobby, watching people as they checked out the poster. (The theaters around town put the posters in the COMING SOON display, right alongside the posters featuring the real attractions.)

When not at the theater, Greg spent most of his time on the set. He had lined up an enormous 'cast'. His friends, his students, the Lunch Lady, the accountant, restaurant managers -- they all offered to step in front of the camera to help turn Greg's dream into a reality, and he gladly accepted -- regardless of their acting skills (or lack thereof).

Of the more than one hundred parts in the cast, there was one role in particular which led to a few laughs behind the scenes.

Charlie cracked, "This was supposed to be a documentary-style film about the Foundation, but my idiot friend insisted his character had to have a love interest. It made no sense."

Greg was happy to explain his reasoning.

"Every great story has a love interest. Rocky had Adrienne, Forrest had Jenny, Roy Hobbs had Iris. So, I had to have one, too."

The hitch, of course, was that Greg was very private about his personal life and didn't want to cast any of his actual ex-girlfriends in the role. So, instead, he decided to have an actress play the part.

(Amusing side notes: Greg insisted her role was *'ex'*-girlfriend -- a self-deprecating nod to the fact his relationships rarely lasted more than a month -- and he only gave her two lines in the whole script. He didn't want her to steal the show from the ad hoc cast and the film's intended focus on philanthropy. It was just the principle he cared about -- if Rocky, Gump and Hobbs had love interests in their big-screen tales, he wanted one, too.)

(Interesting side note: Another person with just a couple of lines in the script? Greg. He had been with the Foundation every step of the way since its inception, and it seemed odd to have its story told without him having a prominent role in the process. But just as was the case with the Galas, he was content being in the back, orchestrating the show, creating the platform from which others could shine.)

As the days passed, Greg continued to have the time of his life.

"Quiet on the set!" he hollered as he walked down the street.

"Action!" he blurted out in an elevator filled with strangers.

He even got his very own Director's Chair (Rocky, the kid in the tux, wrote *Director* on a piece of tape, stuck it on the back of a stool, smiled and said, "If it's a film to you, it's a film to me.").

Unfortunately, Greg's Hollywoodesque honeymoon would not last long. His journey had always been riddled with roadblocks -- and these last hundred days would be no different.

The first day on the set, he nearly started a fire. Then, a camera temporarily disappeared. One day, an entire box of tapes was misplaced. The editing machine broke down twice. For three days, Greg filmed people without realizing he had not turned on their microphone. And that's just what happened *on* the set.

Off the set, like always, his path was no straight line, either. On one occasion, a truck rammed into his car while it was parked on the side of the road. A few weeks after that, he flew out of town to give a speech. On the way back, he was taken to the wrong airport and stranded a thousand miles from home. His apartment got so cluttered with boxes that, more than once, he slept underneath a counter at the 24 Hour store down the street just so he could stretch out a little. He was eating so little that, with fifty days to go, he already lost nine pounds. And to make matters worse, just like always, he had to endure the doubters -- people who thought his grand dream was out of whack.

"You have no business making movies. You ought to stick to helping kids," said one 'expert' who Greg tried to contact for help.

As the date drew near, things went from bad to even worse.

With just barely thirty days to go until 11-10-02, Little Jarrett died. The brave boy from Kentucky finally lost his fight with cancer.

Despite all the setbacks and the grief -- and despite not having his Grandma to call for advice any more -- Greg refused to quit. He was determined to make his vision a reality. From time to time, the stress did get the best of him and he fired off another one of his angry, rambling notes, but more often than not, the lessons of the past thirty years about teamwork and perspective carried the day.

To make sure he stopped losing track of equipment (let alone nearly setting it on fire), Greg brought in a top film student to make sure it got done right. When the edit machine kept jamming, he turned to a top-level production company to lend a hand. And instead of giving up because some people wouldn't teach him anything, he found others who would. So, no matter what happened, Greg just rolled with the punches and stayed focused on his goal.

And eventually, it all paid off.

On the 98th night, he somehow completed his task. Greg stuck the finished tape in a cereal box and headed home.

When he arrived, he poured himself some juice and pulled up a seat near the window. The past fourteen weeks had been a blur, and now he finally had a chance to sit and reflect. As he did, his eyes welled with tears. He raised his glass and toasted his ability to prove yet again there was no challenge too daunting or obstacle too big for the kid willing to wake up earlier and stay up later than smart people.

As he gulped down his juice, Greg knew he was asking for trouble. All his life, when he became a little too proud of what he was on the verge of achieving, the moment proved to be a fleeting one. Almost without fail, whether it was a car crash, a broken thumb, sudden pain in his feet, or a mentor who wrote a letter of recommendation that was anything but, something or someone appeared out of nowhere to knock him off his course.

But, on this night, after all these years, bravado pumping through his veins, he was certain there were no more obstacles that could be thrown in his path. With the film draft finished and just 48 hours to go until its grand premiere, there was not enough time for anyone or anything to derail him. He was too close to the finish line.

Or so he thought.

Earlier in the fall, Greg had received a call out of the blue from Louisiana. The woman introduced herself as a representative of the school he had attended long ago. She said Greg's old friend, The Dean, stepped down after a decade, and the man filling the post wanted to take him to dinner.

"He's very impressed by what you've accomplished," she said.

At the time of the call, with the 100 day film deadline looming, the last thing Greg felt he could afford was to set aside time for a social visit -- but the invitation was just too tempting to pass up.

After repeatedly being dismissed as unworthy of the Froehmann Whitfield name, the notion of being feted by officials from Louisiana seemed like particularly sweet vindication.

At least, he thought, *I am good enough for one alma mater.*

He scheduled the dinner for the night of November 9 -- hoping he would have the film done by then.

"I bet the head of Harvard isn't flying in to dine with Charlie," he squealed with delight, having clearly lost sight of his Grandma's talks about making such comparisons.

November 9, 2002

For the first time in nearly three months, Greg showered, shaved and put on a suit. Given the weight he had lost over the last 98 days, he was a shell of his self, his outfit engulfing him -- but he stuck out his chest and tried to fill out his jacket as best he could.

At the appointed hour, he went downstairs and waited on the corner for the entourage from Louisiana to pick him up.

And he waited. And he waited. And he waited.

It would be two full hours, before he finally accepted the harsh reality that nobody was coming.

At first, Greg thought the worst -- had the school set up the whole charade just to get him back for walking out on them years earlier? -- but, in reality, it was not nearly so malicious nor personal.

As it turned out, the Dean's replacement was coming to town to drum up support for the school. The invitation extended to Greg, no more special than ones presented to many other alums who lived in the area. When the administration received more RSVP's than expected, they simply prioritized them on a sliding scale of perceived importance. And as such things go, a guy in his twenties who left the school after two short years and had never been back since was not exactly high up on that list. The failure to call Greg and cancel? According to a written apology he received a short time later, it was just an innocent oversight, a small task lost in the shuffle of many others.

It was the same old story, really.

Just as Greg was beginning to get too big for his britches or losing his focus, something or someone humbled him back to reality. Here he was, thinking he had become so important that a top university official wanted to fly into town just to meet *him* for dinner. And then the cold, harsh reality check -- he was still so unimportant that they not only didn't show up, it slipped their mind to call and cancel.

In the past, these moments had humiliated Greg. In some cases, they had even left him depressed. But in this particular case, on the eve of 11-10-02, the night when his thirty year journey was going to culminate in one extraordinary, grand night, even he knew the turn of events was apropos.

For better or worse, Greg's story was not the story of a gold medalist who shattered world records with ease. It was not about the Homecoming King who got the girl and lived happily ever after.

To the contrary, Greg's was a story marked as much by setbacks as it was by success, as much by relationships lost as it was by those that were cemented for life. And, in that up-and-down context, it seemed fitting -- if not altogether poetic -- that just twenty-four hours before the biggest triumph of his life, he spent the night alone, standing outside on the corner for hours, in a suit that no longer fit, waiting for a ride that would never come.

The Movie Theater - November 10, 2002

With the name of Greg's one-night-only film -- 11-10-02.com -- up on the marquee, his friends and students came streaming into the theater where they enjoyed the reception with the 'stars' of the film -- *themselves.*

Elliott laughed, "We wore dark shades and signed autographs for each other. And not just the kids. The adults, too. For one night, we all really did feel like *stars.* "

At precisely seven-thirty, with popcorn in one hand and soda in the other, the would-be matinee idols and the others in attendance filed in and took their seats. A few moments later, the lights went out and the 'film' began to play.

A critic would say what was shown that night was not very good, and that critic would be right. By any standard, it was an amateur production. A truly *rough* draft pieced together in a hundred days by a guy who didn't know what he was doing, with a cast that had no idea how to act. But the audience didn't care, and neither did Greg.

For, in that theater on that night, if only for one night, he did what he always dreamed since he was a boy visting his godfather, the projectionist. He made the wall *come to life.*

And in the process, he told the exact kind of story he always vowed to tell. A story about underdogs. A story about someone who stuck up for others who were treated differently. A story about a world where it was okay to dream.

But, ironically, it wasn't the story playing on the screen that made him so emotional. It was the audience. Like any real director, more than the sight of his own work on screen, it was the reaction of the crowd that he craved. To know his product was pressing buttons, touching lives and making people think.

And sure enough, the audience laughed at the parts that were supposed to be funny. They sighed at the parts that were intended to be sad. And through it all, they munched away on that popcorn just like they would at any real movie.

Better yet, thanks to the sponsors and those ticket sales, the event was raising more money for the Foundation than any night ever had.

In every sense, the night was perfect -- the ultimate way to spend the final night of this thirty year journey. Two minutes into the show, Greg already had tears running down both cheeks -- and he made no effort to wipe them away. It was not long until a few others were swept up in the emotion and crying, too.

Little did they know, the best plot twist was still to come.

After the final credits rolled, the Principal of Blue Academy rose from his seat, walked to the front, took the microphone and introduced himself to the audience.

The soft-spoken school administrator talked about the efforts Greg made to help his staff and students over the years, and how they knew Greg sacrificed his own dreams along the way to do it.

Mr. Brooks said his school was a small one, and there was never much they could do to express their gratitude. But, he noted, on this night -- 11-10-02 -- there was a way they could say thanks. He said he knew Greg's most deeply held dream was to make films and to win 'an Academy Award' for his very first one. And, he said, as fate would have it, that was the one dream he could help make come true.

Nobody seemed sure what Mr. Brooks meant, but they started to figure it out when he smiled and said, "Because, as the Principal of Blue Academy, I am, technically speaking, the head of *an Academy*."

He paused for a moment to let his words sink in.

Then he cleared his throat, smiled one more time and said, "Without further adieu, it's my pleasure to present the *Blue Academy* Award for Best Director of a film that does not yet exist."

As the audience simultaneously laughed and applauded, the substitute teacher-turned-director-for-one-night walked down to the front of the theater and accepted the trophy -- a milkshake glass that had been painted gold by the kids.

As he looked out at the crowd giving him a standing ovation, Greg noticed his mother, father and sister leading the applause. His road had been so unpredictable over the years -- he walked away from the kind of certain future that parents usually want for their child -- but his family knew this was his dream. And in the end, even if they didn't understand it, they just wanted to see him achieve it and be happy.

With tears in his eyes, Greg raised up the gold milkshake glass and gave the acceptance speech whose first six words he had been practicing all his life -- words that had taken on a whole new meaning:

"I'd like to thank the Academy...."

When he finished his remarks, the audience launched into an impromptu rendition of *Happy Birthday*. And then, they all headed back out to the theater's lobby where the reception had taken place.

As members of the 'cast' basked in the afterglow of their big-screen debuts, posed for pictures and signed some more autographs, the film's director approached his father to thank him for being there.

However complicated their relationship during the thirty years, even Greg could not deny the man had been there in the beginning and was still there in the end -- and, if nothing else, that was something to appreciate. As he'd come to learn over the past few years, a lot of kids would've been happy just to have a father figure present -- even if it was one they didn't always care for or agree with.

The substitute teacher who still had no couch looked eye-to-eye with the stockbroker who now had several homes, and said, "I know we don't have a lot in common, and I know we probably never will. But I just want you to know I've been giving a lot of thought to stuff you've tried to tell me over the years, and I reached a couple conclusions, and I thought this might be a good time to share them."

Mark smiled and replied, "This should be interesting."

"Well, the first thing is my name. I know you gave me the name Forbes because you wanted me to kind of follow in that family's footsteps. And I know you think I haven't. But, here's the thing. You always said an investor invests not just in companies, but in the people who are part of them. And I think that is what I've ended up doing --

investing in people -- and, so, for whatever it's worth, I have, I think, in my own way, followed in the Forbes footsteps after all."

Mark smirked but said nothing.

Greg continued, "The other conclusion I reached -- when I was a kid and you were talking to me about stocks, you always said 'return is a function of risk'. I never got that. Well, after all the time I've spent working in the schools and helping students with scholarships through the Foundation, I get it now -- and I think it's a hundred percent true. The risk may be greater when you invest in something or someone else few others believe in, but the return is too."

In a more conciliatory mood than usual given the occasion, Mark chuckled and said, "Not exactly how I expected you to apply the lesson, but I'm glad to hear that you remember something I tried to teach you at the dinner table."

That was as close as Greg was going to get to a stamp of approval from his father, and he knew it. He smiled warmly and began to walk away -- when he suddenly spun back around to add one final thought. He just couldn't resist.

"By the way," he said to his father. "I almost forgot, there was one other conclusion I reached. Those cartoons you give me to try and get your points across about what really matters in life. When I was a kid, they didn't make any sense to me. But now, looking back, in at least one case, it makes sense now."

"Which cartoon was that?" Mark asked.

Greg looked down at his milkshake trophy, smiled from ear to ear, and said, "The one that said, *Life is about who owns the glass.*"

**

After the celebration died down and the crowd went home, Greg headed over to The Tempo Cafe. As he walked in, the manager asked, "How'd the movie go?"

Greg smiled and said, "It went well -- except that I was supposed to meet an old friend here a while ago, and I lost all track of time."

With that said, he joined me in a booth by the window, set down his lunchbox briefcase and milkshake glass trophy, took off his shoes, said he was sorry for being late, explained that he had been at a movie, ordered the same thing he'd been having all his life -- grilled cheese and a vanilla shake -- and then told me I could ask him one question.

As the clock struck twelve and 11-10-02 came to an end, Greg began to tell me the story of the first thirty years of his life.

The dreams he had. The goals he set. The books he read. The movies he watched. The teachers he admired. The one who betrayed him. The rejections he faced. The mistakes he made. The obstacles he overcame. The kids he taught, the ones he learned from. The friends he found, the ones he lost. And above all else, a sense of what he thought others could learn from his unusual journey.

I had asked Greg just one question.

Can you start at the beginning?

By the time he finished his answer, it was past five o'clock in the morning. The late-night crowd at the Cafe had long since left, and the early risers had not yet arrived. It was just about the only time of the day that the restaurant was not alive and hopping. In fact, there was only one other customer in the whole place -- a woman, probably in her mid-forties, sitting alone in the booth right next to us.

As I packed up my things, I apologized to Greg for asking a question whose answer required so much of his time.

He laughed and said, "Don't worry about it. I've watched the sun rise more than once over the last few years."

You might think he was just being polite, but he really didn't seem to mind. Because, at some point, shortly after finishing the shake and the sandwich, he had opened up his lunchbox, pulled out a pencil and paper and started drawing a picture of me while he told his story.

Every so often, he looked up -- studying my face intently, double-checking every crease, every shadow -- before turning his attention back to that paper and getting lost in the details of his work.

I am a self-conscious person and don't like being drawn, but in this instance, I didn't say a word -- knowing Greg was more likely to stick around and finish the story as long as there was something to distract him from thinking about how many hours had passed.

And so, I sat silent as he sketched away while sharing one chapter of his life after another. Until, finally, by the time it was five o'clock in the morning, he finished two portraits simultaneously.

The picture of his life that he painted for me, and the picture of me that he drew while doing it.

When he was done, I thanked him again for the chance to tell his story and promised I'd do my best to tell it well.

"I know you will," he said. "I always have believed in you."

With that, he put a tip on the table, tucked the paper and pencil into his lunchbox, slipped on his shoes, picked up his gold milkshake glass, rose from his seat, wished me well and turned to leave.

As he did, the lady next to us waved and said, "You too."

"Excuse me?" Greg responded politely.

"Just now," she replied with a smile, "You said *take care of yourself.* You were looking out the window, but there's nobody else here, so I assumed you were talking to me, so I said *you, too.*"

The woman was trying to be nice, but I didn't think Greg was going to take it that way. When we were little and people said they didn't see me, he launched into a tantrum loud enough to wake up the neighbors. But I should point out, in fairness to him, that on this night, he didn't get upset at all. In fact, he didn't even correct her. He just smiled nicely and headed out the door.

Yesterday, if you would've told me that would be his reaction, I wouldn't have believed you. But now that I know where life has taken Greg in the twenty-five years since I last saw him, I'm not surprised. Because I think if there's one thing he learned from his own story, it is that those who dare to dream -- those who recognize value where others see none, those who see the potential in something that does not yet exist -- will *always* encounter a person or two who don't see their vision. And if *you* are a dreamer, I hope you remember that.

I hope you remember that no matter how many people doubt what you can do, no matter how many doubt what you can see, you should never give up on your vision.

Because anything your mind can think of can become a reality -- a film, a foundation, a friendship, *anything* -- if you're willing to spend the time it takes to make it come to life.

And if *you* have a dream, and try to make it come to life like Greg did, and run into more obstacles than you expect along the way like he did, try to remember what his Grandma always said:

If life was nothing but straight lines, it wouldn't be worth living.

*****

AFTER THOUGHTS

The Milkshake Scholars attended schools across the nation.
None of them washed the glasses.

The next year, the Foundation had another Gala.
It was back at the Restaurant. There were no assigned seats.

At the event, the Foundation announced its largest grant ever. The grant was awarded to Blue Academy.....to help their students learn how to make films....Greg named the grant after the school's clerk.

He eventually raised the price of his milkshakes to $10,000. To justify the increased cost, he added one final ingredient which he said captures the true essence of his Foundation. A single nut on top.

When some people said Greg's shakes had gotten too expensive, he created an alternative. For $1000, you could meet him for a photo with a used coffee cup. No actual coffee. Just you, him and the cup.

To this day, the Foundation continues to receive unsolicited donations -- and, in turn, continues to provide grants and scholarships to students, schools and programs around the country.

To this day,
Greg has still never taken a salary from the Foundation.

He still wears mismatched socks every day.

When Grandma passed away, she left Greg a number of things. One of them was a briefcase, but she didn't leave him the combination to open it....As of 11-10-02, he still had no idea what was inside.

Three decades after first moving in, Mark and Rose sold their house. They now live on a golf course in a private gated community.

The Silhouette Man and The Ladder Horse stayed behind.

Before the old house was sold, the jar holding Tug's ashes was dug out of the backyard and then given to Greg.

On his 30th birthday, Greg announced
his Logo has a *fourth* meaning...
but as of this book's printing, he still has not revealed what it is.

Shortly after Greg's 30th birthday, Rocky -- the 'kid in the tux' --
gave him a gift. His bow tie.... A few months later, with Rocky's
blessing, Greg framed it and auctioned it off for $1,000 -- with the
proceeds going to the Foundation.

On his 31st birthday, Greg returned to the gym
and now once again exercises on a daily basis.

In 2005, in the aftermath of Hurricane Katrina, he launched a new
site -- www.ProjectThankYou.com -- to help recognize some of
the many devoted police officers, firefighters and other First
Responders who make a difference.

That same year, he also started a new tradition. When he visits
different cities, he invites complete strangers to meet up for dinner.
Up to 40 people at a time have joined him.

The Club is no longer in business....The movie theater outside
Greg's window was closed....Over the objections of students, parents,
staff, faculty and administrators, Blue Academy was shut down.

The Bully passed away.
Mr. Welton did, too.

After Blue Academy was closed,
Greg 'retired' from substitute teaching.

He now speaks at schools, nonprofit organizations, companies,
events and conferences...At some events, after he's done speaking,
he goes for a walk to get a milkshake...When he does,
more often than not, the audience gets up and goes with him.

He now writes for a variety of magazines as well.
Most of the time, he is asked to write about the stories of
people who have taken unusual paths to success
and/or who have devoted their lives to making a difference.

He is also currently at work on his own first book and film.

He continues to draw portraits in his free time.
In 2006, he began accepting invitations to have
his art put on display at events around North America.

That same year, he moved to a new community.

In Greg's new apartment, a number of things are framed on the
walls including: some of his portraits, some of the cartoons from his
father, the honorary degree from PSC, the splinters of the rocking
chair, the leftover stitches of the foul ball, a poster from the film that
does not exist, the receipt from the day he took two kids for shakes,
the scrap of paper with the original, hand-written Brunch Bunch
Mission Statement, the letter of certification confirming that he had
been accepted for the study abroad program in England, the letter of
'recommendation' from Mr. Welton, a sketch of The Silhouette Man,
and a picture of his late Grandma.

An extensive collage he made with excerpts from thousands
of rejection letters is framed on one of the walls as well.

The book about Harriet Tubman sits on Greg's shelf...along with
The Brick, the menu from Harvard's, the BOARDROOM sign,
the jar with Tug's ashes, and the gold-painted milkshake glass.

As was the case with Greg's first two apartments,
there is one light outside his window which shines
all night long each and every night without fail.

** To Be Continued **

POST SCRIPT

Since this story first was shared (in its condensed version, *The First Thirty*), many people have tried their best to unravel its ending. The question, at least, is a relatively straightforward one: On the night of 11-10-02, at The Tempo Cafe, the woman at the next table said Greg was sitting by himself. Was Greg really sitting with someone named Jillip -- or was he actually sitting by himself?

Ever the storyteller, Greg has refused to address the question -- insisting that the answer is truly, literally irrelevant.

As for me, well, if I do exist, I'm sworn to secrecy. (And if I don't, good luck finding me to ask the question in the first place.)

I know our silence makes it harder to answer the question, but you really shouldn't need either of us to answer it. After all, the meeting happened in a public place and lasted all night long.

Surely, there is a witness or two who can answer the question.

Well, at least, you would think so.

As it turns out, the situation is a bit more complicated than that.

You see, Greg had so many late-night meals at the Cafe that the servers and busboys could not possibly pull out a calendar years later and tell you who he was or was not eating with on any particular night.

The manager knew 11-10-02 was a special occasion, and so, perhaps, he could recall that particular night and therefore be able to answer the question -- if not for the fact that he sadly passed away.

The lady sitting at the next table that night -- the one who told Greg to "take care of himself, too" -- she obviously would have some insights to offer. If you could find her, that is. Nobody has a clue who she is or even what she looks like. (Well, nobody except me and Greg, and like I said, we're not talking).

So, it seemed the question would go unanswered -- the mystery would remain just that -- until one resourceful reader looked between the lines and realized the riddle could still be solved.

The reader wrote: "I figured out that all you need to do is look at that drawing -- the one Greg drew at the Cafe on the night of 11-10-02 . If it's a portrait of Greg, then the woman was right -- he was sitting by himself, talking to himself and drawing his own reflection. But, if it's a portrait of someone else, that means Jillip *was* there with him -- that there were two people at the table -- and, the woman, for whatever reason, simply could not see one of them."

It appeared the reader was right. Find that drawing, and you've got your answer. Easy enough. But, as with everything in Greg's life, there was an unexpected wrinkle.

That night, 11-10-02, the lights in the Cafe were dimmed. So, the image Greg drew on that paper turned out looking less like someone's portrait and more like someone's shadow -- their *silhouette* -- making it all but impossible to determine who he was drawing.

When Greg was a child, The Silhouette Man was a loyal friend -- always there, standing at attention outside his window.

Over the next couple decades, whenever the easily distracted boy was about to get too far off-track, The Silhouette Man reappeared, seemingly right on cue. There was the photo from the hotel balcony in Hawaii just before Greg's final semester of high school. Then, he showed up again, five years later, in the photo taken during Greg's post-college trip to California. And then, after another five years, he reappeared in Greg's bathroom mirror.

And now, here he was, another couple years later, showing up one more time, seemingly out of nowhere, in a portrait drawn in the middle of the night in a twenty-four hour cafe.

In the past, The Silhouette Man had been there to help Greg, to keep him focused and moving in the right direction. But, this time around, when The Silhouette Man reappeared on the night of Greg's thirtieth birthday, he didn't come back to protect his old friend.

This time around, The Silhouette Man returned to help *you.*

For if he did not return on the night of 11-10-02, in the exact way he did, at the precise moment he did, you would have been able to see if Greg had drawn me or if he'd drawn himself. You would have been able to figure out whether I was 'really' there that night at The Tempo Cafe or whether Greg was all alone.

And that would have been a shame.

For if you sincerely embrace the spirit of this story, you know it is a question best left unanswered. You know the answer *truly* does not matter. To dreamers, there is no such thing as *real* and *not real.*

As Greg likes to say:

Imaginary does not mean something doesn't exist.

It means something doesn't exist *yet.*

*****

CONTACT

Send us your thoughts about *The Silhouette Man* or *The First Thirty*
Email **Feedback@TheFirstThirty.com**
**

For more on this book, go to **www.TheSilhouetteMan.com**
**

For more on the condensed version of this book,
go to **www.TheFirstThirty.com**
**

For more on the Companion Journal Workbook,
go to **www.APlaceToSit.com**
**

For bulk orders of the books, workbook, or products based on them
e-mail: **Books@IdeaListEnterprises.com**
**

For more on Greg, go to **www.GregForbes.com**
**

To book Greg for a speech or event,
e-mail **Events@GregForbes.com**
**

To see a sample of Greg's artwork and learn more about
having it exhibited in your town or at your school or event,
go to **www.MySleeplessNights.com**
**

For more on his brunches, dinners and milkshakes,
see **www.ShakingUpAmerica.com**
**

www.WorldsGreatestName.com
Because the most important word in the world is your name
**

www.WorldsGreatestGrandma.com
Because everybody's got one.
**

www.ProjectThankYou.com
Because small acts of kindness matter
**

For more information on The 11-10-02 Foundation,
go to **www.ShakingUpAmerica.org**